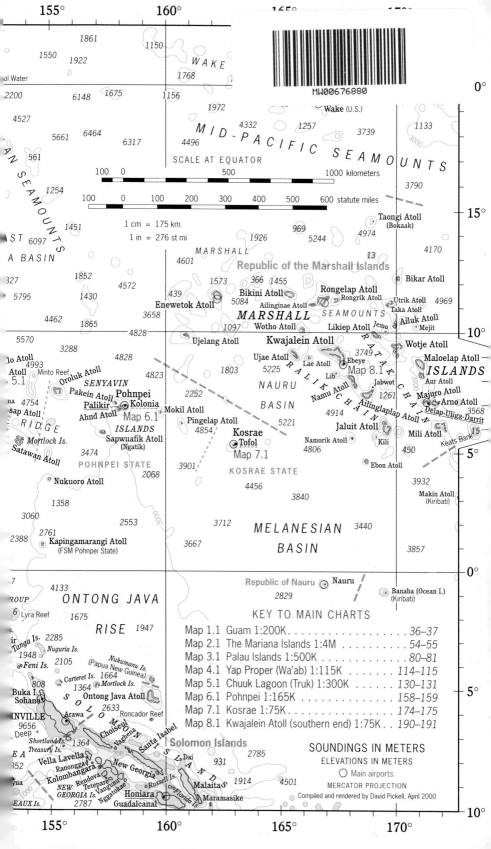

Diving The Pacific
Volume I

Micronesia

and the Western Pacific Islands

INCLUDES GUAM, THE MARIANAS,

PALAU, YAP, CHUUK, POHNPEI,

KOSRAE, AND THE MARSHALLS

David Leonard

Editing and Cartography by David Pickell

PERIPLUS

Published by Periplus Editions (HK) Ltd.

Copyright ©2001 Periplus Editions (HK) Ltd.
ALL RIGHTS RESERVED

ISBN 962-593-499-5
Printed in Singapore

Publisher: Eric Oey
Series editor: David Pickell
Photo and text editing: David Pickell
Cartography: David Pickell
Interior design: David Pickell with Peter Ivey

DISTRIBUTORS

ASIA-PACIFIC   Berkeley Books Pte. Ltd.
5 Little Road, #08-01
Singapore 536983
Tel: (65) 280-3320
Fax: (65) 280-6290

INDONESIA   PT Java Books Indonesia
Jl. Kelapa Gading Kirana
Blok A-14 No. 17
Jakarta 14240
Tel: (62-21) 451-5351
Fax: (62-21) 453-4987

JAPAN   Tuttle Publishing
RK Building, 2nd Floor
2-13-10 Shimo-Meguro
Meguro-Ku
Tokyo 153
Tel: (81-35) 437-0171
Fax: (81-35) 437-0755

USA   Tuttle Publishing
Distribution Center
Airport Industrial Park
364 Innovation Drive
North Clarendon, VT 05759-9436
Tel: (802) 773-8930, (800) 526-2778
Fax: (802) 773-6993

COVER   Fairy basslets on the reef face, Kosrae. Tammy Peluso.
PAGES 4–5   *Dendronephthya,* Chandelier Cave, Palau. Tammy Peluso.
FRONTISPIECE   *Carcharinus melanopterus,* Rongelap Lagoon. Mike Severns.

Contents

95   122

89   30

149   101

Part VII Kosrae

Part VIII The Marshall Islands

Part V Chuuk

Part IX Practicalities

Part VI Pohnpei

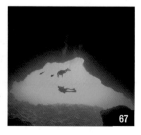

Preface
and Acknowledgments

David Leonard

All travel has its advantages. If the passenger visits better countries, he may learn to improve his own, and if fortune carries him to worse, he may learn to enjoy it.
— Samuel Johnson

MAY YOUR FORTUNE ONE DAY LEAD YOU TO Micronesia. The first time I went there I traveled alone, exploring my heart and soul at the same time as these islands. I found some answers, and I found peace of mind. I learned that there are other ways of getting through these lives of ours. The Micronesians have a respect for their land and seas that is reflected in their respect for one another, a lesson we can all benefit from in this crazy world. If happiness and success can be measured in self-assured contentment, then they are among the most successful people on earth.

This book is for divers, but whether you are a sportsman, family vacationer, adventurer, honeymooner, or sailor, these islands hold fascination, relaxation, self-realization and education in store for you. Descend and explore.

Though Micronesia is a complex of islands divided into many different republics, states, principalities, commonwealths, territories, trusteeships, protectorates, and possessions, this book is set up to aid the dive traveler in more easily navigating the most fascinating locales.

Micronesia's diving world is constantly expanding. New operators are exploring new reefs and newly discovered wrecks every day and adding them to your choice of dive sites. I have attempted to find and describe the most interesting underwater destinations available at the time I was doing my research. I have also tried to recommend those operators who offer the best service and who, most importantly, value your business.

There are certainly more hidden corners than I could ever hope to shed light upon

within this short volume. I encourage you to explore on your own. Please do let me know of any gems you uncover, so that I may include them in the next edition. Good luck. Safe travels and safer diving.

THE AUTHOR

David Leonard was born, bred, and continues to live in New York City. The Big Apple, itself offering a great deal of fine cold-water diving (a prodigious sunken fleet of World War II and 19th-century wrecks dot the coast), serves as home base for his worldwide diving and travel adventures. He has logged several hundred dives in Micronesia, and long ago stopped counting dives in the Caribbean, Cocos Island, the Gulf of Mexico, the Red Sea and the Great Barrier Reef. He has written travel and dive articles for *Scuba Network, Asian Diver, Dive Log New Zealand, Undercurrent,* Australia's *Scuba Diving, American Way, The New York Times, Pacifica, The Village Voice,* and *Musician.* He is currently working on a book on the global village and its disastrous effect on culture and tradition. Leonard is also the founder of StarDive, an annual dive adventure to raise money for child abuse prevention programs.

THE PHOTOGRAPHERS

Tammy Peluso began her love affair with diving in 1986, abandoning a New York design career to open a dive shop in Mexico. She learned underwater photography while living on Cozumel, and began working as an underwater photojournalist several years later. Since then, her work has appeared in

Tammy Peluso

numerous books and magazines, as well as on CD-ROMs, and in brochures, and calendars. Peluso lives in Kimbe, on New Britain Island in Papua New Guinea, where she works part time as a photographer and full time as manager of Walindi Photo, Papua New Guinea's first underwater photo facility, which she established in 1997.

Mike Severns is one of the foremost underwater photographers working in the Indo-Pacific today. He has photographed extensively in the Hawai'ian islands, including Kure and Midway, as well as in some of the most remote parts of the Marshall Islands. For the last fifteen years, he has concentrated on Indonesia. His work has appeared in Periplus Editions' *Diving Bali, Diving Indonesia,* and *Diving Southeast Asia,* as well as in several books on marine life. He photographed and co-authored, with his wife, biologist Pauline Fiene-Severns, the large-format *Sulawesi Seas,* a photo book based on seven years' work in this very rich corner of Indonesia, and *Molokini Island,* now in its third printing, which documents the underwater life of a sunken volcano off Maui, Hawai'i. His photography has appeared in numerous magazines, including *Ocean Realm, Natural History,* and *Islands.* He lives on Maui.

Robert Ricke and **Maria Hults** are a well-known underwater photography and writing team who have collaborated on several books, including the soon-to-be-published *Great Dive Destinations of the World.* Bob and Maria continually travel the world in search of the perfect photograph. Maria is also a world-class scuba instructor who, when not circling the globe, teaches scuba diving privately and through New York's Pan Aqua Dive Shop. They live in New York City.

Bill Beckner spends as much time underwater as he can, and it shows in his work. He and his wife Suzanne, a nuclear physicist, both valued friends of the author, live in Washington, DC.

Gui Garcia is known as a photographer who will always go the extra mile to achieve a photograph that will tell a story. He is also an experienced captain and dive instructor, and you never know where on the globe you will find him.

AUTHOR'S ACKNOWLEGEMENTS

For their advice, direction, and generosity I extend special thanks to the following people. Without them this book would simply not have been possible:

Dave Furlong, Lex Rathbun, Bob Rogers, Ben and Ki Concepcion, Gretchen Young, Christina Pierro, Shelley Donow, Rainer Sigel, Julia Goh, Elijah Ma'asud, Wayne Hasson, Capt. Buck Beasley, Stacy Babaz, Captain Gui Garcia, Maria Hults and Bob Ricke, Jennifer Covington, Dan Ruth and everyone at Aggressor Fleet, Peter Hughes Diving Inc. and the Palau Sun Dancer, Navot and Tova Bornzovski and the Ocean Hunter, Carl Roessler and See and Sea, Steve Conte of Rowdy Rock Divers ("This is another fine mess you've gotten me into!"), Lance and Narinda Higgs and the crew of the SS *Thorfinn*; Kelly Ward, Rick Saul and Dean Tinker at the Palau Pacific Resort; John and Dot Blair, Joanne Dreyfuss, Juan Casanova, Stan and Flora Fillmed, Jesse Faimaw, David Vecella and the staff of Beyond the Reef Charters, Bob, Patty and Janet Arthur at The Village, divemaster extraordinaire Maurice Tudong, Madison Nena, Steve Gavegan ("Gavegan's Island"), Yoshi, Joab and Albon, and the Sun Leader and his crew (the "Coconut Crab Cwajalein Crew").

Also, I'd like to offer a special thanks to the wonderful people of Guam, Saipan, Tinian, Rota, Palau, Yap, Chuuk, Pohnpei, Kosrae, and Kwajalein, who despite the onslaught of everything from Magellan to MTV have been able to maintain their dignity and self respect.

And for contributions both spiritual and physical, I would also like to thank Pete Peterson and John Ryan of the Micronesian Divers Association in Guam, Jimmy and Ricky at the Senyavin in Pohnpei, Hubert Anton, Chris Berger ("All de vay!"), Cecile and Philippe Brawerman, Doug Beitz, Jack Reinke, Gary Mark, Kenny Omura, François Weber, and Cordelia McIntyre.

TAMMY PELUSO   A reef channel in southern Palau

This book is dedicated to my mother and
father, Marion and Albert Leonard, who
long ago instilled within me a deep passion
for travel and a sincere appreciation for
people of all cultures, and to my best
friend and guide, Sam Leonard, for his
unconditional love, help, and balance.

Gray reef sharks in the Marshall Islands. The Micronesian region in general is an excellent place to see sharks, particularly grays and reef whitetips (and in the lagoons and boat channels, reef blacktips).

MIKE SEVERNS   *Carcharhinus amblyrhynchos*   Rongelap Atoll

ROBERT RICKE and MARIA HULTS   Fujikawa Maru   Chuuk Lagoon

Chuuk, formerly called 'Truk,' is arguably the best wreck diving site in the world. For two days in February 1944, in 'Operation Hailstone,' aircraft from nine U.S. carriers rained destruction on the Japanese fleet at Chuuk, sinking sixty ships.

P EOPLE WHO DON'T DIVE FIND IT PUZZLING THAT divers will travel vast distances to exotic places just to spend three hours a day underwater. (And it doesn't help our case much that some of us dismissively refer to our time on land as a "surface interval.") These non-divers will have a hard time with this book. Why would anyone eagerly fly thousands of miles across the Pacific to Micronesia, a place that few people have even heard of and which is, after all, just three-hundredths of one percent land? The reason, of course, is that the other 99.97 percent of Micronesia consists of the warm, clear waters of the tropical Pacific, which bathe some of the richest reefs and finest wrecks in the world. These are places of diving legend: Palau, Chuuk Lagoon, Yap.

And Micronesia, though its land area may be modest, offers an exceptional diversity of terrain, cultures, and traveling experiences. Your "surface intervals" here can be magical. Some islands are jungle-covered peaks; others are dry, sandy cays. Some of the island cultures here are traditional and isolated; others are as twenty-first–century American as a decaf latte.

You can "do" Micronesia in as many ways as there are islands: book an expensive hotel or camp on the beach; dive from the shore or from a luxurious live-aboard; travel in a group or adventure on your own; plan an epic, two-month-long dive series, or a long weekend get-away. Because of this miscellany of options, it's important to plan ahead just a little. There's enough here to fill up a lifetime of vacations, so you have to decide what you have time to see and do.

SPECKS IN THE PACIFIC

Micronesia consists of three huge archipelagoes—the Caroline Islands, the Marianas, and the Marshalls—as well as tiny Nauru Island, and the three scattered island groups that make up the Republic of Kiribati: The Tungaru Islands (formerly Gilbert), the Phoenix Islands, and the Line Islands. This book covers the Carolines, Marianas, and Marshalls, where you will find the region's best (and only organized) diving.

Of the thousands of islands scattered across Micronesia, only 135 are inhabited. A few are small, and the rest are tiny. The largest islands are Guam at 541 square kilometers (209 sq. mi.) and Babelthuap in Palau at 396 square kilometers (153 sq. mi.). Every piece of dry land in Micronesia, taken together, amounts to just 3,224 square kilometers (1,245 sq. mi.), barely larger than Rhode Island. Yet the ocean area, nearly 12 million square kilometers (4.5 million sq. mi.), is almost twenty percent bigger than the land area of the entire United States.

Micronesia's three-thousand kilometer sweep of the Pacific Ocean includes the deepest point yet discovered, an 11,033 meter (36,198 ft.) sounding in the Mariana Trench south of Guam, and the world's largest atoll, Kwajalein in the Marshalls, which has a lagoon encompassing 2,173 square kilometers (839 sq. mi.). The islands, while small, are geologically varied, ranging from sharp, volcanic peaks (some active) to flat, crushed-coral sand bars. Some are blanketed in thick jungle growth; others are sandy deserts.

MIKE SEVERNS Pseudanthias pascalus Rongelap Atoll, Marshall Islands

Marshall Islands reefs are wild and mostly unexplored, and often rich in fish, like the purple queens shown here. But because of their isolation, coral diversity in the Marshalls is modest, as can be seen in this reef face dominated by the algas Halimeda and Padina.

One constant in these islands is the climate. The temperatures are steady, averaging a warm 27°C (81°F) year-round, with the Northern Marianas and the northern atolls in the Marshalls being just a bit cooler. Everywhere the evening brings cooling breezes. Water temperatures are similar to air temperatures, and relatively constant year round. The northeast trade winds blow steadily across Micronesia, and these planetary winds carry some of the cleanest air on Earth, allowing the thick canopy of midnight stars to shine more brightly in Micronesia than anywhere else I've been.

The wet season runs from May through December, but the difference between this and the drier season is marginal, and it rains year-round. Rain showers are usually welcome, brief, and refreshing, and often occur in the evening. The northernmost of the islands are drier than those nearer the equator. Kosrae and Pohnpei, the southernmost of the islands covered here, are among the wettest places on earth. Pohnpei receives a measured 4,917 millimeters (more than 16 feet) a year on the coast, and this is only half what falls in the mountainous interior. Islands with a lot of fruit trees (Kosrae and Saipan, for example) are covered with black flies during the summer ripening season; they don't bite, but they *are* relentless and supremely annoying.

For diving, each season has both advantages and disadvantages. During the dry season, December through March, the northeast trades blow steadily, making offshore and seaward diving difficult. This is also the high season for tourism, and the more popular sites can get crowded. The rainy season—May through December—can produce worsened underwater visibility, as the rains flood the rivers which tend to wash sediments into the lagoons and over the reefs. But the difference is slight at most sites, and during this season you will encounter fewer tourists, pay slightly lower prices, and find unusually still ocean side waters.

THE WORLD'S GREATEST SEAFARERS

The first people to reach these is-

TAMMY PELUSO Subergorgia mollis Palau

lands came from mainland Southeast Asia at least 4,000 years ago. They were Austronesians, part of the same group that populated Malaysia, Indonesia, and the Philippines. The Marianas and western Caroline islands seem to have been settled first, and from there the rest of Micronesia.

Reconstructing this early histo-

Palau's combination of clear water and a wealth of underwater life—including gorgonians, soft corals, reef fish, and pelagics—makes these reefs among the most popular in the world for photography.

ry requires considerable specula-
tion, as these early seafaring people
worked in wood and other perish-
able substances, and no hard evidence exists of their material culture. Anthropologists believe that
they cultivated taro, breadfruit, coconuts, pandanus, and on the more
fertile, volcanic islands, yams. They
brought with them three domesticated animals—pigs, dogs, and
chickens—but fish likely provided
most of their dietary protein.

The Micronesians were the
greatest seafarers in the world, sailing large outriggered canoes across
thousands of kilometers of open sea.
Their navigational techniques involved reading the stars, the wind,
the weather, the currents, and the
pattern of the open ocean swell,
which could bring evidence of an island still hundreds of kilometers in
the distance.

The remarkable stone ruins at
Nan Madol in Pohnpei, Lelu on
Kosrae, and the monoliths on Babelthuap in Palau, as well as the
great *latte* stones of the Marianas
and Yap's huge stone money, are evidence of a time when Micronesia
held great seafaring kingdoms, with
elaborate systems of patronage and
trade. The islanders flourished
during this period, beginning early
in the first millennium A.D., and
they cultivated unique social systems, architecture, language, art, and
tools.

The feats of engineering, transportation, and social organization
reflected in these stone artifacts are
nothing short of remarkable. For example, Yap's huge *rai*, stone money
disks weighing up to five tons,
were quarried and shaped on
Palau, then hauled across 400 kilometers of open ocean to Yap.

Today the memory of the golden
age of Micronesian cultures survives
in stories, and on some of the islands—Palau, Yap, Pohnpei, parts of
the Marshalls—traditional leaders

who trace their roots to this period
are still respected. But in much of
this area, the old cultures have
been forgotten.

With the arrival of the Europeans
in numbers in the 19th century
came disease, which decimated the
population of the islanders, who
had no resistance to smallpox, influenza, and syphilis. The entire
population of Kosrae, for example,
was reduced to just 300 by century's
end. Fully half of Pohnpei's population died in a single 1854 outbreak
of smallpox. With the coming of aggressive Christian missionaries, the
survivors soon learned to forget
their traditional past.

FOR GOD, GOLD, AND GLORY

"The Spanish came for God, the
Germans came for gold, the Japanese came for glory, and the Americans came for good" is a popular,
slightly tongue-in-cheek shorthand
for the four waves of European and
American colonialism that have
swept through Micronesia. It is not
entirely inaccurate.

The European Age of Exploration was driven by the search for
a sea route to the source of the
spices of the East, particularly the
three supremely valuable "fine"
spices of Indonesia's Maluku islands: nutmeg, mace, and cloves.
The Portuguese were the leaders in
this race, although by the early 16th
century, to avoid conflict between
the two Catholic countries, the
pope split the globe into two separate hemispheres of influence. The
islands of Micronesia fell into the
Spanish half, and to get there the
Spanish would have to sail west, and
reach the Pacific by rounding Tier-
ra del Fuego.

Ferdinand Magellan, a Portuguese navigator sailing for the
Spanish crown, was the first European to land on what is now Micronesia, reaching Guam in February of 1521. Remarkably, this was

TAMMY PELUSO Palau

Magellan's first landfall since he had rounded the South American cape, and his crew was by this point starving and wracked by scurvy.

This first meeting between Micronesians and Europeans did not go well, and in retribution for the theft of a skiff and some petty items, Magellan killed seven men and burned 50 Chamorro houses. (Soon after, Magellan himself was killed in Mactan Island in the Philippines.)

For a long time the Spanish were not particularly interested in the islands of Micronesia except as supply and water stops for their "Manila Galleons," which followed the seasonal winds back and forth from Manila (loaded with silk, spices, and tea) and Acapulco (loaded with New World silver). They didn't set up a permanent station on Guam until 1668. At this time they brought missionaries, the Spanish language, and all the other trappings of colonial rule. Although a few Spanish missionaries reached the western Caroline islands in the early 1700s, only the Marianas felt any substantial European influence until the 19th century.

The first British whale ships began arriving in the region in the early 1800s, and Yankee whalers out of Nantucket, in much greater numbers, followed two decades later. By mid-century, hundreds of whale boats were working these waters. Although these entrepreneurs had no interest in colonizing the islands, they opened the way for traders, and more tragically, left behind a range of devastating diseases.

Flouting Spanish claims to the region, traders began moving in from Germany's New Guinea colony. First an office was established on Yap, and in 1878, after negotiating with the traditional leaders of Jaluit Atoll, Germany declared the Marshall Islands to be a German protectorate. Spain was nonplused by what they considered an incursion on their territory, but could do little about it.

Although Palau—and Micronesia generally—is most famous for its drop-off reefs and channels, snorkeling the reef crests and lagoons can also be rewarding. Even a tough old knob of Pocillopora in a meter of water on the reef flat can hide some interesting animals. Please do remember to apply plenty of waterproof sunblock, and a dark-colored T-shirt wouldn't hurt, either. This gentleman looks like he is heading for an uncomfortable night.

In 1898 the United States declared war on Spain, and as part of the settlement at the end of the Spanish-American War, Spain was forced to turn over the Philippines, Guam, and Wake Island (as well as Cuba and Puerto Rico) for $20 million. Seeing this result coming, and not wanting to sell all of its colonial possessions at the point of a gun, in

such as a large one on Ngeaur Island in the Palau group—and developed the infrastructure on the islands. They also used forced labor in their operations, and caused huge disruptions in traditional land use. German rule lasted just 15 years. At the start of World War I the German Pacific fleet returned to Europe, and with the blessing of the European Allied powers, Japan moved into Micronesia.

THE JAPANESE AND WORLD WAR II

When the war ended, the Japanese were awarded the German territories, with the stipulation that they not build fortifications. In 1935 Japan left the League of Nations, and unilaterally annexed the islands the Empire called Nanyo Gunto. Japan fortified Micronesia, and developed phosphate and bauxite mines, copra and sugar plantations, and fisheries and agricultural operations.

The Japanese encouraged emigration to the islands, and by 1940, two-thirds of the population was Japanese, Korean, and Okinawan. The Japanese held the government positions and best private industry jobs, with the Koreans, Okinawans, and Micronesians providing labor.

Canoe travel between the islands was prohibited and traditional clan structure was thwarted as Micronesia now existed only to service and supply Japan's growing needs. The Empire frantically snatched up and stockpiled resources which would be used to fuel Japan's burgeoning economy as it began gearing up for war and conquest.

On December 7, 1941, the Japanese launched their famous attack on Pearl Harbor, and in 1942 attacked the Philippines and Indonesia from their Palau bases, and the Solomons and New Guinea from Chuuk Lagoon. When they took Guam, tiny Nauru, and Kiribati, Micronesia was offi-

TAMMY PELUSO Lutjanus kasmira Palau

Blue-lined snappers are common throughout the Indo-Pacific. They school on reef faces and around rocky points during the day, and spread out at night to feed. They are easy to catch on a handline at night, and like the rest of the snappers, make a fine table fish.

1899 Spain secretly negotiated the sale of the Carolines and the remaining Mariana Islands to Germany for $4.25 million.

Germany quickly began developing these new possessions, chiefly by planting coconut trees. At the time, dried coconut meat or copra was quite valuable as an ingredient in soap and cosmetics. The Germans set up phosphate mines—

cially united under a single flag for the first time in its history.

World War II was an unmitigated disaster for the Micronesians. Starved, beaten, enslaved, and bombed, at least 5,000 of them died in the conflict (and probably many more, as histories rarely record their deaths).

Pearl Harbor, of course, was not the fatal blow that Admiral Isoroku Yamamoto had hoped. American factories shifted rapidly to building war matériel, and finally the United States simply out-produced Japan. Eventually American factories were turning out three hundred new warships each month.

In mid-1943 General Douglas A. MacArthur and Admiral William F. "Bull" Halsey began working their way back through the Solomons and New Guinea, and by the end of the year, Admiral Chester W. Nimitz was fighting back up through Kiribati (then called the Gilbert Islands). By February 4, 1944 Nimitz took Kwajalein. Two weeks later, in a surprise attack, Chuuk Lagoon—"The Gibraltar of the Pacific"—fell in the two heaviest days of bombing of the war. In June, the largest group of fighting ships every assembled, with a quarter of a million American soldiers on board, left the Marshalls for Saipan and Tinian.

The fighting over the Marianas was some of the most brutal in history. Thousands of soldiers died, on both sides. When it was clear the Allies would prevail, Japanese soldiers and citizens committed mass suicide rather than surrender. In November 1944 the Americans began bombing Japan from Micronesian airstrips, and in August 1945 the planes containing the world's first atomic bombs left from Tinian airfield for Hiroshima and Nagasaki.

BASES AND BOMBS

After the war, the United States Navy argued for the wholesale an-

nexation of Micronesia, but the Truman administration opted for a United Nations trusteeship, managed by the United States, and this came to pass in 1947. The Trust Territory of the Pacific Islands included what are now the Commonwealth of the Northern Marianas, the Republic of Palau, the Federated States of Micronesia,

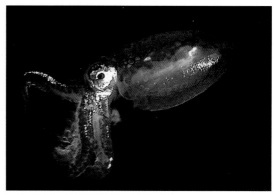

MIKE SEVERNS   Unidentified juvenile octopus Kwajalein Atoll

and the Republic of the Marshall Islands.

This was considered a "strategic" trust, and the United States immediately established military bases in the region. In fact, the trust was run by the U.S. Navy up until 1951 for most of the area, and until 1962 for Saipan and Tinian.

During this period the United States used the atolls of the Marshall Islands for atomic testing, exploding 66 nuclear devices in the area from 1946 to 1958. This program obliterated some islands, left others uninhabitable, and irradiated hundreds of Marshallese.

The most powerful was the 1954 hydrogen bomb called "Operation Bravo," with more explosive force than the total of all the bombs dropped in World War II. Bravo spread radioactive fallout over a 130,000 square kilometer area. The Bikinians are now back on their islands, but the effort required years of negotiation, and came with what

A group of these tiny octopuses washed up on the swim platform of the photographer's dive boat in Kwajalein. This character is about the size of a honeybee.

TAMMY PELUSO Phyllidia ocellata

This nudibranch is a conspicuous, and widely distributed species. It prefers shallow reefs, almost always less than twenty meters, and can often be found crawling brazenly out in the open.

many consider paltry compensation.

By the 1960s, anti-colonial sentiment was building throughout the world, and the United States government came under growing criticism for its Micronesian "colony." President John F. Kennedy began to explore ways of improving agricultural development and social programs to benefit Micronesia, but most of these simply made the islanders even more economically and culturally dependent upon the United States. The bureaucracies built to oversee improvements sucked up all the money allocated to fund the very programs they were intended to administer.

In 1966, Micronesia was targeted by the Peace Corps, and at the height of the program, there was one volunteer for every 100 Micronesians. This program did not work out quite as its designers hoped, as many of the volunteers sympathized with the Micronesian plight, and actually helped them litigate against the United States government (this led Richard Nixon's administration to cut the Peace Corps legal services program). Today a few of these politically involved expatriates still live here, some having married Micronesians, some developing trade, service, business and professional careers.

A FRAUGHT INDEPENDENCE

The Trust Territory came to independence status in pieces. The Northern Marianas left the trust in 1978 and opted for U.S. Commonwealth status. After a failed vote the same year for a unified, independent territory, the other districts also went their separate ways. In May 1979, the Marshalls became an independent republic, and the same month, Yap, Chuuk, Pohnpei, and Kosrae voted to join together as the independent Federated States of Micronesia. Palau's independent constitution went into effect in 1981. (The Trust Territory was not formally dissolved by the UN Security Council until 1990).

In its trusteeship, the United

TAMMY PELUSO Manta birostris Mi'il Channel, Yap

States for the most part respected Micronesian land rights, and today the land previously seized by the Germans and Japanese has been returned. In 1945, the Micronesians were a minority in their own lands, while today—with the exception of Guam—they are in the majority.

But overall, Micronesia has not fared well with respect to gaining full self-sufficiency. Decades of U.S. aid have also created an atmosphere of dependency, and distinct local cultures have been thoroughly crushed by stateside exports. American educators teach Americanized curricula; television networks broadcast reruns of American sitcoms and advertise American products; American and Asian canned goods substitute for seasons of hard work farming taro and breadfruit and fishing.

On some islands, domestic crop cultivation has almost ended, and people live on Spam, canned Vienna sausage, frozen beef, canned vegetables, and unbelievably in a place that exports almost $1 billion worth of fresh-caught tuna, *canned* tunafish.

THE MICRONESIANS TODAY

Although scattered across a huge expanse of sea, Micronesia has very little land mass, and its population of 532,694 (1999) makes it one of the most densely populated places on earth. The population is also growing fast, and is extremely youthful, with fully half under the age of 15. Outside of Guam, perhaps half the population is rural.

Racially, today's Micronesians are a mixed group, with notable Polynesian and Filipino influences. Eleven major languages are spoken, including Chamorro and Palauan (both Malay-based); Ulithian, Chuukese, Yapese, Pohnpeian, Kosraean, Nauruan, Gilbertese, Marshallese (all Micronesian); and Kapingamarangi (Polynesian). After many years of U.S. influence, nearly everyone speaks English, and most of the countries designate both English and the local tongues as their official languages.

Mantas are the great attraction of the Yap Islands. The reefs around this island group are broken up by long channels, which the great rays frequent, seeking the plankton funneled into the channels by the changing tide. The water in these channels is not as crystalline as at Palau or many of the other Micronesia sites, which of course is why the mantas are here. Modest visibility is a small price to pay for seeing these majestic creatures at such close range.

Almost everyone here is now a Christian. There are many denominations, most of them American Protestant. Mormons and various evangelical groups have been particularly successful here.

The literacy rate in the islands varies considerably, but educational opportunities are generally good. There are Jesuit schools, U.S. col-

Research on the commercial propagation of Tridacna, the so-called 'giant clams,' began in the seventies at the Micronesian Mariculture Demonstration Center in Palau. Since then, successful clam farms have been established in Micronesia, the

lowed their breadfruit orchards and taro patches to grow wild, but in others farming for personal consumption is on the increase. Pandanus (which has a rich and tasty nut), coconut, and areca palm and betel pepper are widely grown for domestic needs. Kosrae has a great deal of citrus and other fruits that are fully harvested.

Many islands, especially Saipan, Pohnpei and Kosrae, are blessed with rich, volcanic loam and showered with abundant rain. The occasional entrepreneur here will plant corn, vegetables, and other crops usually not found on these islands, and this produce is quickly snatched up by hotels and tourist restaurants.

Per capital gross domestic product in Micronesia is fairly high in Guam ($19,000), and decent in the Northern Marianas ($8,300) and Palau ($8,800), but very low in the Federated States of Micronesia ($1,760) and the Republic of the Marshall Islands ($1,680). Fishing, tourism, copra, pepper, *Trochus* shell products, and garment manufacturing are the major industries, but they are relatively small-scale, and often grossly mismanaged.

A CULTURE IN TRANSITION

Micronesians are shy (certainly by New York standards), and may even seem sullen when you first pass them on the streets. But once you smile and volunteer a "hello" their faces light up, and you will receive a warm greeting in return. This is, first and foremost, an island culture. No one is in a hurry in Micronesia. Relaxation is the key to enjoying your trip to the Pacific. Crime is rare, though it is cropping up more and more on certain islands (it rarely consists of anything more than minor theft).

The Micronesians, as a rule, are a family-oriented people who have learned that the key to their survival

MIKE SEVERNS Tridacna farm Majuro Atoll, Marshall Islands

Philippines, Australia, and Melanesia. Originally begun to replenish diminishing stocks on the reefs, the farms now seek to turn an ecologically sound profit by selling live, captive-reared clams to the seafood markets of East Asia, and, more recently, to aquarium hobbyists in the United States and Europe.

leges, the Micronesian Occupational College, and the Community College of Micronesia here. Many students study abroad in the United States or Japan, and there are now more educated workers than jobs to fill. A growing number of these are moving overseas, particularly to Hawai'i and California, where there are more opportunities.

In some areas, farmers have al-is to look out for one another. But remember that through the centuries their experience with the outside world has been one of exploitation and broken promises, and though they generally appreciate tourism and the income it brings, you will run across people who are suspicious of you.

The islanders, only recently in charge once again of their own affairs, are still in the process of sifting through the wreckage of the past 500 years. The Chamorros of Guam and the Marianas show a renewed sense of ethnic pride. The Chuukese now can look to their history as wide-ranging sailors and merchants with pride. There is a real effort to maintain—and restore—cultural identities through native dancing and singing, traditional craft work, and the passing down of traditional values.

This effort can produce some startling moments for a visitor. While shopping for groceries one afternoon on Yap, I glanced to my left to see a woman dressed in a traditional *lava-lava* with no top standing next to her daughter, also in the *lava-lava*, but with a Motley Crüe T-shirt on top. (Now that Yap is wired for cable TV, I can't help thinking that in this clash of cultures, it is Motley Crüe that is going to come out the winner.)

One of the most disappointing changes brought by modernization is architectural. Traditionally, most Micronesians used local materials to build their shelters, and even today many of the more charming hotels and inns are constructed of wood frames lashed together with sisal, sheathed in palm fronds, and roofed with thatch. This design does a fine job of keeping out the wind, rain, and heat. Often constructed on platforms to foil insects, these houses featured tall, steep roofs, which are brilliantly effective in attracting cool breezes.

MIKE SEVERNS Tridacna derasa at Tridacna farm Majuro Atoll, Marshall Islands

ROBERT RICKE and MARIA HULTS Tridacna gigas Palau

These houses are not often built anymore. Television has introduced "modern" housing to Micronesia, which means flat-roofed and hot. Now, expensive electricity is vital to keep the houses cool. A German expatriate I met in Palau built an immense traditional style house, raised on concrete legs and with an extra tall roof. The Palauans laughed at the old-fashioned construction when it was going up, but on hot summer nights these same detractors now bring their warmest blankets to sleep inside this natural refrigerator.

ISLANDS OF LIFE

From the unique mushroom-shaped Rock Islands of Palau to the flat, one-palm desert islands of the Marshalls, Micronesia is blessed with a wide range of natural beauty.

At least three of the nine known species of Tridacna clams are seriously endangered, despite being protected by law. The flesh of these clams, particularly the sweet adductor muscle, is highly prized, and the shells are used as basins or even crushed for building material. The two species above are the largest, and among the most endangered. T. derasa reaches a shell diameter of a half-meter. The largest known specimen of T. gigas, the biggest clam in the world, was discovered in 1817 off Sumatra, in Indonesia. The shells, now held by Arno's Vale museum in Northern Ireland, measure 137 centimeters, and together weigh 230 kilograms.

TAMMY PELUSO   Sosanhaya Bay, Rota, Northern Marianas

MIKE SEVERNS   Harbor, Kwajalein Atoll, Marshall Islands

The odd, two-layered topography of Mount Taipingot, at the end of a peninsula of the same name in South Rota, has earned it the nickname 'Wedding Cake Mountain.' The bay shown here offers Rota's finest diving.

Probably the easiest way to dive Micronesia is off a live-aboard or large day boat. Fast, comfortable vessels work nearly all of the sites including Kwajalein, as shown here.

High, forested peaks crown Pohnpei and rolling fields of vegetation carpet Yap and Guam. From all the islands, coral elbows reach far into the sea, turning the deep blue of the Pacific to a pale aqua. Beaches, cliffs, caverns and caves are scattered over the landscape, offering divers and hikers unlimited variety in their adventure.

Though beautiful in their isolation, island ecosystems are less diverse than those on the mainland. Before people reached Micronesia, the largest land species were monitor lizards, crabs, and birds. The only land native land mammals were bats. The horses, cows, pigs, deer, goats, monkeys, dogs, cats, rats, and mice you can now find on the islands were all introduced by people—some intentionally, the others by accident.

Plant life, though limited for similar reasons, can still be lush. On the wetter, more fertile islands, torch ginger, hibiscus, orchids, and hundreds of other flowers color the landscape. Some of the Micronesian islands are ringed with mangrove forests, which are important breeding areas and sources of nutrition for the offshore reefs.

And then there is the underwater world of Micronesia. These reefs harbor as many as 1,500 species of fish (see table opposite), and hundreds of species of coral. Sea turtles are common here, and whales and dolphins live in these waters. In Palau, if you are very lucky, you can still see the threatened dugong, or sea cow.

THREATS TO THE REEFS

Marine conservation is fast becoming a critical issue in Micronesia. In Chuuk the government does not seem able—or willing—to stop its people from removing unexploded shells and mines from the historic sunken fleet to use for making fish bombs. Yap is selling fishing rights to Taiwanese tuna boats that are removing fish at a rate well beyond what is sustainable. Palau is guilty of "sacrificing" reefs with reef hooks and anchors in order to allow novice divers the chance to participate in dangerous drift dives that yearly kill a half dozen tourists. Saipan refuses to stem the flow of sewage from visiting yachts and cruise ships. People with the power and responsibility to prohibit or at least monitor these destructive activities do nothing.

There is also some progress, however. Pohnpei has instituted a nickel-a-can recycling program that has almost overnight made the island virtually spotless. Kwajalein Atoll Development Authority has built a coral road connecting five islands north of Ebeye, to relieve the incredible crowding on that west

Marshalls capital. Yap has worked to control development in an effort to grow slowly, which should help maintain the island's precious cultural identity. Palau has banned spear fishing on scuba.

Palau has also set aside a fairly large and especially beautiful area known as Seventy Islands as a natural preserve and wildlife sanctuary. Though you will often pass it while motoring to a dive site, no boats or people are allowed within its perimeters. And on Kosrae, Madison Nena is working diligently on a plan to set aside long sections of the southwestern shore as a marine park. By prohibiting fishing and other destructive activities there, it is hoped that the reef will maintain its natural health. Other parts of Micronesia would benefit from similar efforts.

As visitors, it is our duty to be responsible in our own activities, and wherever possible to encourage—without arrogance or anger—the people of Micronesia to pursue policies that will preserve their

Micronesian Reef Fish Diversity

KNOWN SPECIES *by island group*

Southern Marianas	862 (756)
Northern Marianas	315 (287)
Palau Islands	892 (837)
Yap Proper	385 (370)
Ifalik and Ulithi	416 (413)
Chuuk Lagoon	208 (205)
Pohnpei	471 (445)
Kosrae	363 (351)
Kapingamarangi	437 (434)
Northern Marshalls	773 (762)

EXPECTED SPECIES *by region*

Mariana Islands	904 (817)
Palau to Yap	1,357 (1,223)
Eastern Carolines	1,149 (1,040)
Marshall Islands	875 (824)

*Parentheses note species found shallower than 60 meters.

Source: Myers, Robert F., 1991. *Micronesian Reef Fishes,* 2nd edition. Guam: Coral Graphics. Page 14.

world-class coral reefs. These are resources not just for future generations of foreign divers, but also for their own children.

Divers don't often notice damsels, but they can have a subtle beauty. I like the blue lips on this one.

MIKE SEVERNS Dascyllus reticulatus Majuro Atoll, Marshall Islands

The dorids are a large and colorful family of nudibranchs, and their striking, almost absurdly wild hues and patterns are always a shock—and joy—to encounter. This species is one of the most dazzling.

TAMMY PELUSO Chromodoris kuniei Micronesia, unspecified

TAMMY PELUSO   Pterois volitans   Micronesia, unspecified

This grizzled old soldier looks like he has been around the block more than once. Lionfish, even old ones, are very easy for a diver to approach. With their great ruffles of venomous spines, why should they be afraid?

This island, the largest and most developed in all Micronesia, is usually ignored by divers in a hurry to head to Palau or Chuuk. But Guam has its own cosmopolitan charms, and a fine hard coral—dominated fringing reef sweeps down the length of its western coastline.

Guam

ALTHOUGH ALMOST EVERY FLIGHT into Micronesia stops first on Guam, most divers never even leave Won Pat airport, immediately transferring to an "Air Mike" (the universal nickname for Micronesia's airline) flight to their final destination. This is unfortunate, because Guam has a great deal to offer the diver or adventure tourist.

This island is completely different from the rest of Micronesia. From Agana to Asan, Guam is a little piece of America, with ultra-modern high-rise hotels, sprawling beaches, espresso bars and hamburger outlets, luxury department stores, and even rush hour traffic. But in the south, the heartland of local Chamorro culture, there is only rough-hewn natural and historical beauty, ideal for sightseeing and exploring: jungles, waterfalls, sleepy villages, dramatic coastline, ancient churches, and Spanish ruins.

Unfortunately, the entire northern third of Guam is a U.S. military installation that is both off-limits to civilians, and very unpopular with the islanders. The long-running dispute over the navy and air force installations, particularly over land confiscated just after World War II, was settled out of court in the mid-eighties with a $39.5 million check, but not all Chamorros are happy with the deal.

There are practical reasons for beginning your Micronesia visit with a few days on Guam. As part of the United States, you can access your bank account here and take care of any last-minute U.S. business, and you'll be able to pick up any supplies you may have forgotten. Also, Guam is quite a resort area, particularly for Asian tourists, and if you are in the right mood, can be fun in a mai-tai and karaoke kind of way. And last, but certainly not least, there's some wonderful diving here.

FROM LATTE STONES TO B-52S

Guam is thought to have been first settled 5,000 years ago, by ocean-faring people from what is now Malaysia. Evidence of the aboriginal Guamanians can be seen today in the huge *latte* stones that can be found throughout the Marianas Islands. These stones, some as tall as seven meters, were used to support the huge houses of the elite. You will see the silhouette of the *latte* on flags, tattoos, doughnuts, and doorknobs in Guam, but the largest surviving stones are on Tinian, two hundred kilometers to the northeast.

The first European to land on Guam was Ferdinand Magellan, who arrived at Umatac in 1521. The encounter was not pleasant, and after the islanders appropriated one of his tenders, Magellan's men killed seven Chamorros and burned a village. This incident prompted him to rename the Marianas "Islas de los Ladrones"—"Islands of Thieves"—a name that stuck for four hundred years. (The navigator's karma caught up with him soon after his visit to Guam, when he was killed in a similar incident in the Philippines.)

In 1656 Miguel Lopez de Legaspi claimed the island for Spain, and the Jesuits arrived in 1668. Over the next hundred years, punitive colonial wars, syphilis, and smallpox reduced the island's original population of 80,000 Chamorros to 1,500. In the 19th century, Guam began to serve as a rest stop for American whalers, and after the Spanish–American War of 1898, the island was "purchased" by the United States and turned into a naval base. In 1941, two days after the surprise attack on Pearl Harbor, Guam's under-armed U.S. Naval forces surrendered to Japan.

Renamed Omiyajima by the Japanese, the island again became the scene of misery for its native population, particularly toward the end of the war. Twenty thousand Guamanians were put into concentration labor camps. Beheadings and torture were frequent.

In July 1944, 55,000 American troops landed at Asan and Agat and retook the island in less than three weeks. The Allies lost 2,124 men, with another 5,275 wounded; the Japanese lost some 17,000. After the war, 200,000 U.S. soldiers occupied the island, and for the next four years the military held war crimes trials there, leading to the conviction and execution of fifteen Japanese defendants.

In 1950, Guamanian residents were offered U.S. citizenship (and the opportunity to pay U.S. income taxes). Throughout the Cold War, Anderson Air Force Base was of critical strategic importance, housing the nuclear B-52s. In recent years, the military has drastically reduced its presence here, although the island remains the navy's communications center for the western Pacific. The future relationship between Guam and the U.S. military is unclear, but the islanders would seem to prefer an economy based on Pacific Rim business and tourism rather than use payments (up to $50 million a year) from the armed forces.

A LARGE, DIVERSE ISLAND

Guam, though just fifty kilometers long and fifteen across, is the largest island in Micronesia. The island is a flat, coralline limestone plateau, with steep coastal cliffs and narrow coastal plains in the north, hills in the center, and high mountains in the south. Like the other Mariana Islands, Guam is surrounded by shelving coral reefs. On the eastern shore you are swimming in the Western Pacific Ocean; on the western shore you are

DAVID LEONARD Agat Invasion Beach, Guam

swimming in the Philippine Sea.

Ironwood and pine trees, sword grass, palms, and ferns cover much of the island. Some 75 percent of the island is left to forest, woodland and other rough terrain, and only 11 percent is farmed. After the war, American planes dropped tons of seed to protect the war-torn island from erosion, and as a result, in the north the aggressive wild tamarind tree *Leucaena leucocephala* grows in dense thickets.

Lizards, snails, crabs, huge frogs and toads and a wide variety of insects (including the ubiquitous and damnable stinging ant) form Guam's typical Pacific island fauna, and these join pigs, chickens, ducks and other introduced domesticated animals. The only indigenous mammals are two species of bats.

The bird life of Guam has been decimated by the introduced catsnake *Boiga irregularis*. This animal, called the brown tree snake, appears to have originally found its way to Guam aboard a packet ship or the landing gear of aircraft. Since the only snake found on the island before this was a small and inoffensive blind snake, the island's avifauna had evolved no defenses against an agile predator like *Boiga*. (Although mildly venomous, the rear-fanged catsnakes are not generally a hazard to people.) It is believed this snake has managed to gain a foothold in other Micronesian islands as well as in Hawai'i.

The U.S. government has set aside $1 million to study this reptile, and you'll notice ground personnel spraying and inspecting landing gear at the airports.

Guam's waters are not as densely populated as those of some of the other islands described herein, but are nonetheless rich. Green turtles, hawksbill turtles, pelagic fish and sharks of a dozen species can be found, as well as 756 different kinds of reef fish. Scientists have counted 325 species of coral on Guam's fringing reefs.

Guam enjoys a generally warm

Looking toward Agat Invasion Beach, off western Guam. There are several good shore diving sites off this beach.

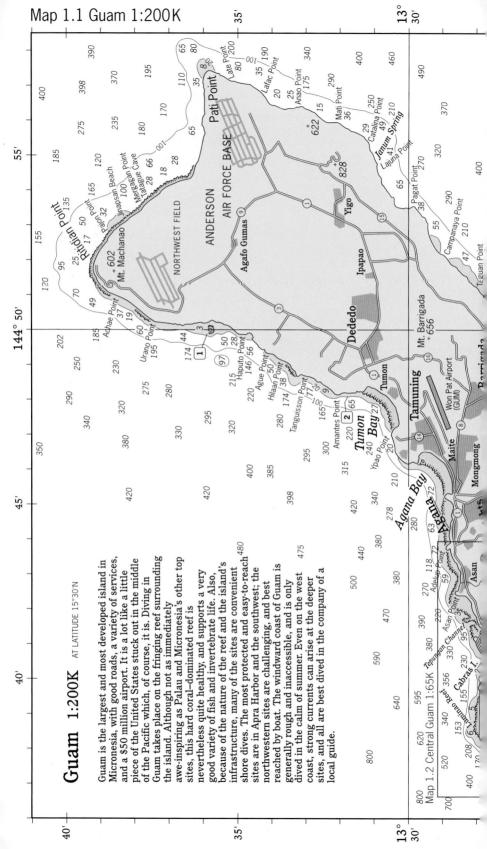

Guam 1:200K

AT LATITUDE 15°30'N

Map 1.1 Guam 1:200K

Guam is the largest and most developed island in Micronesia, with good roads, a variety of services, and a $50 million airport. It is a lot like a little piece of the United States stuck out in the middle of the Pacific which, of course, it is. Diving in Guam takes place on the fringing reef surrounding the island. Although not as immediately awe-inspiring as Palau and Micronesia's other top sites, this hard coral-dominated reef is nevertheless quite healthy, and supports a very good variety of fish and invertebrate life. Also, because of the nature of the reef and the island's infrastructure, many of the sites are convenient shore dives. The most protected and easy-to-reach sites are in Apra Harbor and the southwest; the northwestern sites are challenging, and best reached by boat. The windward coast of Guam is generally rough and inaccessible, and is only dived in the calm of summer. Even on the west coast, strong currents can arise at the deeper sites, and all are best dived in the company of a local guide.

Map 1.2 Central Guam 1:65K

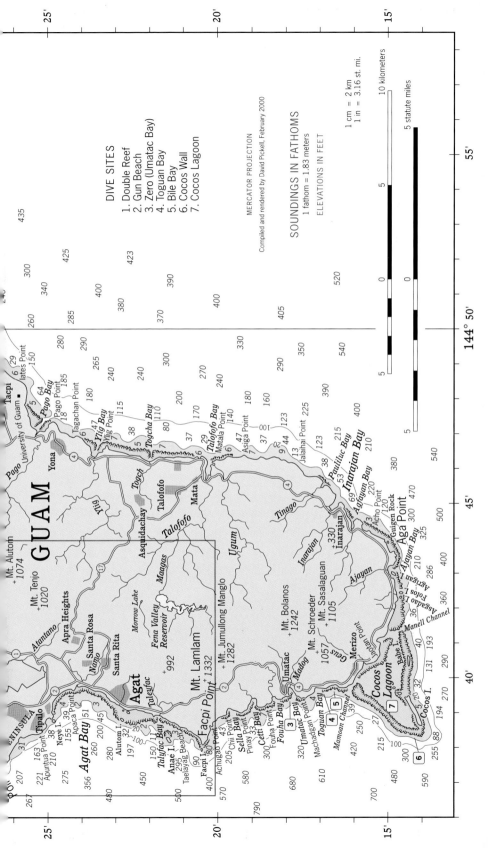

DIVE SITES

1. Double Reef
2. Gun Beach
3. Zero (Umatac Bay)
4. Toguan Bay
5. Bile Bay
6. Cocos Wall
7. Cocos Lagoon

MERCATOR PROJECTION
Compiled and rendered by David Pickell, February 2000

SOUNDINGS IN FATHOMS
1 fathom = 1.83 meters
ELEVATIONS IN FEET

1 cm = 2 km
1 in = 3.16 st. mi.

10 kilometers

5 statute miles

GUAM

Mt. Alutom
+1074

Mt. Tenjo
+1020

Apra Heights

Santa Rita

Santa Rosa

Nanso

Agat

Taleyfac

Mt. Lamlam
+1332

Facpi Point

Morrow Lake

Fena Valley
Reservoir
+992

Mt. Jumullong Manglo
+1282

Maagas

Asquidachay

Talofofo

Togcd

Yiig

Ylig

Talofofo

Mata

Pago

Yona

University of Guam

Tacpi

Pago Bay

Pago Point

Tagachan Point

Ylig Bay

Ylig Point

Togcha Bay

Talofofo Bay

Matala Point

Asiga Point

Jalaihai Point

Pauliluc Bay

Inarajan Bay

Agfayan Bay

Acho Point

Gugen Rock

Aga Point

Ajayan Bay

Agrisan I.

Fotos I.

Assadao I.

Cocos
Lagoon

Cocos I.

Babe I.

Manell Channel

Merizo

Geus

Mt. Sasalaguan
+1105

Mt. Schroeder
+1057

Inarajan

+330
Inarajan

Ajayan

Tinago

Ugum

Mt. Bolanos
+1242

Madog

Umatac

Toguan Bay

Machadgan Pt.

Mamaon Channel

Cocos I.

Fouha Bay

Pinay Point

Fouha Point

Cetti Bay

Sella Bay

Chiii Point

Achugao Point

Facpi I.

Taelayag Beach

Anae I.

Talujac Bay

Alutom I.

Apaca Point

Apuntua Point

Tipalo

Neye I.

Agat Bay

Atantano

PENINSULA

"PO"

This common, and beautiful commensal shrimp is found on a number of hosts. The coral on which this particular specimen lives is a Fungiid that has the largest tentacles of any known species of coral. The skeleton of this coral is nearly identical to mushroom corals of the genus Fungia, and it was placed in this genus until scuba allowed scientists to observe the live animal. Once they did, Heliofungia's dramatically large polyps, which, unlike other Fungiids, open during the day, necessitated the creation of a new genus for this animal.

and humid, tropical marine climate. The dry season runs from January to June; the rainy season, from July through December. Guam's rainy season has often been marked by ferocious typhoons—nearly 150 have passed within a few hundred kilometers of the island since World War II—and May and June can be ferociously hot. The winter, which lasts from November through March, is moderated by northeast trade winds, and the best time to visit would be December through April.

PACIFIC RIM TOURISM CENTER

Guam has a limited self-government that controls local agencies such as utility and port concerns, and almost half the population works for the government—Gov-Guam. Red tape and conflicting interests, and sometimes corruption have long deadlocked any progress and expansion in many industries. Most food and other consumables are produced elsewhere and shipped in, causing prices to be

ridiculously high. The large U.S. military population shops at the government-run, tax-free PX, and rarely contributes to Guam's local economy.

Tourism brings almost one million people and $1 billion a year to Guam, and is responsible for a third of the job market. In the Pacific, only Hawai'i gets more visitors than Guam. More than three-quarters of the tourists are Japanese, and most arrive on Japanese planes, stay at Japanese hotels, ride on Japanese buses, and eat Japanese food, making their contribution to the local economy less than it might otherwise be. A booming service industry caters to mostly Asian tourists (Koreans are second in number to the Japanese; Americans are a distant third). Oil refineries make up the bulk of local industry, with garment and component manufacturing filling in the gaps. The economy is relatively healthy and there are many jobs available, although pay scales remain low and housing costs high.

TAMMY PELUSO Shrimp: Periclimenes holthuisi; Coral: Heliofungia actiniformis Micronesia, unspecified

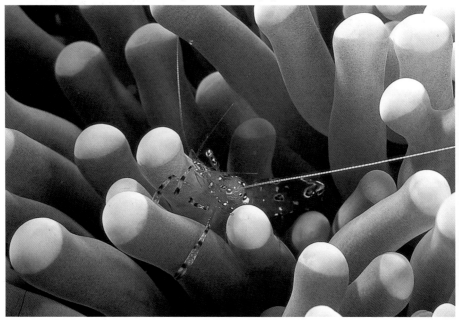

Two Tanks and a Pickup
(and a Cooler of Beer Wouldn't Hurt)

WHETHER YOU'RE CONTINUING ON into Micronesia or remaining on Guam, this island is a great place to adjust to the pace and feel of the western Pacific. Guam's abundance of beach-access shore dives makes it an inexpensive and hassle-free way to both do some exploring, and get some light diving under your belt. I did just this on my first trip, borrowing a pickup from my friend Lex Rathbun—professional fun-seeker, generous friend, and excellent chiropractor—and looping around the island with only a U.S.O. tourist map to guide my way. If you rent a vehicle and some tanks of your own, you can do the same thing. As an alternative, the local dive shops offer safe and enjoyable trips to all the classic dive sites, either by land or by boat, at a fair price.

The diving on Guam is not considered truly world-class when compared to Palau or Chuuk, but the visibility is excellent, and you will see some beautiful undersea vistas filled with many typical Micronesian reef fish and large pelagics. There are even some interesting sites for wreck divers, although not on the scale of Chuuk Lagoon or Kwajalein Atoll.

DECEPTIVELY EASY CONDITIONS

For a diver, water is Guam's greatest asset, but unfortunately, the beauty of these tropical beaches and deep blue seas hides many dangers. Do not underestimate Guam's waters. They claim as many as twenty people a year—this is not the place to be cocky. Most victims were oblivious to the strong currents lying beneath the apparently benign surface. Even Apra Harbor, which would appear from a map to be well-protected, claimed five divers one year.

Although the waves on the lee side of Guam do not seem large or rough, the currents sweeping past the fringing reefs are very powerful, sometimes enough to pin a swimmer or diver against the razor-sharp reef. Stay away from the reef edge, and *do not* make open-water entries directly over the reef.

The Air Force command has expressly prohibited all of its person-

With healthy hard corals, shipwrecks, and even a blue hole, Guam's west coast holds enough good diving— both from shore and by boat—to keep any diver happy.

nel from walking, fishing, standing, or climbing on any of the reefs surrounding Guam. At Anderson's Pati Point, water entry even by non–Air Force personnel has been prohibited by order of the wing commander.

Shore entry should be avoided by all but the most experienced divers at certain sites, including Shark's Hole, NCS Beach, Tanguisson Beach, Ritidian Beach, Asan Bay, Cabras Cut, Bingot, Agfayan Bay, UOG Beach and Pagat

The well-known manta is not the only free-swimming ray to see in Micronesia. The white-spotted eagle ray, found circum-globally in the tropics and warm temperate seas, is also common here. This animal has been known to reach three meters in wingspan, as big as some mantas, but most specimens are about a meter and a half across. Although it swims in the open, the eagle ray is not a planktivore like the manta. It possesses tough tooth plates, and is a specialist for clams, oysters, and other benthic mol-lusks. Aetobatus, again unlike the manta, also has a stinging spine. Many, like this one, seem to lose most of their tails through wear and tear. If complete, the tail is at least twice the length of the body. Like the manta, this ray is a fine eat-ing fish, although few other than the French like to hear this.

Point. Breakwater Tip, Luminoa Reef, Blue and White, and Mc-Gundis Beach can also be danger-ous. Scuba Cut at Tarague is open only to specially certified divers, and then only for six months of the year, and at full slack tide; it is otherwise off limits.

As elsewhere, experience counts when diving Guam. It is always best, the first time you dive a new site, to do it with someone who's familiar with it. The east coast of Guam can be dived only in the summer, and even then only with extreme care. The tides are extreme and the cur-rents powerful. The sites listed below, all on the leeward coast, are listed in order roughly from north to south. The precise locations of the sites listed below can be found on MAP 1.1, pages 36–37 and MAP 1.2, pages 42–43.

GUN BEACH

My introduction to the beach ac-cess diving on Guam was an excit-ing (solo) stroll into the surf at a beach named for the nine-inch can-

non whose barrel protrudes from the thick, brushy thorns edging the shore. Gun Beach is in Tumon, on the northwest side of the island, be-hind the lavishly appointed Nikko Hotel (if you ask nicely they will let you use their pool shower facilities after your dive).

The beach is a long strip of sand that sweeps out from the foot of Two Lovers Point. You can walk along Gun Beach for miles into the next village of Tamuning to Ypao Beach Park, where there is an engaging flea market and inter-island craft and culture fair. The scenery along this short trek is like passing by Newark, New Jersey, then Fort Dix, then Disneyland, then across the Pa-cific to the Ginza, and then Kansas, before finally you arrive in Holly-wood on the set of a fifties war movie. That's Guam, and I love it.

Ah yes, the dive. Lex explained the dive profile to me the preceding evening during happy hour at the Okura Hotel:

"They built that cable to facili-tate communications between all the

TAMMY PELUSO Bryaninops youngei (?) on Cirrhipathes sp.   Micronesia, unspecified

island nations in the Western Pacific. Follow that bastard out to the shelf. Then, work your way along a broken wall that drops a hundred meters. Lots of fish, an occasional pelagic; friendly cuttlefish and the occasional oddity. Used to go off the beach and pull five-pound bugs [spiny lobsters] outta those caves."

Enough said. There is heavy surge at times off Gun Beach, and you should check the tide tables before diving—dive here on incoming or slack tide only.

After diving, watch the sun set over the Philippine Sea from the Okura Hotel. They offer a bang-up happy hour between 5 and 8 where they serve *gratis pu-pus* (free munchies) such as sashimi and teriyaki chicken. Bee is a wonderful hostess, and no matter how short or how long your stay in Tamuning, she will never forget what you drink (even if you do).

DOUBLE REEF

With a borrowed truck and a pair of rented tanks from Coral Sea Divers (Guam has many good dive shops, and I recommend them all), I had already tasted a varied sampling of the diving available here. Then Bob Rogers (semi-retired University of Guam history professor, diving legend, brilliant conversationalist, and all-round good guy), Dave Furlong (esteemed editor of *Pacific Crossroads*, ardent fan and fact collector of Guam), Lex Rathbun, Tom (another chiropractor—always bring two, just in case) and I (smiling freeloader) sailed Bob's boat up the coast a few miles towards Pugua Point to a wonderful little dive on Double Reef.

We set out two long lines to troll for wahoo, one of the tastiest game fish in the world (skipjack and mahi-mahi can also be caught here). Bob piloted until one of his rods bent double, whereupon he vaulted the length of the boat to attend to it. A quarter of an hour later he pulled a 15-kilogram wahoo out of the blue.

As we motored along the coastline of Anderson Air Force Base, the

Black coral gobies are not rare, but it takes a good set of eyes to see them. Their ventral fins form a kind of suction cup, which gives them the ability to hang on to their host. Hiding on the black coral whips gives them a way to lurk safely a meter or more out into the plankton stream, away from benthic predators and right in the thick of the passing plankton stream. When approached closely, and clumsily, they are very adept at keeping the black coral strand between you and them.

Map 1.2 Central Guam 1:65K

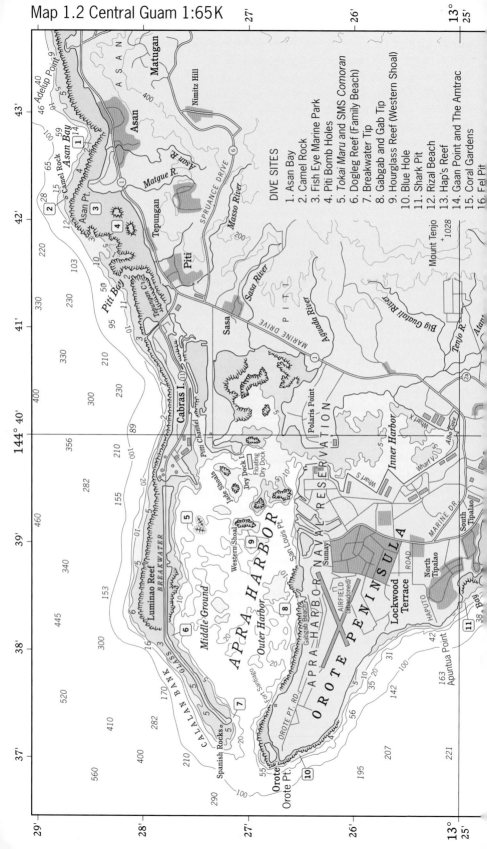

DIVE SITES

1. Asan Bay
2. Camel Rock
3. Fish Eye Marine Park
4. Piti Bomb Holes
5. Tokai Maru and SMS Comoran
6. Dogleg Reef (Family Beach)
7. Breakwater Tip
8. Gabgab and Gab Tip
9. Hourglass Reef (Western Shoal)
10. Blue Hole
11. Shark Pit
12. Rizal Beach
13. Hap's Reef
14. Gaan Point and The Amtrac
15. Coral Gardens
16. Fel Pit

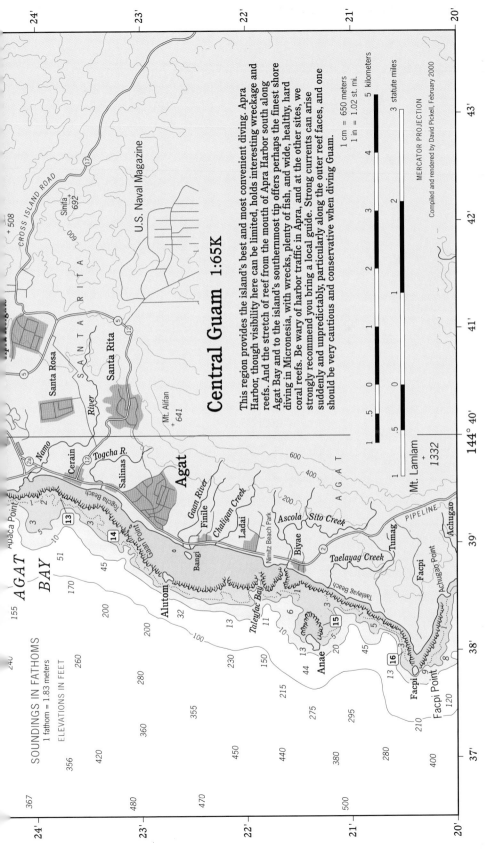

Central Guam 1:65K

This region provides the island's best and most convenient diving. Apra Harbor, though visibility here can be limited, holds interesting wreckage and reefs. And the stretch of reef from the mouth of Apra Harbor south along Agat Bay and to the island's southernmost tip offers perhaps the finest shore diving in Micronesia, with wrecks, plenty of fish, and wide, healthy, hard coral reefs. Be wary of harbor traffic in Apra, and at the other sites, we strongly recommend you bring a local guide. Strong currents can arise suddenly and unpredictably, particularly along the outer reef faces, and one should be very cautious and conservative when diving Guam.

1 cm = 650 meters
1 in = 1.02 st. mi.

5 kilometers
3 statute miles

MERCATOR PROJECTION

Compiled and rendered by David Pickell, February 2000

SOUNDINGS IN FATHOMS
1 fathom = 1.83 meters

ELEVATIONS IN FEET

AGAT BAY

U.S. Naval Magazine

SANTA RITA

Santa Rosa

Santa Rita

Mt. Alifan
+ 641

Sinifa
+ 692

+ 508

CROSS ISLAND ROAD

Namo

Cerain

Salinas

Agat

Togcha R.

Gaan River

Finile

Chaligan Creek

Ladai

Ascola

Sito Creek

Biyae

Nimitz Beach Park

Taelayag Creek

Tumag

PIPELINE

Achugao

Facpi

Facpi Point

Achugao Point

Taelayag Beach

Anae

Taleyfac Bay

Bangi

Alutom

Apaca Point

Togcha beach

Gaan Point

Mt. Lamlam
+ 1332

Mt. Alifan

largest in the world, we savored the welcome view of the most unpeopled area of the island.

For security reasons, the upper third of the island is still inaccessible by land, though, curiously, the U.S. Air Force doesn't prohibit boat landings on their territory. If you're lucky enough to have access to a boat during your stay, there are many unspoiled beaches and fascinating hikes in this area.

Then, we noticed a thousand shades of blue in the water and dropped anchor behind Double Reef. As the name implies, the reef has two spines which run roughly parallel in water three to fifteen meters deep. Interspersed among the coral heads are wide sand flats fringed by small caves, where lobster and reef fish thrive. Along the perimeter of these sand fingers is a wall of coral so thick and varied that the many species have actually grown into and over one other.

We saw several large grouper, some octopus and a reef shark who followed me for a short time before heading back into deeper water. There is a bit of surge here, but this was a satisfying dive, and I highly recommend the site.

SOUTH OF TAMUNING

Next, I headed south out of Tamuning, having added to my inventory a local dive map and the expert direction of another diving legend, Pete Peterson of the Micronesian Diver's Association (MDA), whose advice, followed closely, assured me three days of consistently interesting and safe shore diving along the entire coast of Guam.

The dive at RIZAL BEACH, in Agat, is reached via an old boat ramp and its attendant channel. At a maximum depth of 15 meters, this spot can be a bit mundane, but many divers have seen eagle rays and mantas here in the early morning. Rizal is considered more satisfying as a night dive. The bay, well protected from ocean currents, is normally calm.

Although many of Guam's shore entries have been widely ex-

The ribbon eel is certainly the most graceful of the morays, and these strange, gulping, fragile-looking creatures are always a pleasure to encounter. As juveniles they are black and yellow, and don't acquire the blue until they become sexually mature. The amount of yellow in the adult eels varies, and some are almost completely bright yellow. These animals appear as delicate as flowers, but the lavish color and frills on their nose and chin seem to be designed as a distracting disguise, and they are are as effective as other morays at snatching up passing fish.

TAMMY PELUSO   Rhinomuraena quaesita   Micronesia, unspecified

plored, AGAT BAY, off Agat Village, is often overlooked. I shadowboxed a small octopus and sparred with some of the many clownfish and spotted damsels who guarded the large anemones flourishing on this open reef.

Down the coast a few miles (and also infrequently dived), are a Japanese bunker and cannon marking AGAT INVASION BEACH. At a maximum depth of ten meters, above a king-sized bed of staghorn coral teeming with reef fish, you'll see acres of schooling snapper.

This is one of many dives in Guam where you will have a chance to encounter leftover ordnance and artifacts. Please note that some of these shells are still live, and even after decades of neglect can and occasionally do explode. Do not even touch them.

GAAN POINT and THE AMTRAC, TOGUAN BAY, BILE BAY (pronounced like "Billy"), UMATAC (where there is a Japanese Zero), and COCOS LAGOON are other wonderful shore entries offering easy access and safe, yet engaging diving.

DAVID LEONARD   Agana Beach, Guam

DAVID LEONARD   Dog casualties of war monument, Guam

FISH EYE MARINE PARK

Newly built, and long controversial, this is an underwater conservatory built right in the middle of Piti Bay. There are those, I suppose, who prefer to stay dry when they explore the underwater world. The park is connected to the shore by a long boardwalk. Fish Eye Marine Park is of only passing interest to the dive community, though a great deal of work was done to repair the coral and keep the fish happy, so that visitors would at least have something to see.

PITI BOMB HOLES

In the village of Piti, just north of Apra Harbor (near MDA), these "bomb holes" are remnants of collapsed caves, and not collateral damage from World War II. They can be seen easily from the road, as the water changes from turquoise to circles of deep and even deeper blue. Wade or snorkel to the pits, then dive down to a 15-meter maximum depth.

The craters are fascinating, and filled with a lots of of fish, many of which have become quite tame and expect handouts. Soft corals, anemones and hard corals offer shelter to morays, octopus and reef fish, including Moorish idols, butterflyfish and lionfish.

Be prepared for some drastic thermoclines here. Stay in the lagoon and away from the reef, and be wary during windy or rainy weather conditions, which can bring tricky currents. Piti, protected and interesting, makes an excellent night dive.

Agana Beach is just a couple of kilometers from the airport. This is the first part of Micronesia that most people encounter.

A monument to the twenty-five dogs lost by the Marines on Guam. Note the names—an interesting, but not in every case pleasant, reminder of the America of 1944.

APRA HARBOR

At the mouth of Apra Harbor is the island's ultimate "industrial" dive: BREAKWATER TIP. The path down to the water is charmingly enigmatic, and you must be alert and agile as you descend over the truck-sized boulders that stud the cliff. It's not as bad as it sounds, but when I told Lex that I left his truck parked on the access road, he was genuinely annoyed. The site is apparently famous for vandals. He chalked my mistake up to the ignorance of a visitor, but now you know better.

This isn't a great dive, but there are many varieties of fish and hardy coral along the banks of the channel. Nearby, a similar, but easier dive can be had at DOGLEG REEF, about a mile or two down the breakwater.

The harbor bottom is carpeted with ammunition casings, unexploded shells, armor, and most of all, Spam cans. Guam is considered the Spam capital of the world, although there is a lot of competition for this honor throughout the Pacific Islands. Apparently, Guamanians became fond of the GI's ration during the war, and grew so addicted to it that they neglected their breadfruit and yam plantations. There is a Spam sculpture contest here every year, and 1993's winner carved his block of canned pork shoulder and ham into a miniature bust of Elvis.

Boat dives inside Apra Harbor are enjoyable and include two wrecks. The *Tokai Maru*, a sunken 150-meter Japanese freighter that was downed by torpedo in 1943, and the SMS *Cormoran*. In a curious twist of fate, the *Tokai Maru*, now at 25 meters, sank right on top the *Cormoran*, which lies on its starboard side in 25–45 meters. A local T-shirt proclaims this "The only dive in the world where you can visit two wrecks from two different wars!" At night, beautiful golden-crowned *Tubastrea* corals blossom here.

Penetration of either of these wrecks is strongly discouraged, and there is little to see inside. Several people have died trying to do so. Even without entering the wrecks, you should closely monitor your depth and time when diving these sites.

The harbor floor is a vast bowl of fine sand and volatile mud, so be very careful not to stir up the bottom. It can be extremely disorienting here. It is also important to note that while most of Guam's shipwrecks are not yet protected by law, it is up to us as the only visitors to these international treasures to ensure that these fragile memorials are left intact. Don't scavenge.

Sadly, Herb Ward, the man who discovered this interesting wreck, drowned here in 1975 during one of his many, many return trips.

GABGAB AND GAB TIP

Well inside Apra Harbor and thus protected, Gabgab is a lovely dive on a reef bed that starts in five meters and slopes out to more than 35 meters. You can enter here from the beach, or by boat. Beautiful coral growth including a large bed of table corals decorate one vista; large crevices and coral shelves offer hiding places for hawksbill turtles, which camouflage well against the algae-dominated reef. A small cave is home to several large pelagics and shimmering sweepers. Look for lots of interesting little creatures among the coral heads. The current here is generally light or absent.

BLUE HOLE

Just south of the tip of Orote Peninsula, you'll see the deep blue hole just behind a large marker buoy. Often a dive boat or two are also around to mark the spot. Here there is a naturally formed tunnel that cuts into a sloping reef at 20 meters, and exits at 40 meters and again at 100 meters (I recommend using the first one). Visibility is excellent, and the light pierces the water down to 60 meters.

When you emerge from the tunnel onto the outer wall, look immediately for large tuna, rays and sharks. At night, you're sure to see flashlight fish here (grab onto a rock and keep your light off for a few minutes). Watch out for the strong current that can sometimes arise.

SHARK PIT

There are no sharks here, at least when I visited, but plenty of abandoned military equipment. This is a boat dive off the northern point of Tipalao Bay, on the outside of the Orote Peninsula. Among some of the garbage that's been dumped here over the years are Amtracs and rusted steel that offer cover to lionfish, schools of silver sweepers, humphead parrotfish, and larger predators.

HAP'S REEF

Usually calm, the reef starts in seven meters of water and drops to about 20 meters. This is a fun boat dive among tame reef fish who will expect a handout. Although spearfishing is legal at any site on Guam, a gentlemen's agreement exists at Hap's, where the tame fish have become the attraction. Many sea anemones with clownfish cling to the rocks, while a confetti of small tropicals swirls around them.

CORAL GARDENS

This site, on a reef growing out from the eastern flank of little Anae Island, south of Agat, requires a boat ride. Coral pillars, sandy flats, and blocks of healthy coral reef all make this site interesting. Sleeping reef whitetips and other reef sharks seek cover in the varied terrain, while morays, lionfish, large shells

and soldierfish feed on the bluffs. I've had dolphin come in close here—perhaps they feel particularly comfortable in the calm, protected waters of this clear lagoon.

MANY POSSIBILITIES

The west coast of Guam is literally packed with dive sites. Other spots to visit include: EEL PIT, the

TAMMY PELUSO Octopus sp. Micronesia, unspecified

Japanese Zero at Umatac Bay, ASAN BAY, DOGLEG REEF and HOUR GLASS REEF. Also interesting is Camel Rock, strewn with 500-pound bombs.

In the far south off Cocos Island, COCOS WALL, recently discovered, is a great place to see lots of pelagic action. It's a 20-meter shelf on the windward side, so it can often be quite rough.

With their lively eyes and an intelligence that belies their taxonomic status (a snail with arms), the octopus is one of the most surprising animals on the reef. Octopods are sensitive, and should be approached gently. Start by touching an ungloved fingertip to one of their very arms. Flirt with them.

The Northern Marianas are blessed with some of the clearest water found anywhere in the world. They also offer excellent diving, including this wreck of a Japanese freighter, in Sosanhaya Bay off Rota.

Great columns of pyramid butterflyfish are a hallmark of clear, current-swept seaward reefs, particularly walls and steep slopes, off the islands of the western and central Pacific. They like islands, and are not found on continental shelf reefs.

Rarely visited, particularly by American divers, these islands—rich in often tragic World War II history—are one of Micronesia's best-kept secrets. Visibility is astounding, and there are wrecks, caves, healthy reefs, and absolutely no crowds.

The Northern Marianas

THE COMMONWEALTH OF THE Northern Marianas is a chain of fourteen islands sweeping almost 700 kilometers north from Guam. Only the southernmost and largest islands in the group—Saipan, Tinian, and Rota—have any appreciable population and amenities, and a few of the northern islands contain still-active volcanoes.

Although they appear to be mere specks on the sea, with an elevation of no more than 1,000 meters, these islands (and Guam) are actually among the tallest mountains on Earth. The Mariana Trench, which parallels the island arc to the east, is the deepest in the world, reaching 11,033 meters at its most abyssal point (Mount Everest's elevation is 8,945 meters).

BALMY AND BEAUTIFUL

The Northern Marianas are fringed with coral and limestone ter-races that form their protective reefs. On the plains spreading down from Mount Tagpochau on Saipan, the limestone has eroded into excellent, well-watered topsoil that is thickly overgrown with the invasive wild tamarind *Leucaena,* called *tangan-tangan* locally, a tropical American tree planted by the military after World War II. Along the roads, the strikingly beautiful flame trees (*Caesalpinia,* a West Indies import) bloom bright red in the late spring and early summer. In places, the island's impressive basalt cliffs erode into black sand beaches. The western shore is buffered from the waves by a barrier reef which forms a broad and usually calm lagoon, offering optimal conditions for swimming and water sports.

From January to April, the weather is most predictable and inviting, but the Marianas are truly a year-round destination. Temperature rarely fluctuates from 26°C (78°F), though the humidity at times can be high. Annual rainfall averages 2,182 millimeters (86 in.) making these the driest islands in Micronesia.

The brown catsnake *Boiga irregularis* has been found in Saipan, but the invader has not done as much damage here as on Guam. Saipan's skies are filled with a dizzying array of beautiful birds, most notably the white tern—sometimes these are said to be the souls of the Japanese who jumped from Saipan's Banzai Cliff during World War II. The tasty coconut crabs and fruitbats have been heavily hunted here, and are now threatened. Guam's unique flightless rail, nearly wiped out on its native island by the catsnake, has been introduced to Rota in an effort to save it from extinction.

The reefs off Saipan, Tinian, and Rota are nearly pristine. The islands are outside the typhoon belt, and the coral is largely whole and unbroken. Though it has been the centerpiece of family feasts for many years, the sea turtle is still frequently seen. Sharks, especially juveniles, are plentiful, as are many pelagic species which come in close to shore to feed on the clouds of reef fish that thrive here.

Near the main docks on Saipan, there is far less life. Unscrupulous yacht captains empty their sewage tanks into the harbors. Factories, as well as the public utility companies also pump into the lagoon millions of gallons of raw sewage every day. Better to dive in more remote locations along the shores of northern and eastern Saipan, or better yet, Tinian or Rota.

ARRIVAL OF THE CHAMORROS

Saipan and the nearby Mariana Islands are believed to have been first settled 4,000 years ago by the ancestors of today's Chamorro people, and about 1,000 years ago a second wave brought in the Carolinians. The Europeans arrived in the 16th century, and in 1669, Charles II of Spain named these islands after his mother, Queen Maria Ana of Austria. The Chamorros resisted colonization for three decades, but finally were defeated and relocated to Guam. There they intermarried with Spanish sailors, missionaries, and colonists, leading to the mestizo Chamorro language and culture of today.

Afraid of losing the Marianas in the Spanish–American War, Spain sold the islands to Germany in 1899 for $4.25 million. The Germans did much to improve the infrastructure, building roads, improving land, and required the natives to farm both sustenance and export crops, particularly copra (dried coconut meat), which as an ingredient in soaps and cosmetics was then quite valuable in Europe. In 1914 Japan took over the islands. The Japanese planted sugarcane and fruit, and laid down narrow-gauge rail to connect the farms and orchards with the processing plants and docks.

Japanese, Koreans, and Okinawans immigrated to the islands during this period, and by the outbreak of World War II, as many Northeast Asians as Chamorros and Carolinians lived here.

WORLD WAR II

During the summer of 1944, in a horrific battle that left 3,500 Americans, 30,000 Japanese, and at least 400 Chamorros dead, the United States took the Marianas from the Japanese Empire. The Americans landed at Chalan Kanoa on the southwestern shore of Saipan on June 15, 1944, and in 24 days, swept north and east, clearing out the entire Japanese force. The Japanese forces were outnumbered two to one, and the U.S. forces sunk

DAVID LEONARD Maigo Fahang, Saipan

three Japanese carriers and de-stroyed 402 planes at the cost of just 17 U.S. aircraft. This lopsided battle has been nicknamed "The Great Marianas Turkey Shoot." Without artillery or armor, 5,100 Japanese infantrymen charged against Allied troops in suicide attacks across the northern plains of Saipan. All but a handful were killed.

The final holdout was at Banadero, and you can visit the site today. A pair of boulders formed a natural lookout for the Japanese command under General Yoshitsugo Saito, and using concrete blocks, the Japanese fortified and extended a huge natural break in the rock to create their command post. Today, there is a gaping hole where an American missile found its mark on July 9th, 1944. The anti-aircraft and machine guns still stand out front, and the wreckage remains. During the battle, being inside this post would have been like being in hell. Japanese visitors have left small offerings—photos, incense,

sake bottles—to their relatives who died here in the war.

Even though he could see all hope was lost when the overwhelming U.S. force invaded, General Saito was unwilling to surrender. After ordering his men each to "Take seven lives for the Emperor," he committed ritual suicide. Historian P. F. Kluge, in his *The Edge of Paradise*, describes the horror of this period well:

"Japanese died by the thousands on Saipan, thirty thousand in all. They died on the invasion beaches, in trenches and bunkers, they died in the rubble of Garapan and Chalan Kanoa, they died in the ravines and gullies that lead up to Mount Tagpochau. The battle lost, invaders pressing north, they still died. They were incinerated by flame throwers, they were entombed in blasted shut caves, they committed hara-kiri in bunkers and command posts. Toward the end, they poured down out of the hills, onto the plains of Tanapag and San

This little island, in Fañonchuluyar Bay off northeast Saipan, is a seabird rookery, hence its name, 'Bird Island.' The dive site called The Grotto lies just off the far point in the photo.

Map 2.1 The Mariana Islands 1:4M

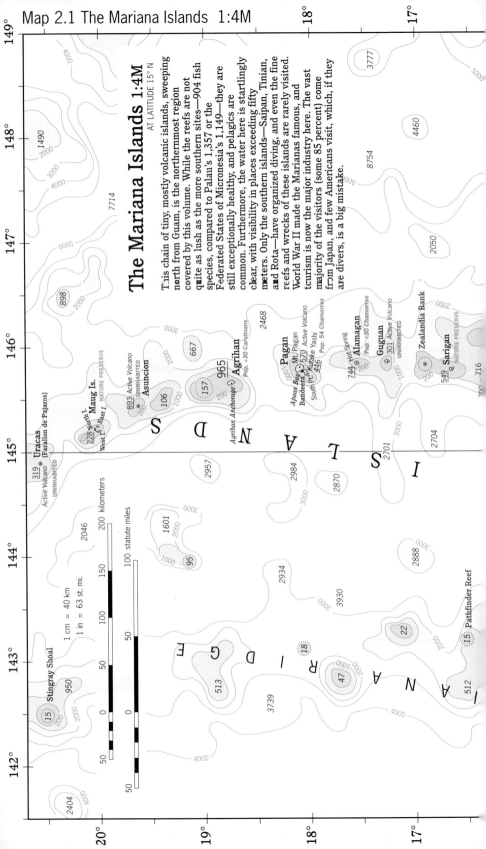

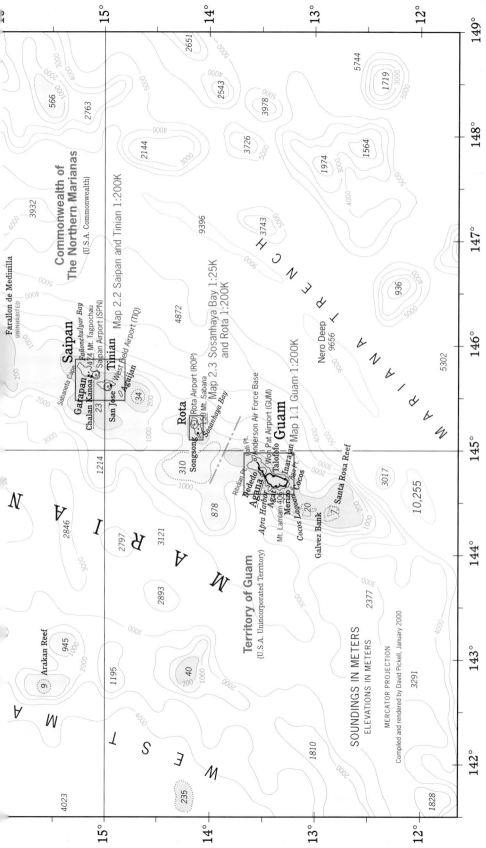

Commonwealth of
The Northern Marianas
(U.S.A. Commonwealth)

Farallon de Medinilla
UNINHABITED

Saipan
Flores
Garapan
Chalan Kanoa
San Jose
Tinian
West Field Airport (TIQ)
Fañonchuluyan Bay
Mt. Tagpochau
Saipan Airport (SPN)
Sabaneta Cape
Aguijan

Map 2.2 Saipan and Tinian 1:200K

Rota
Songsong
Rota Airport (ROP)
Mt. Sabana
Sosanhaya Bay

Map 2.3 Sosanhaya Bay 1:25K
and Rota 1:200K

Guam
Anderson Air Force Base
Ritidian Pt.
Pati Pt.
Dededo
Agana
Apra Harbor
Agat
Won Pat Airport (GUM)
Mt. Lamlam
Talofofo
Merizo
Inarajan
Cocos Lagoon
Cocos
Galvez Bank
Santa Rosa Reef

Map 1.1 Guam 1:200K

Territory of Guam
(U.S.A. Unincorporated Territory)

MARIANA TRENCH

Nero Deep
9656

Arakan Reef

SOUNDINGS IN METERS
ELEVATIONS IN METERS

MERCATOR PROJECTION
Compiled and rendered by David Pickell, January 2000

M A R I A N A

W E S T   M A

TAMMY PELUSO Last Japanese Command Post, Saipan

DAVID LEONARD Last Japanese Command Post, Saipan

The Last Command Post of the Japanese forces on Saipan, in the far north of the island near Puntan Sabaneta, is now a tourist attraction. At this site in the summer of 1944, with American troops at Chalan Kanoa, General Yoshitsugo Saito instructed his remaining men to each kill seven enemy soldiers. Then, to make sure his command sunk in, he committed ritual suicide. Although the Japanese could not defeat the Americans, the general's instructions were taken to heart. Of 30,000 Japanese soldiers on Saipan, only 600 survived, many committing suicide rather than being taken by the Allies.

Roque, armed with guns and clubs, a human-wave banzai charge, right out of the movies. At the last, they died jumping off cliffs, eight hundred feet, the biggest mass suicide till Jim Jones dispensed Kool-Aid in Guyana."

The Japanese did not formally surrender until December 1, 1945, when Colonel Sakae Oba, along with 45 troops, presented his sword to Colonel Scott of the U.S. Marines. Oba was "The Last Samurai," and his little band had for 16 months waged an effective guerrilla war against the occupying force. The surrender is fabled for the respect that was shown to Oba.

These islands were vital to the American effort in the Pacific as a launching pad for the invasion of Japan. Every hour, one hundred and sixty B-29 bombers took off from

Tinian's North Field for the ten-hour flight to Japan, where they caused widespread devastation. Finally, in August 1945, the *Enola Gay* marked the dawn of the atomic age—and the beginning of the Cold War—when it departed Tinian for Hiroshima with the bitter fruit of the Manhattan Project in its bay.

After the War ended, in 1947, all of formerly Japanese-held Micronesia became part of the U.S. Trust Territory of the Pacific Islands. In 1975 the Northern Marianas, through a popular vote, left the Trust Territory to became a U.S. Commonwealth, like Puerto Rico, trading military access for U.S. citizenship and monetary aid, including medical, welfare, retirement and educational programs.

VISITING SAIPAN

Saipan breathes of its past everywhere you look, but being the business, government, and tourism capital of the Northern Marianas, the island—with 45,000 hardworking and friendly residents—is also a vital part of the present.

Saipan, like Guam, has amenities like ATM machines, metropolitan shopping centers, and full-service luxury hotels. While taxis, tour guides and buses made a car rental not strictly necessary, if the independence of having your own transportation appeals to you, you can rent a car here. Hotels in Saipan vary widely, as do the restaurants and night life, but I promise that you'll enjoy yourself immensely.

Children play in the fields as your taxi takes you north on Beach Road along the island's west coast, past the stately hotels and commercial activity of Chalan Kanoa and the hectic construction in Susupe, through quiet San Jose to arrive at Garapan, where most of the tourist hotels and activities are centered. Here you'll stop to check in before you explore the northern corner of Saipan (see MAP 2.2, pages 62–63).

Head north to Micro Beach and Charley Dock, where the pathways to the public amphitheater, museum, and dock wind past abandoned and rusted artillery. The road curves out of town past Capitol Hill and the old Peace Corps training facility, then through the Aqua Sports Club (with its alluring brewery). Three hundred rooms of the Nikko Hotel surround a water park and a mall full of high-end boutiques. Korea World, next door, is only minutes from the Last Outpost.

As you continue north into Marpi, you pass the site of the infamous Naval Technical Training Unit (NTTU). Here is where Nationalist Chinese, Indonesian, Korean, and possibly Vietnamese operatives, brought to the top-secret site in blindfolds, were trained by the Americans. This is also the area where Colonel Oba led his band of renegades. Oba returned to Saipan in the 1970s to aid the so-called bone hunters who were attempting to locate the remains of the Japanese who died here so they could be given proper burial.

Passing the memorial park, you will see in the distance the majestic, emerald face of Suicide Cliff. Here Japanese soldiers jumped 820 feet to their deaths rather than suffer the shame of surrender. Also at Banzai Cliff, on the island's northern tip, hundreds of civilian Japanese women, children, and men leapt to their deaths rather than face captivity by the Americans, who they were told would rape, torture, and enslave them. Families lined up single file, the younger being pushed by the older, until the father, after pushing the mother, ran backwards so he would not know which would be his last step over the ridge. Some families were seen huddling around hand grenades, waiting for the father to pull the pin. Many were buried by

the Americans in mass graves dug along these cliffs. The remains of others were either repatriated to Japan or cremated many years later in memorial services.

DON'T MISS TINIAN

This beautiful, windswept island lies just five kilometers south of Saipan. A long surface interval be-

TAMMY PELUSO Sosanhaya Bay, Rota

tween dives will afford you ample time to take a quick, enjoyable tour, but it will take much more than this to understand this island's dark mysteries. From Tinian's plains, the *Enola Gay* and hundreds of other B-29 Flying Fortresses took off for Hiroshima, Nagasaki and the rest of Japan, ten hours to the north and west. The pits from which the bombs were loaded into

Sunset in Rota. The Northern Marianas are blessed by the sunniest climate in all of Micronesia.

Mystery of the Cannon

I WAS IN SAIPAN, IN A FIELD IN SAN ROQUE, ADJA-
cent to the Nikko Hotel. Offshore the wind was
blowing, and the clouds were tall and snow white
in the sky. Standing in this place, a newfound
friend told me an intriguing story:

*When I was a little boy, my grandfather told
me that when he was little, he would stand here,
watching his family's cows in the pasture by the
ocean. One day, he saw some German soldiers
landing a small wooden rowboat on the shore.*

*The officer stepped onto the beach and ordered
the men to a small clearing; two of them were carrying what looked to be a very heavy box. Some of
the men were carrying shovels and another
shouldered a rifle. Grandfather left his small herd
of cows and crept closer, hiding behind a rock to
watch. There he saw the men dig two holes, about
twenty yards apart. The heavy box was placed in
one, and in the other, a cannon, carefully angled
so its barrel was aiming at the box. After replac-
ing the dirt, a bronze rod was driven deeply into
the ground.*

*My grandfather know the box must have been
important, because as soon as it was buried, the
captain drew a pistol and shot all but one of the
men, who appeared to be the captain's mate.*

*The two men left the site, and walked very near
to where grandfather was hiding. He heard the
captain say that the cannon pointed directly to the
site where all the gold was buried. They dragged
the dead into the brush, ran to the rowboat and
oared back to their ship which was lying to in the
blue water off the reef.*

*For many years, my grandfather spoke of the
buried gold, but no one would believe him, and no
one could check out his story because the land he
spoke of belonged to the government of Germany.
I often dreamed myself of going to see in which direction the cannon pointed.*

*Then, many years later in the 1980s, the
Japanese broke ground for their new resort hotel.
I was reading the morning paper with a cup of coffee, when one of the stories hit me like a brick: a
worker had found a cannon barrel while exca-
vating the hotel foundation, and was arrested
when he tried to smuggle it back to Japan.*

*I would love to ask this man if he ever noticed
which direction the cannon was pointing.*

the bellies of the flying beasts remain
and are marked with monuments to
the era. Tinian is peculiar; so quiet
it's deafening, so desolate it presses
upon you like a crowd.

The weeds Hawaiʻian planters
seeded to eliminate competition in
the sugarcane business now blanket
the island, but breadfruit, Pacific al-
monds, bananas, and coconuts also
flourish. Tinian beef is raised on the
Bar-K Ranch and distributed widely in the Marianas. The sea is as
clear as Russian vodka.

The ride south from Saipan
takes about an hour. Off the coast of
Tinian, the invasion beaches appear
tiny as you blow past in the skiff, and
it is difficult to believe that thousands of American GIs waded
ashore here, or died bleeding on this
sand. Strange altars dot the cliffs.

One commemorates a Filipino
man who drowned while fishing
from the high cliffs on the western
shore. Another, on the northwest
point just across the channel from
Saipan, was built in memory of eight
men who drowned here while
bringing a cow to a family feast.
These waters are unpredictable
and unforgiving, and should be approached with respect.

Along the western shore are
many fascinating dives—wrecks,
reefs, holes and caverns—and the
water is so clear, you'll never forget
it. Between dives, you'll want to
spend a few hours on island, eating
lunch and sightseeing.

Rounding the southern horn,
you pass the rusting hull of a large
tuna fishing vessel upended in a typhoon several years ago. She held a
full catch which, unsalvageable,
rotted. The acidic waste that re-
sulted killed fish for miles. On the
shore, just behind the wreck, is a
huge tuna processing plant.

Tinian's harbor is old, but still
navigable. It was built by the U.S.
Army Corps of Engineers to facili-
tate the unloading of millions of

pounds of ordnance transferred from ships to the B-29s.

With a touch of whimsy, the soldiers on Tinian named all the roads and features after Manhattan: Fifth Avenue, Central Park, Greenwich Village. Tinian's Fifth Avenue and Broadway run down the center of the island, each one-way in opposite directions. This was a precaution to eliminate the chance of a head-on collision between trucks that were, after all, transporting munitions.

Once ashore at San Jose, walk three blocks to JC's restaurant where you'll drink a very welcome ice-cold beer while waiting for your delicious sizzling squid. I've spent a lot of time in America's West—Arizona, Colorado, New Mexico—and JC's took me right back there in a flash. Here you might be able to find someone who can give you a tour of the island.

As you leave the fiercely air conditioned restaurant, the hot blast of Tinian awaits you. The air hangs heavy and still on a July afternoon, fanned only by millions of dragonflies and butterflies. Get a ride to the Bomb Pits, where "Little Boy" and "Fat Man" were loaded into the *Enola Gay* for the last trip past Mt. Fuji. Now the pits are planted with *Plumeria*. In San Jose, visit the huge *latte* stones that used to support Chamorro lodges, here called the Taga House.

In the thirties, the Japanese used Carolinian labor to cultivate sugarcane on Tinian, and remnants of the railway can still be seen. This was a fairly sophisticated Japanese outpost, and evidence of this period is everywhere. Even the post office retains its old Japanese sign.

THE CHARMS OF ROTA

Located about halfway between Tinian and Guam, Rota is a quiet and ruggedly beautiful island, instantly recognizable by Mount Taipingot, called "Wedding Cake Mountain" for its unusual shape (see MAP 2.3, pages 70–71). It is one of the friendliest places in Micronesia. Rota's main village of Songsong is a good place to expe-

The humphead, or Napoleon wrasse is one of the largest fishes to be found on Micronesian reefs, and specimens have been recorded with a total length (including tail) of 229 centimeters, or seven and a half feet. The weight of a specimen this size can approach 200 kilograms. In areas where these fish are regularly fed (a dubious practice, in the editor's opinion) they can become quite tame, but otherwise they are rather wary fishes, and with good reason. This species is extremely valuable in the live fish trade, particularly in Hong Kong, where its flesh commands $60–$90 a kilogram, wholesale. To get the highest price at market, the fish is butchered live, laid on a table and cut carefully to expose the still beating heart, so each customer knows his steak came from a still living animal.

rience traditional Chamorro life, but you better hurry, because tourism is about to sweep through this lush, idyllic paradise.

Although spared Saipan's horrific fate, Rota still has many reminders of World War II here, and some are quite interesting. Tonga Cave, filled with stalagmites and stalactites, served as a Japanese hospital, and is still used as a typhoon shelter. Japanese cannons and infrastructure dot the landscape.

Evidence of early Chamorro life exists here at the *taga* stone quarry, where you can still see huge *latte* stone pillars and capstones where their masons left them unfinished. Rota has one of the Pacific's finest seabird sanctuaries, as well as natural limestone caves, refreshing swimming holes, and long, pristine beaches.

TOURISM-DRIVEN ECONOMY

Since The Royal Taga, Saipan's first hotel, opened here many years ago, tourism has thrived here. The current total is something like 500,000 visitors a year, 85 percent of them Japanese. There are more signs around the island in Japanese than in English. How is it then that with the exception of Mañagaha Island, the beaches are still roomy and uncrowded?

Tourism has brought considerable wealth to Saipan and the Marianas, and the services and infrastructure here are well-maintained. But even though the Japanese spend $150 million each year, since most of the tours are bought and sold as packages through Japanese operators—including hotels, transportation, restaurants, and tours—a lot of this money stays in Japan.

The tourist industry provides 37 percent of the commonwealth's budget, and the Marianas receive $250 million in U.S. aid. Other than these, the biggest local business is the garment industry in Saipan. Few of the islanders will work in what are low-wage, sweatshop conditions, however, and most of the workers are visiting Thais and Filipinos on short-term permits.

The anemonefishes are perennial favorites with divers. The orange-fin anemonefish is one of four species found in Micronesia. It is rather catholic in its taste in hosts, having been found with at least six species of anemones.

MIKE SEVERNS Amphiprion chrysopterus in Heteractis crispa Kwajalein Atoll

Saipan, Tinian, and Rota

Where the Water is as Clear as Air

SAIPAN HAS LONG BEEN OVERLOOKED by dive travelers, and this is a big mistake. The gin-clear waters, wide range of underwater vistas, large numbers of pelagics, and reefs thick with fish make a perfect dive experience. Even further off the beaten track is nearby Tinian, with some of the most beautiful diving I've experienced. Again, the water is unbelievably clear. And at Rota, which is only a 20-minute flight from Guam, there are still many virgin reefs easily accessed via local dive operators.

All three of these islands offer pristine reefs. But if you are seeking a real adventure, and have the connections and time, you might want to head north with a compressor onboard. Anatahan, Sarigan, Guguan, Pagan, Agrihan, and the rest of these pinpricks on the map are almost never visited by anyone, not to mention scuba divers, and none has more than a few dozen inhabitants. Check with Ben Concepcion in Saipan (see Practicalities), and he may be able to arrange something for you.

Unlike most of the Micronesian region, June through August is the best time to dive in the Marianas. The rest of the year, diving is limited to the more protected parts of the leeward coasts of the island.

Saipan

In my experience, Ben Concepcion (of Ben and Ki's Watersports) is the only man who can truly show you the best of Saipan underwater. Decades ago, in the German days, Ben's grandfather quit his job on a whaler and settled on Saipan.

"My grandfather, like all the people here, was attracted to the fancy uniforms, guns and polish of the German soldiers, so they were made honorable Germany army," Ben said. "Every Sunday they would march back and forth on the beach and in the villages. One day, a warship sailed up to the island and flew the Rising Sun. Suddenly, no more honorable German Army."

This is Ben's short version of how Germany lost Saipan to Japan without a fight.

Ben was raised on a cattle farm on the site of today's Nikko Hotel,

Though not as rich in coral as the southern Micronesian sites, these islands offer empty, pristine reefs with rugged formations, lots of fish, and glowing blue water.

and today he and his lovely wife Ki run a large, but personalized water sports service from a kiosk on the beach right between the Hyatt and Dai'ichi hotels.

The sites below are listed in geographic order, running clockwise around the island from the northern point, and are keyed to MAP 2.2, ages 62–63.

BANZAI DROP-OFF [1]

Off the coast of the Last Holdout at Banadero is Puntan Sabaneta,

Map 2.2 Saipan and Tinian 1:200K

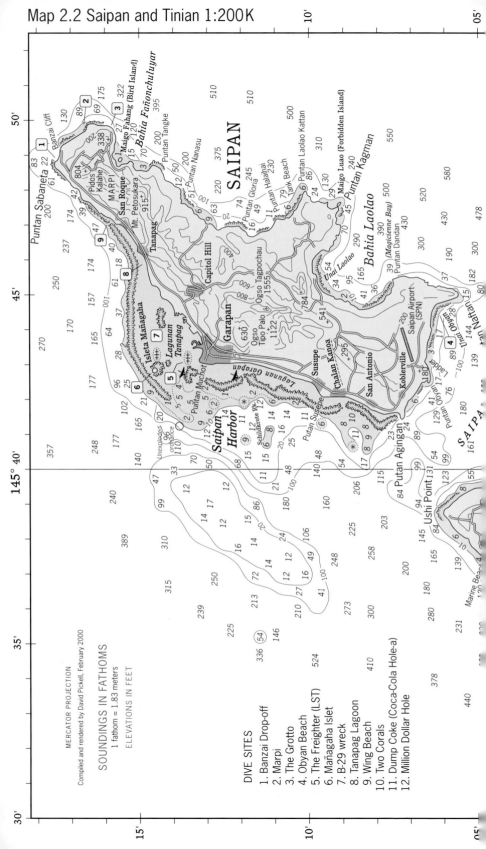

MERCATOR PROJECTION
Compiled and rendered by David Pickell, February 2000

SOUNDINGS IN FATHOMS
1 fathom = 1.83 meters
ELEVATIONS IN FEET

DIVE SITES
1. Banzai Drop-off
2. Marpi
3. The Grotto
4. Obyan Beach
5. The Freighter (LST)
6. Mañagaha Islet
7. B-29 wreck
8. Tanapag Lagoon
9. Wing Beach
10. Two Corals
11. Dump Coke (Coca-Cola Hole-a)
12. Million Dollar Hole

SAIPAN

Puntan Sabaneta
Banzai Cliff
Bahia Fañonchuluyar
Maigo Fahang (Bird Island)
Pidos Kalne
San Roque
Mt. Petosukara
MARPI
Tanapag
Puntan Tangke
Puntan Nanasu
Puntan Gloria
Puntan Halaihai
Tank Beach
Puntan Laolao Kattan
Maigo Luao (Forbidden Island)
Puntan Kagman
Bahia Kagman
Bahia Laolao
Unai Laolao
(Magicienne Bay)
Puntan Dandan
Capitol Hill
Garapan
Ogso Tagpochau
Ogso Tipo Palo
Isleta Mañagaha
Lagunan Tanapag
Puntan Muchot
Saipan Harbor
Laguna Garapan
Susupe
Chalan Kanoa
San Antonio
Koblerville
Saipan Airport (SPN)
Unai Obyan
Puntan Obyan
Putan Susupe
Schizkrate Rk.
Putan Agingan
Ushi Point
Unexploded ordnance
Unai Nattan
SAIPAN
Marine Beach

TINIAN

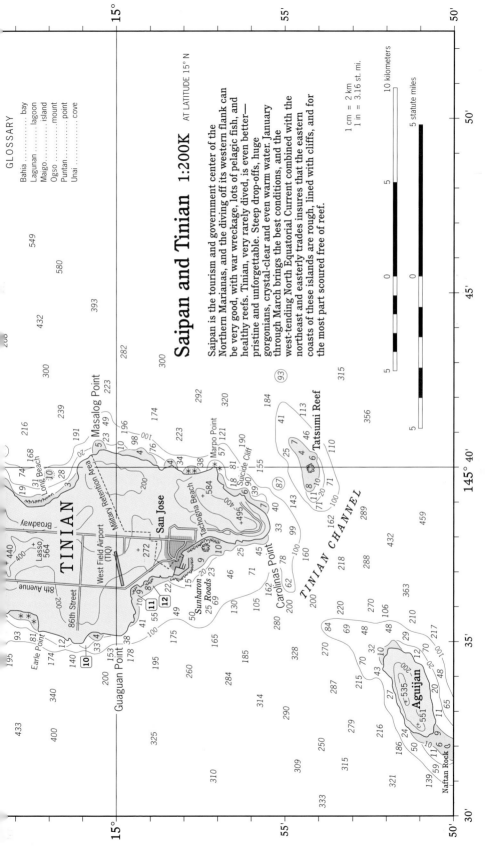

Saipan and Tinian 1:200K AT LATITUDE 15° N

Saipan is the tourism and government center of the Northern Marianas, and the diving off its western flank can be very good, with war wreckage, lots of pelagic fish, and healthy reefs. Tinian, very rarely dived, is even better—pristine and unforgettable. Steep drop-offs, huge gorgonians, crystal-clear and even warm water. January through March brings the best conditions, and the west-tending North Equatorial Current combined with the northeast and easterly trades insures that the eastern coasts of these islands are rough, lined with cliffs, and for the most part scoured free of reef.

GLOSSARY

Bahia .... bay
Lagunan .... lagoon
Maigo .... island
Ogso .... mount
Puntan .... point
Unai .... cove

1 cm = 2 km
1 in = 3.16 st. mi.

10 kilometers

5 statute miles

TINIAN

Broadway

8th Avenue

Lasso
564
440
400

West Field Airport (TIQ)

Military Retention Area

86th Street

200

272

San Jose

Earle Point

Guaguan Point

Masalog Point

Long Beach

Tachogna Beach

Marpo Point

Suicide Cliff

584

Sunharon Roads

Carolinas Point

TINIAN CHANNEL

Aguijan

551
535
200

Naftan Rock

The beautiful mandarinfish is locally common, but rarely seen. It likes shallow, rubbly habitats, sometimes with leaf litter and algae, although it can also be found in dense stands of lettuce corals. Quiet, shallow, dirty habitats around Palau's rock islands

known to divers as Banzai Drop-off. At the foot of the Banzai Cliffs is a reef elbow cutting deep into the sea. Visibility in excess of 35 meters allows you to survey what, a half-century ago, was a watery grave for hundreds of terrified and heartbroken Japanese.

At the time of the suicides, U.S.

TAMMY PELUSO Synchiropus splendidus Micronesia, unspecified

are said to be a good place to look. The fish scoot slowly about the bottom in search of small invertebrates, and are always found in pairs. Because of their modest size, shyness, and chosen habitat, they can make an infuriating subject for photography.

PT boat and subchaser captains cruised the shore beneath the cliffs, using bullhorns to plead with the Japanese not to jump. Some of the jumpers survived, including a woman named Betty who hid in a waterline cave until the Americans discovered and rescued her. She now lives in Guam.

"We were told the Americans

would torture us, and we believed this, since our own soldiers had been so brutal to the people living on Saipan; if your skin was light in color, you were told to face Japan, get on your knees and hail the emperor. Then, unsuspecting, you were beheaded with the captain's sword. So, we believed we would be treated the same way in revenge."

When diving the Banzai Drop-off, a strong current can sweep you along the reef, but if you descend quickly you will have plenty of time to enjoy the wall. Watch your buoyancy—the flow wants to roll you up and over as it nears the breakwater.

A huge Napoleon wrasse greets you at about 12 meters, but the plateau is primarily home to juveniles of hundreds of species. Pillow stars dot the wall in many different colors. Groupers, triggerfish, and other reef species stay in close, while off in the blue water, you will usually see a passing turtle as well as a shark or two.

On a clear day, the blue water sparkles, revealing abundant pelagic action—this is Saipan's premier site for seeing large open ocean fish. Before turtles were protected by law, this was a favorite place for local fishermen to harvest a holiday centerpiece. The turtles look much happier hunting for their own dinner. In the summer, you'll see them on every dive.

What you will also see at Banzai are vestiges of the tens of thousands of tons of leftover military hardware that the Americans bulldozed off the cliffs above. This site (like another dump site off Tinian) is sometimes nicknamed "Million Dollar Hole." The military calculated that it was cheaper to abandon the equipment than to bring it home, and of course leaving it intact was not an option.

Swim away from the wall for an effortless safety stop, and surface into waves that usually peak at about a meter, so get some air into your BC and be prepared to bob a little while the boat fishes you out. It's not difficult; just be prepared for conditions that can get a little rough on the surface. I would suggest that for the most part, only experienced divers attempt this site.

THE GROTTO [3]

Off Saipan's northeastern hook, southwest of Banzai, is the reason divers come to Saipan: The Grotto. This is shore dive—of sorts. You park your car in the lot and put on all your gear except for your mask and fins. Then you walk through the portico (it has "The Grotto" written on it) and descend 104 concrete stairs cast into the steep and rocky hillside to the water. These stairs were recently rebuilt—the originals having been constructed by prisoners sentenced to hard labor.

At the bottom is a huge tide pool, framed by a monstrous natural arch carved into the volcanic rock, and in the middle of the pool is a large boulder. There used to be a footbridge to the boulder, but a typhoon knocked it out. To get out to it today, you'll have to watch the waves and wait for the ebb before carefully stepping across the narrow gap. To the left is a smooth (and slippery) platform cut in the rock. Walk down the three short steps and put on your fins and mask. As you step into the pool, swim out quickly to avoid the surge that will slide you back onto the boulder. It's a bit tricky, but more a matter of timing than anything else.

Descend ten meters into crystal clear water and you'll be facing three large openings in the wall. It's better to have a guide here since the return trip in particular can be confusing (and thus dangerous). As you clear these arches, keep the wall on your left and continue along at about 20 meters. The floor will slope away from the ridge gently to a maximum of about 30 meters.

Even just a few meters down the wall is deep purple from encrusting coralline algae and sponges. It's gorgeous. In the arches you'll be attended by hundreds of reef fish that are actually a bit tame and always on the lookout for a handout. Large spotted groupers can often be seen here, mating in the summer

TAMMY PELUSO   Shoun Maru wreck   Rota

months. Clowns, butterflies, Moorish idols and the occasional batfish come in close to watch, voyeurs all. A jack or two sails by, as do occasional sharks. Young coral colonies are everywhere. There is a very large cavern here at 18 meters in which grow big yellow gorgonians and sponges. In the far corner here is a spindly black coral

One of the great attractions of Rota, and in fact all of the Marianas, is its extremely clear water. The glowing blue background in the photograph above tells it all. Rota has Hawai'i class visibility, sometimes seventy meters or more.

TAMMY PELUSO   Unidentified Calappid and Gymnothorax javanicus   Micronesia, unspecified

This box crab and moray seem an odd couple, indeed, but hiding places on a reef can be like apartments in San Francisco—unless you're lucky, or a dot-com millionaire, you're going to have to share.

tree that towers over the room.

By this point you are probably running low on air, so head back to the grotto entrance. As I stated earlier, it is best to use a guide here. But if you insist on being a cowboy, then be very careful that you've chosen the correct entrance—since there are several choices which can really foul you up. Be sure to look up to see the crashing surf above you. The generous visibility makes it sparkle brilliantly.

Upon returning to the cave, feel the surge, and get a sense of its periodicity. If you time things just right, it will gently lift you and practically place you back atop the boulder.

OBYAN BEACH [4]

On the south coast of Saipan past the airport are two beaches, Ladder and Obyan. The first one you come to is Ladder Beach. Skip this one, but just beyond, turn in and park. This is Obyan Beach. Here there is a large concrete Japanese bunker on the shore

which marks the optimal entry point for a dive. A sand bottom slopes out to 10 meters where the reef begins. The coral continues on a slope to about 20 meters.

This site is home to a phenomenal number of rays, as well as soldierfish, triggerfish, garden eels and parrotfish. Occasionally you'll see smaller reef white-tip sharks. The coral formations provide endlessly changing scenery, which keeps this site interesting. You can swim through all the cuts and tunnels. Bring a buddy, four tanks and a picnic for a fun, leisurely afternoon of shore diving.

THE FREIGHTER (LST) [5]

This wreck, in Tanapag Lagoon is almost completely destroyed. On top of the shot that originally sank it, it was subsequently used for target practice in CIA training classes. Still later, the government dismantled it further so no passing ships would hit it.

Despite its rough condition, the wreckage provides excellent cover

TAMMY PELUSO Puntan Senhanom Rota

for the reef fish, which in turn attract the schooling fish, which in turn attract the sharks and other predators. This is an excellent place to photograph resident lionfish, since the sunlight penetrates easily through the 15 meters of clear blue water. A few artifacts remain on the ship—bicycles, portholes, and the like—but it's been pretty thoroughly scavenged. Next to the ship are its engines. Have a look in this area for a docile adult turtle who calls this home.

MAÑAGAHA ISLET [6]

This miniature resort island is a lesson in the freakish economics of tourism. Despite that there are plenty of free, uncrowded beaches on Saipan, every day boats deliver thousands of tourists here, who each pay an admission charge before buying lunch and souvenirs, renting towels, snorkel gear, and water toys, and using the crowded beach and walking the short paths among some relic artillery, including a Japanese cannon rather ominously pointing west.

Other than a somewhat silly and very regimented beginner's mini-course (which can be sort of fun to watch) there is no diving here, although there are bits of a Japanese Zero, Betty bomber, and sub-chaser. Even snorkelers will feel as though they are in well traveled—even well *trampled*—territory. Unless you're with your non-diving family, skip it.

Diving, snorkeling, fishing, boat rides, waterskiing, and banana boat riding, are available at reasonable prices, but, snorkeling and tanning on the crowded beach are the main activities at Mañagaha.

TANAPAG LAGOON [8]

The west side of Saipan is bounded for most of its length by Beach Road, which follows the shoreline closely. At Tanapag, a narrow dirt road leads to the wide and sandy beach, where you can picnic, swim, fish, or just lie in the sun. The beach itself is actually the shore of a lagoon, formed by a long, long strip

The sea cave at Senhanom Point, on the western side of Rota's Taipingot Peninsula, is one of the island's most distinctive and famous sites.

of reef that acts as a breakwater. In this lagoon, people play among the abandoned and destroyed vehicles of war. Jetskiers slalom around a partially submerged tank; snorkelers hover over the ruins of airplanes and landing craft.

The brutal unwillingness to surrender displayed by the Japanese on Saipan was demonstrated here by an officer who, during the final U.S. assault, beheaded his men on the breakwater.

Only rarely deeper than ten meters, the lagoon is filled with interesting sites and productive natural cover for the fish who live here. While you may dive from the shore, boats will take you out beyond the limits of a comfortable swim from the beach. Coral grows thick and a white sandy bottom reflects abundant sunlight making everything sparkle brightly.

The *Suehiro Maru*, a sub-chaser, lies here waiting to be explored by sport divers. A dozen tanks, planes, bombs and subs also lie nearby. There is a large freighter, mostly stripped and salvaged, that is a haven for fish. Extending slightly above the surface at low tide, it's easy to spot and fun to explore. Be careful of the numerous jagged steel plates caused by bomb hits. Tanapag Lagoon is a rather tame dive, but enjoyable nonetheless.

WING BEACH [9]

At the point where the barrier reef protecting Tanapag Lagoon meets the shore of Saipan, a few kilometers south of Banzai Drop-off, lies the most northern beach in Saipan—Wing Beach. Here a cliff-line arises, heading north to Puntan Sabaneta. Enter the water at the beginning of the cliffline, descend to eight meters and then follow an easy slope down to 20 meters. Here you're over a short drop that leads to a small wall swarming with thousands of reef fish.

It's always different at this site. One dive will excite you with turtles, large wrasses, and jacks. Another will be filled with a full spectrum of reef fish. Look for a crevice in the

It was in the early 1960s that Austrian ethologist Konrad Lorentz came up with the term 'plakatfarben'—literally poster colors—for the strikingly bright and saturated markings of tropical reef fishes. Like posters, the job of these colors is advertising, and in the great American tradition, what most of them are selling is sex or violence. Only old, sexually mature big-nosed unicornfish exhibit the striking blue tattooing of this specimen.

TAMMY PELUSO Naso vlamingii Micronesia, unspecified

reef. Right at the mouth of this cut is a large rock pointing straight up, on top of which is a wide crater. It's an unusual feature, and this one displays a multi-colored halo of crinoids and coral.

Tinian

Only a few thousand people live on this beautiful, breezy island, its limestone plateau covered with scruffy vegetation and clumps of wild sugar cane. Its harbor and freezing plant make it a major transshipment point for tuna, but compared to Saipan, Tinian is a quiet backwater.

One reason for this is that the island does not have enough hotel and restaurant space to accommodate Japanese package travelers. Or at least, it doesn't yet. Some Tinian islanders, eager for their share of the money that pours into Saipan, have suggested building a casino and 300-room hotel on the island.

Not many divers have visited Tinian, and its reefs are unscathed. The water here is as clear as anywhere in the world.

TAMMY PELUSO   Amblyglyphidodon aureus   Micronesia, unspecified

TAMMY PELUSO   Amphiprion perideraion in Heteractis magnifica   Micronesia, unspecified

TWO CORALS [10]

This beautiful dive, off the west coast of Tinian near the terminus of 86th Street, can be repeated over and over again because there are so many ways to do it. The site's namesake is a pair of enormous coral heads, growing upward from 20 meters to within five meters of the surface. These are huge, and very impressive. Around these is a plain of hard coral, brightly illuminated in the clear water. Basically, just pick any direction and swim slowly; there is much to see in and around the boulders.

Swarming over the corals is a full complement of reef inhabitants, including lots of macro subjects such as shrimp, shells, crabs, tunicates, and sponges. Reef white-tips, barracuda, and other larger animals frequent this site. Triggerfish dig deep nests and parrotfish gnaw on algae and coral.

As you round each new vista, keep your eyes focused on the blue water in the distance for sharks and other shy pelagics. This is a particularly beautiful and peaceful dive. Gray reef sharks also frequent Two Corals, and on my first dive here I happened upon an enormous specimen. Also, be on the lookout for tiger sharks here, as they sometimes come close to shore when the tuna boats offload their spoiled fish.

TINIAN GROTTO

This site, sometimes called The Caverns, is Tinian's equivalent of the famous Saipan site of the same name. It is marked by a mooring, and you will need a guide to get here. Here, in crystal blue water, is

The golden damsel is a common fish on Micronesian reefs, particularly favoring channel walls and seaward drop-offs. This gentleman is guarding a batch of eggs, laid by its mate on a section of gorgonian from which the living 'bark' has been nibbled off. When guarding their eggs these damsels can be very fiesty, bouncing off your face mask or even giving you a nip if they can find some exposed skin.

The beautiful magnificent anemone has a curious habit of periodically blowing its column up into a ball and 'swallowing' its tentacles, which must be an irritation to its tenant anemonefish.

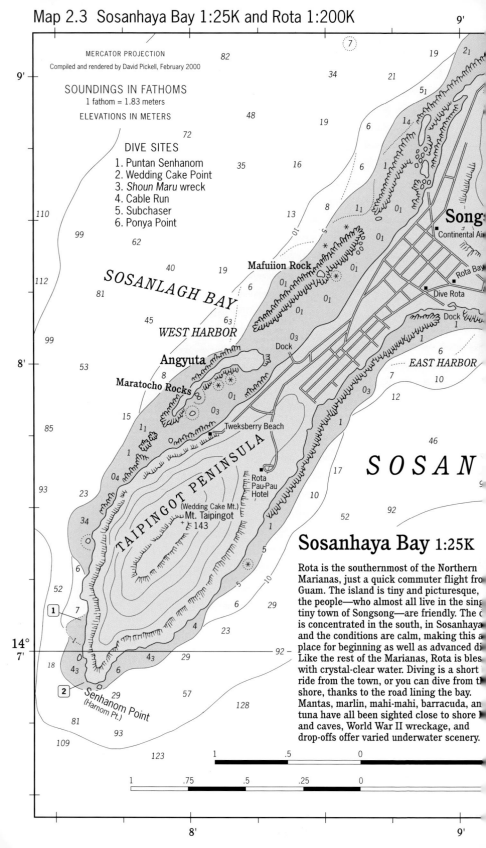

Map 2.3 Sosanhaya Bay 1:25K and Rota 1:200K

MERCATOR PROJECTION
Compiled and rendered by David Pickell, February 2000

SOUNDINGS IN FATHOMS
1 fathom = 1.83 meters

ELEVATIONS IN METERS

DIVE SITES
1. Puntan Senhanom
2. Wedding Cake Point
3. *Shoun Maru* wreck
4. Cable Run
5. Subchaser
6. Ponya Point

Sosanhaya Bay 1:25K

Rota is the southernmost of the Northern
Marianas, just a quick commuter flight fro
Guam. The island is tiny and picturesque,
the people—who almost all live in the sing
tiny town of Songsong—are friendly. The c
is concentrated in the south, in Sosanhaya
and the conditions are calm, making this a
place for beginning as well as advanced di
Like the rest of the Marianas, Rota is bles
with crystal-clear water. Diving is a short
ride from the town, or you can dive from t
shore, thanks to the road lining the bay.
Mantas, marlin, mahi-mahi, barracuda, a
tuna have all been sighted close to shore
and caves, World War II wreckage, and
drop-offs offer varied underwater scenery.

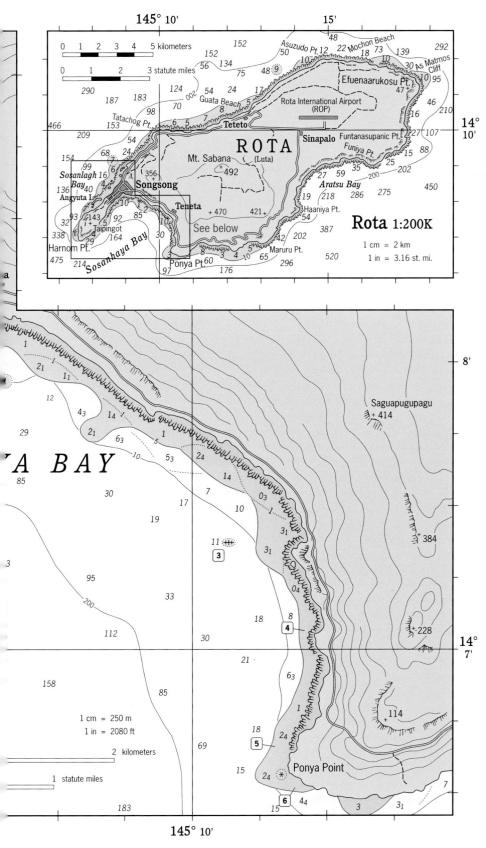

a path through a large archway that opens on a series of cuts into the reef. Two caverns, one at the foot of the mooring, one just to the south, await you.

The best one is the largest, with four openings. Swim into the "courtyard" which is naturally lit by sun streaming through holes cut over millennia in the cavern ceiling

TAMMY PELUSO   Shoun Maru wreck   Rota

The Shoun Maru, on June 23, 1944, had just finished unloading its cargo of ordnance and filling up the holds with phosphate when it was struck by an Allied aerial torpedo. It sank to the bottom within minutes.

by the waves crashing overhead. Millions of bronze sweepers flow through the openings; large lionfish float weightless in the passageways. Look for the many "gardens" of broken seashells, which mark octopus lairs. Lobsters peek out of crevices. Now and again you will find an air pocket in the cavern, into which you can surface. Please use a guide, particularly in order to safely manage

the second cavern. With all the available exits into the surf you can easily get lost, and possibly trapped in a rough cove. The words "scraping," "laceration," and "bruising" should all come to mind.

In these caverns and arches are many unusual fish and formations. The largest lionfish I ever saw—at least a foot long—waited around one bend; a thousand baby squid jetted through the shallows. Towards the back of the main cavern is a cave filled with brackish water fed from above. The water actually changes color here as you swim back and forth—it's quite extraordinary. You'll see big trumpetfish and many varieties of reef fish. Some seem eager for a handout, though you still don't get the feeling that many others have been here. Sergeant majors, goatfish, parrotfish, titan triggerfish, surgeonfish in schools of a hundred or more, and large schools of mackerel cavort in this wonderland. You'll love this dive.

DUMP COKE [11]

Halfway up the west coast of Tinian, above a semi-circular cove, is the former site of a popular GI canteen. The canteen served up cold bottles of America's favorite cola during the U.S. occupation, and when the thirsty soldiers emptied their bottles, they tossed them into the lagoon below, giving the site its name (it is also sometimes called "Coca-Cola Hole-a").

In fact, when the Americans left the island, they threw whole cases of unopened Coca Cola bottles into this hole. And, along with the no-deposit no-return bottles, they dumped a half-track, several jeeps, bombs, tanks, and a variety of other Japanese hardware. The wreckage scattered amongst all these bottles (and sea glass, of course) makes for a surreal dive. Most of the nearby rocks are rust-colored from all the iron in the water. Look for turtles

TAMMY PELUSO   Shoun Maru wreck   Rota

and rays who live among the twisted steel and green glass.

There is also an airplane here:

"An old person who used to work for me was telling me about an American B-29 airplane that he saw go down here," said Ben Concepcion. "We went to look for it. In those days we had a club, teachers and lawyers and other interesting people. We would try to find wrecks and we also searched for this plane. We brought a Clorox bottle to the bottom and marked where we started, and put another buoy where we finished, and swept a tight anchor line across the bottom.

"We kept doing that, and it was the third Sunday when we finally found it. 'This is the four-engine bomber!' we thought. The radios and the seats were all there, but then we noticed that the radios were all marked in Japanese. It was mistakenly called a B-29, but it's not. B-29s have twin fifty-caliber machine guns, but this wreck has machine guns with flared barrels. Later, my theory was confirmed by an old B-29

pilot whom I brought here to dive."

MILLION DOLLAR HOLE [12]

Like Banzai Drop-off on Saipan, this is another spot where the U.S. forces dumped millions of dollars of taxpayer money into the Pacific Ocean in the form of tanks, cannons, planes, and ammunition, rather than incur the expense of bringing it all home.

This is a great wreck dive with lots of photo opportunities, as there's lots of sea life and good visibility. Be very wary of anything that may look like ordnance—there are still unexploded phosphorous bombs here, and these are not to be toyed with.

AGUIJAN ISLAND

You'll see this mysterious island on the map, and it is visible from Tinian's southern point. In case you are wondering, nobody lives on Aguijan. During the Japanese occupation, Okinawan farmers had a schoolhouse on the island, just ten kilometers from Tinian, and today

Bicycles, a truck, and the ship's engine are some of the most interesting features of the Shoun Maru wreck. The vessel's hull fell away during a poorly planned salvage operation more than thirty years ago. The wreckage lies on sand, at 15–35 meters.

MIKE SEVERNS Carcharinus amblyrhynchos Rongelap, Marshall Islands

Gray reef sharks are found throughout Micronesia. More or less fixed populations can be found in deeper atoll lagoons, while nomadic groups frequent oceanic outcrops, the outer walls of deep drop-offs, and atoll channels.

Grays are very curious, and are often the first species to show up at the sign of any disturbance. They will often come over to investigate even a simple sound, like two rocks clacked together.

The species is famous for its elaborate threat display, and though not particularly feared in the Pacific, grays are worthy of respect.

Not all are as beautifully marked as this young specimen, but the species is easily distinguished from similarly shaped requiem sharks (such as the Galapagos shark) by the dark crescent on the trailing edge of its tail fin.

there is a camp there for troubled kids, something like Outward Bound. Although physically beautiful, there are no beaches here, as the entire island is surrounded by cliffs. The island is home to a herd of feral goats, and is sometimes called "Goat Island." Occasionally Tinian islanders will go there to hunt the goats or coconut crabs, which have become scarce on the main islands.

None of the operators seems particularly anxious to take divers here, and it is basically unexplored. Since it is a long trip from the main island, and the map shows little area protected enough to form a good diving reef, Aguijan might just stay that way.

Rota

The sleepy island of Rota had for long seemed content to allow all the regional tourist development to take place in Saipan and Guam. Recently, however, three large resorts have gone up, complete with golf courses. Along with the resorts

have come hundreds of workers, mostly from the Philippines, which threatens to alter the character of this pleasantly isolated island.

Rota has long been a one-village island, with Songsong—the name, appropriately enough, simply means "village" in Chamorro—holding most of the island's population. The new resort just south of the airport has swelled Sinapalo's population, but Songsong, on the neck of a kind of tombolo between Rota and Mount Taipingot, is still the island's main village.

At Dive Rota, on the East Harbor side of Songsong, you'll meet Mark and Lynne Michael, who take great pride in the diving their island offers. They offer a number of economical package deals that can introduce you to Rota in as little time as a long weekend.

Most of the dive sites are within the sweep of Sosanhaya Bay, and thus not far from East Harbor. There is a nice wreck here, and excellent wall dives, caves, and reefs. The visibility is tremendous, and the water just glows blue. The sites are keyed to MAP 2.3, pages 70–71.

PUNTAN SENHANOM [1]

It seems every dive destination has its main attraction, and this exciting sea cave on the southwest side of the Taipingot Peninsula is Rota's. Located near the tip of the southwest plateau, the atmosphere here in this cave changes constantly as the sun and water alter their positions and intensity. While entry is safe, emerging can be a little rough if you happen to scrape the lava rock at the mouth of the cave, but the experience is worthwhile.

It is possible to see just about everything here—reef white-tips, myriad reef fish, lobsters, and the coral and sponges are beautiful. A dive light is necessary, especially when you explore the recesses. Though it is often calm, be wary of surge and current.

WEDDING CAKE POINT [2]

Just southeast of Puntan Senhanom and at the very tip of Senhanom Point, this site offers excellent visibility, a beautiful wall, schooling fish, sharks, and pelagics. It is a wonderful dive. The wall is covered with carpet anemones, crinoids, and corals. Watch the unpredictable currents.

SHOUN MARU [3]

Located in Sosanhaya Bay, this 4,500-ton Japanese freighter sunk just minutes after being hit by an American aerial torpedo in June 1944. The crew had just finished unloading ordnance and re-filling the holds with phosphate from the cable run.

Today, the *Shoun Maru* sits upright in 15–35 meters, on a bed of white sand, and is home to thousands of fusiliers, crinoids, garden eels and batfish.

A botched salvage operation in the sixties left her hull ripped away, exposing a coral-encrusted steam engine, truck, and bicycles. The enormous prop and rudder make an excellent photographic subject. Be sure to look overhead, as there are sometimes mantas here.

CABLE RUN [4]

Along the northwest shore of Sosanhaya Bay is an abandoned cable run which the Japanese used to load phosphate before the war, and just offshore here is the site called "Cable Run." Although it is possible to get here from the shore, a boat will help you avoid the rather precarious shore access.

Thick coral growth frames the many cuts and caves through which reef fish swim. Hard corals cover the reef from six to 20 meters. Sharks, mantas and other pelagics sometimes come in close here.

This site used to be known as the Coral Gardens, one of Rota's main attractions, but an attempt by the U.S. Navy to get rid of old ordnance destroyed what was once here. It's recovering, though, and even now makes a good night dive.

PONYA POINT [6]

This point marks the eastern extent of Sosanhaya Bay. There are several sites here, of which Pearlman Tunnel is the best known. Pearlman is a cave that reaches from three to 30 meters, and is home to large reef white-tips, lots of small and interesting invertebrates, and everything in between.

The upper opening is a great spot for silhouette photos when the sun beams through. Listen for the crashing of the waves as they echo through the tunnel.

At the deep end, the ridge is covered with gorgonians and swarming with reef fish. Large schools of barracuda and batfish are an added treat. If you stare into the blue you can sometimes see cruising sharks, tuna, and even sailfish.

One of the most recognizable images of Palau, this is Ngerukuid or "Seventy Islands," part of the Rock Islands group that decorates the lagoon south of Oreor. Ngerukuid is a wildlife preserve, and off limits to visitors.

TAMMY PELUSO   Dendronephthya (Spongodes) sp.   Palau

Divers sometimes divide Micronesia into soft coral and hard coral 'kingdoms.' This is not particularly useful, and is really a way of saying that the 'hard coral kingdoms'—e.g. Guam and the Marianas—don't have much soft coral. Palau has both, in droves.

This famous diving area almost needs no introduction. Palau's combination of clear water, steep, rich, current-swept walls, and lots of sharks and pelagics makes it the gold standard of world dive sites. A warming event caused some shallow water damage in 1999, but the drop-offs remain one of the diving's most exhilarating rides.

Palau

PALAU IS ONE OF THE MOST ABSORB-ing travel destinations in the Pacific. Besides the arresting scenery—an aerial photograph of the other-worldly green humps of Ngerukuid or the "Seventy Islands" is one of the Pacific's iconic images—and besides offering perhaps the finest dive experience in the world, Palau is also rich in history and culture. As you first leave your plane, it may occur to you that Palau's airport is something out of the Flintstones, but it all works very well and you are treated with respect and courtesy. The Palauans are a remarkable people and I've always enjoyed their companionship during my stays.

Stretching southwest from the largest island, Babelthuap, is a huge lagoon containing an archipelago of three hundred islands and islets. These are Chalbacheb, more commonly called the "Rock Islands,"

Palau's most distinctive geographic feature. Some are tiny limestone mushrooms, eroded at the water line and capped by a scruff of green vegetation; others are large and sinuous, with shapes more random than spilled paint. This area is a cartographer's nightmare, but a diver's dream. The 150-kilometer barrier reef surrounding this lagoon offers what is regularly claimed to be the single finest diving area in the world. Bright white sand, 70-meter visibility, towering coral walls, huge clouds of fish, and raging currents create a thrilling time underwater.

On Babelthuap, the second largest island in Micronesia, the traditional culture of Palau still lives undisturbed. Peleliu, in the south, has as grim a history as Iwo Jima, having been the site of one of World War II's bloodiest battles. Oreor (Koror), the site of the capital, is bustling and lively. Ngeaur, iso-

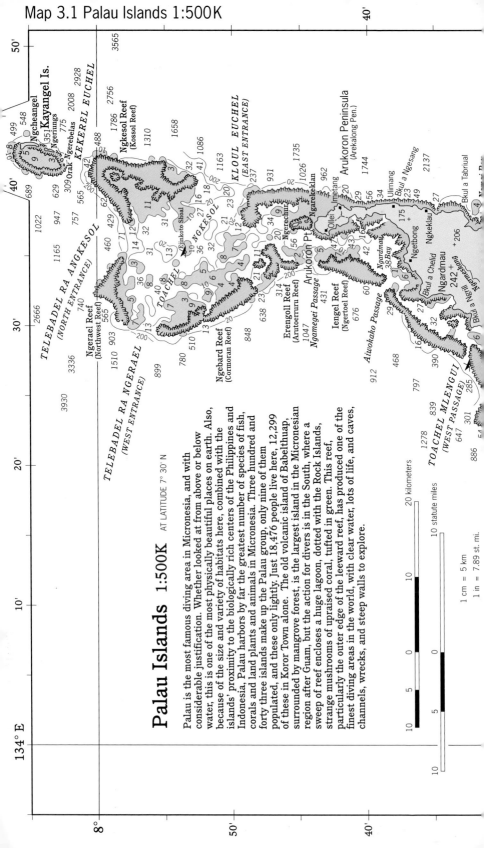

Map 3.1 Palau Islands 1:500K

Palau Islands 1:500K

AT LATITUDE 7° 30' N

Palau is the most famous diving area in Micronesia, and with considerable justification. Whether looked at from above or below water, this is one of the most physically beautiful places on earth. Also, because of the size and variety of habitats here, combined with the islands' proximity to the biologically rich centers of the Philippines and Indonesia, Palau harbors by far the greatest number of species of fish, corals and land plants and animals in Micronesia. Three hundred and forty three islands make up the Palau group, only nine of them populated, and these only lightly. Just 18,476 people live here, 12,299 of these in Koror Town alone. The old volcanic island of Babelthuap, surrounded by mangrove forest, is the largest island in the Micronesian region after Guam, but the action for divers is in the South, where a sweep of reef encloses a huge lagoon, dotted with the Rock Islands, strange mushrooms of upraised coral, tufted in green. This reef, particularly the outer edge of the leeward reef, has produced one of the finest diving areas in the world, with clear water, lots of life, and caves, channels, wrecks, and steep walls to explore.

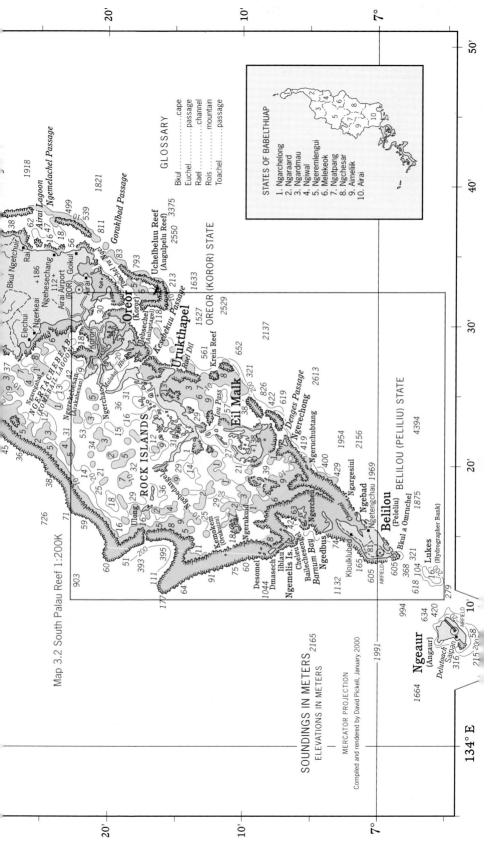

Map 3.2 South Palau Reef 1:200K

GLOSSARY

Bkul..............cape
Euchel............passage
Rael..............channel
Rois..............mountain
Toachel...........passage

STATES OF BABELTHUAP

1. Ngarchelong
2. Ngaraard
3. Ngardmau
4. Ngiwal
5. Ngeremlengui
6. Melekeok
7. Ngatpang
8. Ngchesar
9. Aimeliik
10. Airai

SOUNDINGS IN METERS
ELEVATIONS IN METERS

MERCATOR PROJECTION

Compiled and rendered by David Pickell, January 2000

134° E

OREOR (KOROR) STATE

BELILOU (PELILIU) STATE

Oreor
(Koror)

Urukthapel

Eil Malk

ROCK ISLANDS

Belilou
(Peliliu)

Ngeaur
(Angaur)

TAMMY PELUSO Palau

The reef surrounding the Palau Islands, particularly in the southwest, is considered by some to be the finest diving area in the world.

bacteria, algae, sponges, urchins, chitons, snails and other hungry mouths endlessly scour the splash zone. The most distinctive formation of the Chalbacheb islands is Ngerukuid, which was suffering from visitors and has now been set aside as strict reserve, hoping it will return to a pristine state.

Palau is the most biologically rich of the Micronesian islands. It is in the heart of the tropics—just 7°N—and just 800 kilometers from the southern Philippines and Indonesia's Maluku islands. Ghost-white terns and brightly colored, and endangered, jungle doves join a hundred other species of birds. Fruitbats, monitor lizards, and salt-water crocodiles—though now rare, these can reach over five meters, and are not to be trifled with—also call these islands home. Lots of "boonie" dogs run wild in packs, but they are relatively shy and harmless, preferring to forage through garbage than hunt the wild tourist. Rabies are still unknown here. In fact, there is almost no land animal that can inflict any harm upon you in Palau. (There are some plants here, on the other hand, that can certainly spoil your day—your guide will warn you.)

An estimated 1,357 species of reef fish swim here, and more than 70 genera of coral shared in building Palau's reef. Sharks of a dozen varieties, rays, sea turtles, endless schools of jacks, barracuda, and snapper, *Tridacna* clams, anemones, and myriad colorful reef fish—everything you can think of—live here. To put it mildly, this place is rich. And then, of course, there are the odd jellyfish lakes.

The average temperature is 27.2°C (80.9°F) on land, and surface water temperatures average 27°C (81°F). Visibility ranges from 20 to 80 glorious meters. The dry season runs from February through May, and the wet monsoon is July

lated in the south, is mystical and beautiful, with just two hundred people and thousands of monkeys, the progeny of pets left behind by German scientists a century ago.

LUSH AND STRANGE

The Palau republic includes 343 islands, comprising 458 square kilometers of land. The islands are upraised coral limestone, shot full of sinkholes, caverns, and other karst formations, carved by the humic acids produced by decaying leaves. In some areas the stone, eroded from both sides, has produced razor-sharp ridges. Covering this is a mat of lush, impenetrable jungle.

The distinctive mushroom shape of many of the Rock Islands is a product of biological erosion, as

DAVID LEONARD Rock Islands, Southern Palau reef

through October, though throughout the year it can rain for a short
while each day, and usually the
shower is welcome.

A GLUTTONOUS CHILD

Palauans possess a rich quilt of
traditional narratives, built around
a dozen basic stories explaining
birth, creation, fertility and the like.
One of these describes a voracious
child, Uab, who lived on Ngeaur Island. It is said that he ate so much he
grew too large for his own home—
only his head fit inside. His neighbors, fearing Uab, eventually tied
him up and burned him. With
such force did he rail against his
bonds that he finally tore apart, flying off into the void, forming
Palau's many islands. His torso became Babelthuap, with Ngiwal, in
the northwest, being his stomach—
thus in Ngiwal they eat seven times
a day. (You can use your imagination
for the rest of the body parts.)

Archaeologists suggest that Indonesian seafarers first landed on
Palau 4,500 years ago, and habita-
tion by 3,500 years ago has been
confirmed by carbon dating. The
settlers built many impressive
structures, terraced villages and se-
cluded *bai*s, some of which can still
be seen today. Government was the
job of a council of chiefs, descendants of whom still retain a share of
authority today. The first Palauans
fished extensively and cultivated
taro, *Areca* palm, bananas, pandanus, and breadfruit.

The Spanish and Portuguese
had been stopping in Palau for 250
years before the British East India
Company ship *Antelope* foundered
off Ulong Island, just inside a narrow pass in the western reef, in
1783. Captain Henry Wilson, with
the help of the native Palauans, built
a new ship using parts of the wreck,
and continued on to Macao. One of
Captain Wilson's crew members decided to stay behind in Palau, and in
his place, Prince Lebu sailed back to
England, where he sadly died of the
flu just five months later. Lebu's
presence in London, and George
Keate's *An Account of the Pelew Is-*

The Rock Islands,
with their arches,
cuts, and mushroom-
like profiles, provide
one of the most dis-
tinctive pictures of
Palau. The Palauans
call these islands
Chalbacheb, and
there are literally
hundreds of them,
both large and small,
scattered throughout
the thirty-kilometer-
wide lagoon south of
Babelthuap and Oreor.

Some people
assume that physical
erosion—the inces-
sant pummeling of
waves—produces
these arches and
whimsical shapes. But
the Rock Islands are
on the protected
inside of the lagoon.
In fact, the inter-
tidal notch on these
and similar coral
limestone islands has
been shown to result
chiefly from bioero-
sion by the algas, chi-
tons, echinoderms,
boring sponges, and
various rasping
shelled mollusks living
in the splash zone.

TAMMY PELUSO Subergorgia mollis Palau

Palau
BLUE PARADISE

Huge seafans (opposite), clinging
to steep walls, are one of the
hallmarks of Palau diving.
During the daylight hours, shoals
of sweepers (right) gather in
caves or under coral overhangs,
dispersing only at night to
feed. The Napoleon wrasse
(below) is the largest of its family.
Because of regular feedings (a
controversial practice) this
individual has become quite
tame. Be careful in situations like
this, however, as in their
eagerness Napoleons have been
known to inhale a diver's arm
right up to the elbow. They seem
to know this is a mistake,
however, and I have never heard
of one using its formidable
pharyngeal teeth (i.e., they are in
its throat) to grind up anyone's
hand. Although a fish that routinely
eats sea urchins, shellfish, and even
crown-of-thorns starfish certainly
could do so, of course.

GUI GARCIA   Parapriacanthus ransonneti   Chandelier Cave, Palau

DAVID LEONARD   Cheilinus undulatus with Buck Beasley   Palau

BILL BECKNER   Mastigias papua   Jellyfish Lake, Eil Malk, Palau

DAVID LEONARD   Chelonia mydas   Palau

TAMMY PELUSO   Sphyraena genie   Palau

TAMMY PELUSO   Periclimenes brevicarpalis   Palau

After countless generations locked in an anchialine lake on Eil Malk, these rhizostome jellies (above) have almost completely lost their capacity to sting. Solitary hunters by night, chevroned barracuda (right, above) gather in huge schools during the day, forming balls, columns, and sometimes rings. This commensal shrimp (right) is always found living with sea anemones, in this case the fierce *Actinodendron*. The green sea turtle (left) spends its entire life at sea. Females come ashore only for breeding.

lands and similar popular works, made Palau famous in late 18th-century England.

Britain enjoyed a trade relationship with the islands until the Spanish, in 1885, kicked them out and brought in missionaries to evangelize the Palauans until, with the rest of Micronesia, they sold the territory to Germany in the midst of

TAMMY PELUSO Subergogia mollis Palau

This species of sea fan, reaching up to three meters across, is the largest gorgonian in the Indo-Pacific. Big gorgonians indicate a site that receives a regular and generous supply of plankton, and this is certainly true of Palau's southwestern walls.

the Spanish–American War. By this point, introduced diseases had reduced the population to 4,000, barely ten percent of the number before the Europeans arrived. The Germans set up copra plantations and mined phosphate on Ngeaur using forced Palauan labor, setting up sanitation facilities and providing inoculations so that their work force would not dwindle further.

Japan took over Germany's Micronesian possessions in 1914, and continued to exploit the islands' people and resources, expanding agriculture and mining bauxite. Koror during this period became an island metropolis with a streetcar, concrete block buildings, and paved roads. Because of Japanese emigrants, the population of Koror reached an all-time high of nearly 40,000.

WORLD WAR II

In September 1944, a blistering Allied air attack flattened Koror. Then the Americans invaded and occupied Peleliu, in one of the ugliest and bloodiest battles of the entire Pacific war. Unable to extricate the Japanese from the vast complex of caves and tunnels that wormed their way through the limestone mounts, the Americans decided to drill down through the bedrock, pouring phosphate and diesel fuel into the caves. When the match was struck, 12,500 Japanese burned and suffocated to death. Only Peleliu and Ngeaur were occupied, and the Allies ignored the Japanese on the northern islands. There the Japanese tortured and abused their Palauan wards, and herded them into concentrated areas in Babelthuap, until the final surrender less than one year later.

In 1978 Palauans voted against becoming part of a greater Micronesian political unit, and the move to self-government has been rocky. The first president, Haruo Remeliik, was assassinated, and the second, Lazarus Salii, died in a suspicious suicide. Corruption was rampant. Full independence came in 1994, and today the nation is a republic, in free association with the United States.

LIVELY TRADITIONAL CULTURE

Palau's population of 18,467 lives on just ten of the hundreds of islands, and two-thirds of this total lives in Koror. Native Belauan is spoken in the main Palau island group, and Sonsorolese and Tobian in the remote southern islands. But nearly everyone speaks English, and some, especially many of the older citizens, speak Japanese. You'll also hear Chamorran and a variety of other Micronesian dialects. The U.S. dollar is the currency of choice.

Beautiful, hand-painted *bai* (traditional men's meeting houses) can be seen in many areas. Still used for community meetings and respite from the sun (and wives, I'm told), these buildings are large, airy affairs built on platforms. Open eaves supply air conditioning.

Palau is the home of the storyboard, and I defy you to go home without one. It seems almost anyone who goes to jail here is a storyboard artist, so the Koror jail is the best place to buy. The inmates spend their time whittling away, earning money towards their defense and bail. But these savvy prisoners do not sell their work cheaply, so be ready for some challenging bargaining (conducted through a jailer). Prisoner storyboards tend to be the most expensive—some can cost thousands of dollars—and also the most beautiful.

Contrary to popular belief, the storyboard is not originally Palauan, but a Japanese invention passed on to the Palauans in the 1930s. It consists of a slab of wood, usually mahogany, mangrove, or ideally the now rarer ironwood (if you're not sure, just pick it up— you'll know if it's ironwood) engraved with a scene one of the traditional Palauan stories. The most exquisite one I've seen was two meters long, cut in the shape of a crocodile, and embellished with mother of pearl. Much in demand is the legend of the impossibly endowed fisherman, whose member snakes through the sea, his semen fertilizing the Rock Islands.

THRIVING ECONOMY

Palau has come a long way from the days when its sole export was stone money and its sole trading partner was Yap. The islands have received a recent infusion of Japanese investment, and Japanese com-

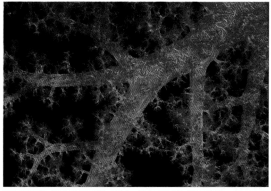

TAMMY PELUSO   Dendronephthya (Roxasia) sp.   Micronesia, island unspecified

panies offer package deals for Tokyo-based divers and vacationers. (Palau has also instituted $15 diving permits, which most operators pay for you.) Almost half of the employed population works for the government.

Fishing is a big industry in here, and 50 tons of Grade-A sashimi flies to Japan every week, earning the government of Palau a million dollars a year in license fees. At least Palauan authorities are diligent in making arrests when captains fish too closely to the reefs. Oddly, few islanders fish themselves.

"Palauans are lovers, they are not fisherman," Palauan millionaire businessman and politician Polycarp Basilius said. "They go fishing for dinner or to impress their girlfriend, but not commercial fishing."

Many Palauans are returning to their fields and orchards to grow bananas, taro, yams, breadfruit, and pandanus, but the only cash crop is marijuana. This is highly illegal in Palau, so be careful.

Dendronephthya— the name means something like 'tree of the goddess'—is undoubtedly the most beautiful of the soft corals. These animals, which do not host symbiotic algae like the shallow water octocorals, favor relatively deep, clean, plankton-rich water, and like big gorgonians, are a sign of a healthy reef. The organization of the genus is a mess, with some 250 species having been more or less haphazardly named, making species identification difficult or impossible. Perhaps, however, like 'Garbo' or 'Marilyn,' beauty of this caliber only needs one name.

A Sleepy, History-Rich Island

MAURIZIO TEBIONG WAS BORN ON A POOL table, discarded in his parents' yard on Peleliu in 1928. He has lived on this strange, isolated island his entire life. Maurizio is a master at reading natural signs—for weather, for direction, for animal life—and his memory is vivid. Everything was damp on the afternoon we spoke about the tragic events of World War II on this island. The wet monsoon was beginning, and clouds filled the sky.

"Those low clouds always make me weep, even after fifty years," Maurizio said. "I was helping my mother strip thatch for our roof, which had been damaged by the fire bombs the Americans dropped, when thick clouds and hollow booms rose up from the ground. I could hear yelling, and muffled screams from behind the hills, and the wind suddenly seemed to pick up, carrying the fumes of chemicals we had not smelled before.

"We knew something was terribly wrong, because the Americans had been here for months, but there was only scattered gunfire and an occasional explosion. American planes had been flying from the Japanese airstrip every day, but this was different. When night fell, the bombs stopped. There was a cold feeling in the still air; there was only the solitary sound of the ghost bird.

"Later, the Americans left most of their half-tracks and tanks behind because they were bombed or broken. We thought the Japanese had prevailed. We didn't yet know that their bodies had been left in the caves and on the sides of the hills where they landed after the phosphorous bombs exploded. They were all dead. We were poor and had nothing, and took what we could. My mother found a bayonet which she sharpened and used for years afterwards to cut meat in the kitchen.

"The bodies started to swell and stink. We dug big holes and said prayers, but we didn't know what to feel. For many years, the Spanish, the Germans, and the Japanese made us work hard under the sword for no wages. It was a long time before we would

truly really understand the meaning of freedom. We had long forgotten that we could live our lives and be ourselves. This was new to us, and we learned to treasure it.

"That is why Palau is a beautiful place. We have a beautiful sea, and beautiful islands and beautiful stars at night. But we have something more—we have a beautiful heart, both as a country and as a people. We have known much pain and sorrow, but now we choose to live without it, as long as we can."

CHARMING AND ISOLATED

This is Peleliu. Only fifty years ago the site of one of the bloodiest battles in the Pacific, today she is one of the sleepiest, most idyllic, least-traveled destinations you will ever encounter. This fabled island lies 50 kilometers (and a half century) southwest of Koror. It is most easily reached by the public boat that will include you among its cargo of livestock, local commuters, and freight for just three dollars. The two-hour ride is very enjoyable, affording you a view of the entire stretch of Rock Islands. There are seats in the back beneath a canopy, where the locals will find it amusing that you're riding among them to this island, decidedly off the tourist track. I was offered home-cooked snacks, cigarettes and beverages in what turned into a community gathering aboard the *Peleliu Star*.

The dive boats that bring you to the dive sites off Peleliu will also take you ashore for lunch and short tours. And Palau Paradise Air will fly you to the island in their propeller plane (a ten-minute flight, for about $20), landing you on the enormous, historic Japanese wartime runway, complete with abandoned bunkers and storage buildings. There is no terminal, but a minibus will take you where you want to go.

There are no hotels on Peleliu, but there are charming, albeit somewhat peculiar, guest houses where you can stay for about $20 a night, usually including two delicious home-cooked meals. I stayed at The Wenty

Inn just outside the main village of Kloul-klubed, choosing to walk the three sun drenched miles from the dock to the village. A car stopped, and the driver asked me where I was going. Naturally, it turned out to be Isabel Wenty, who drove me back to her inn, where I showered and made my plans for the next two days. It's a small, friendly isle.

Set near the ocean on a cozy strip of beach, this white stucco building is an odd pastiche of Micronesia, Las Vegas, and Big Sur. A velvet painting of the Last Supper hangs in the hallway, and a karaoke machine with a ribbon around it stands in the living room, carpeted in bright red shag. The game show furniture was out of place in a community built of open-sided shacks and tree houses. My room was clean, breezy, and comfortable. A few resident geckos kept the bugs at bay. There were no other guests at Wenty's, or in Peleliu, from what I could gather.

I put on a hat, a pair of shorts and a T-shirt and strolled down the road toward a store I'd noticed on the drive in. Here was a wooden platform built into the side of the road, with a roof and railings. Set on the platform was a seven-foot Brunswick coin-op pool table hosting five or six Palauan teens in a spirited game of eight ball. A wooden pathway led to a general store where cold Budweiser was sold among a few other sundry items. I bought a beer and watched the game for a few minutes.

The players greeted me shyly, then realizing I was probably not a snitch, resumed smoking the fat joint they had hidden. It was later that I was informed of the fact that marijuana is Peleliu's only cash crop. In twice traversing the entire island, this one instance was all the evidence I witnessed to that fact.

I walked a few hundred yards further until I reached a sprawling playing field where schoolchildren romped beneath a large billboard announcing that "Palau says 'no' to drugs." Across the street are the graves of the first two presidents of Palau, Haruo Remeli-ik, who was assassinated, and Lazarus Salii, who died in a suspicious suicide. During my first visit, Palau finally signed the historic Compact of Free Association with the U.S.

DAVID LEONARD Peleliu

Peleliu, the southernmost island in the main Palau group, was the site of one of the most brutal and protracted battles of World War II. It cost the Americans more than two months, and many casualties, to defeat the 10,000 Japanese defenders holed up in the rugged interior. Mercifully, the native islanders had been evacuated to Babelthuap before the fighting began. Today Peleliu has four sleepy villages, 600 people, 25 cars, and, as the sign above suggests, only one cash crop.

Back at the Wenty home, I spent the early evening chatting with Ed, the Wenty's neighbor. Experiencing a revelation at the age of 42, Ed cleared out his bank accounts, left his successful business and family roots in Frankfurt, and settled in Peleliu, possibly the polar opposite of Western Europe in every way. With a sober and well-informed viewpoint, Ed gave me the crash-course in the compact, cave networks, war artifacts, fishing, sailing and Palauan culture.

We were sitting in the midst of what could only be called a pile of radios in various stages of disrepair. The community brings to Ed their broken appliances and radios to be fixed, a service for which his charge, though always nominal, varies considerably depending upon the particular neighbor's attitude. Exploring the island, Ed has amassed a large collection of war relics which he displays on the wing of a Japanese Zero that rests in the yard next to the house he's building almost single-handedly.

Ed's house stands five meters off the ground on concrete pillars, and has a steeply sloped, vented roof, both features to insure the structure will withstand anything nature can throw its way. The structure is unusual in Peleliu for that reason. Micronesians, perhaps having watched too much American television, build ranch-style houses with flat roofs. In this climate, houses like these make efficient broilers, while Ed's is always airy and cool. That explains why on the hottest nights all the neighbors climb the stairs to Ed's still unfinished lair, and sleep on the floor. Ed's design, in fact, works so well that they bring blankets.

The sun set nearby, just over the horizon, as I watched the geckos stake out their night territories around a bare bulb. When asked, I told Isabel that I would like to try coconut crab for dinner, but had to settle for regular crab, as these threatened animals are now very rare. Dinner was served at a table next to a washtub exactly the diameter of the hawksbill turtle that resided therein. They had found him as a baby, and have kept him as a pet all these years. Occasionally, they attach a chain to a hole drilled in the back of his shell so he can swim in the surf.

I quaffed a bowl of deliciously spicy fish and vegetable soup. A salad came, and then, baked crab meat. Dinner was splendid and wholesome, the crab accompanied by sublime steamed tapioca, grown locally and wrapped in a palm leaf, red bean bao, and sugar bananas for dessert.

BICYCLING AROUND THE ISLAND

Early morning came with feral roosters cackling insanely at my window. The jungle is full of them. I packed fruit, water, sun screen, snorkel gear, camera, map, and wind-breaker, borrowed one of the Wenty's bicycles—a ten-speed mountain bike affair—and headed for the hills and back country of Peleliu. (If you decide to make this trip one day, leave the wind-breaker at home, and bring your wind-*finder*.)

The heat rose off the crushed-coral road like vapor from a teapot. Though there are only 25 cars registered in Peleliu, (and no readily identifiable means of importing any more), the roads have been widened to accommodate Los Angeles traffic. In the process, they've felled the sprawling pines and palms that once shaded these roadways, and they are now so scorchingly hot that my tires ballooned out over the wheel rims.

First I visited the cave where a renegade troop of Japanese hid while they harassed the occupying Americans well into 1947. Then I cut off onto a shaded avenue that led into the dark jungle. After pedaling for an hour through the wet forest, I stopped to check my map. The old Japanese road, unimproved since the thirties, was draped in towering trees, which blotted out the sun completely. Suddenly, the hardest rain I ever felt poured relentlessly through the leaves, creating an ear-splitting cacophony of rustling and splashing. I stood still in the fifteen-minute downpour, knowing this refreshment would very soon be a wistful memory.

Biking toward the other end of the old Japanese road, I was soon dry again, and then, by the time I reached the foot of Bloody Nose Ridge, soaking wet with perspiration. After a long climb up weather-worn stairs built into the side of the cliffs, I came to Shinto shrines and U.S. Marine memorials draped with artifacts found and left behind by visitors.

From atop this hill, the Americans liberated Peleliu from the Japanese in 1944. Nearly 20,000 Japanese and 5,000 Americans perished here in a battle that would later be deemed unnecessary.

After the Allies repeatedly failed to extract the Japanese from their hiding place in the network of caves that form the island's substrata, they poured a mixture of airplane fuel and phosphate through openings in the cave ceilings, literally blowing the Japanese out through the sides of the hills of forlorn Peleliu. Today, these caves are full of artifacts. I found shoes, holsters, bullets, casings, grenades, helmets, knives, gloves, and canteens (do not collect artifacts anywhere on Palau—the government levies very large fines on anyone caught doing so). The human remains were gathered up much later by Japanese emissaries, who performed ceremonial cremations.

From the top of Bloody Nose Ridge, you can see the main Shinto shrine and cemetery, beyond to Honeymoon Beach, all the way to Camp Beck dock at the other end of the island. You can see, in fact, all the way to Koror across the stretch of Rock Islands to the north. Engraved into the memorial left here in 1947 by the 323rd infantry, U.S. Army, are the names of lovers: "Jim and Sandy, '51," "David and Sherri 1948." Way off in the distance was a blue tarp I'd passed earlier. It sheltered a woman who was working alone in the hemp fields. Next to the memorial is a weather-beaten flag pole, a dried bouquet of wildflowers long ago raised to the top. A single, rusted machine-gun is melted into the concrete. This guards the lizards and beetles, the true kings of this hill, from any pretenders to their throne.

DAVID LEONARD   Eil Malk, Palau

Much of Palau is lowland forest, which on the shore of Eil Malk Lake becomes a mixed mangrove and pandanus habitat.

A WELCOME SWIM

Back in the saddle, I rode up the island's east coast past a score of abandoned tanks and planes, to the Ngermelt swimming hole, an inland sinkhole filled with water that rises and falls with the tides. I recklessly dove in, surfacing to hear the most unusual noise emanating from the surrounding walls. A bit startled at first—the sound of snapping crocodile teeth?—I soon realized it was only the popping and crackling as water surged into and out of from the millions of small holes eroded into the cavern walls. The sound could only be approximated by a hundred small steel drums played lightly and randomly. This was the coolest water I'd found in weeks, and I stayed for some time, repeatedly diving into the five-meter-deep pool.

The long ride back across the Japanese airstrip, past the Peleliu shrine, and up the now familiar Old Japanese Road into Kloulklubed village found me, at the end, face to face with the deep Peleliu night. I heard only the sounds of night birds and insects, the rustling of the palms, and the distant crash of the surf.

Best Ride in the Pacific
and Postcard Beautiful

PALAU IS BEST LOVED FOR ITS RICH, vertical walls, clear water, and wild currents. Huge schools of fish are common. Sharks are everywhere. I saw a giant *Tridacna* here that must have weighed 250 kilograms, its rippled mantle flashing electric blue. And everywhere is a healthy reef of hard coral, soft coral, and gorgonians.

In the spring of 1999 an El Niño warming event (technically it was a La Niña year) hit Palau hard, hold-

> Sharks, mantas, sailfish, huge gorgonians, bright yellow soft corals—the list is endless. Palau's walls, especially off Ngemelis and Peleliu, are rich, swift, and thrilling.

ing water temperatures at about 32°C (90°F) for several months. This had a devastating affect on much of the shallow water hard coral and leather coral, the heat stress causing them to expel their symbiotic algae and die. The deeper areas (greater than about 15 meters) were unaffected, as were the non-zooxanthellate soft corals and gorgonians. The best sites, such as those off Peleliu, were little affected even in the shallows. Perhaps the greatest tragedy was the complete extinction of one of the two species of jellyfish in the famous Jellyfish Lake on Eil Malk (see below). The deep drop-off reefs were un-

harmed, and Palau remains one of the world's premier sites.

Although Chuuk Lagoon is Micronesia's most famous wreck-diving site, Palau—both on land and in the sea—has a world-class treasure trove of planes, tanks, ships, subs, and guns. Among the best preserved are the numerous Japanese Mitsubishi A6Ms, better known as Zeros, because they were built from non-corroding aluminum alloys.

The dive boats leave the dock at 9:30 in the morning, passing Taiwanese tuna fishing ships, strapped together in rafts of fifteen, as they head out to sea. After the first dive, the boat runs ashore on the beach of a deserted island where lunch is served, spread out on a bright white beach under the coconut palms, out of the sun. After a relaxing surface interval spent beach combing, reading, swimming, snorkeling, exploring the island and splitting coconuts, the boat glides across the glassy sea to the early afternoon dive site.

After the day's second dive, on the way back to Koror, you will stop at one of the dozens of fascinating side trips—Jellyfish Lake on Eil Malk, a Japanese Zero wreck, The Mystery Wreck, the *Gozan Maru* or *Iro Maru*, or maybe even Peleliu. The dive boats are quick and agile, affording easy access to most points in the archipelago. The outbound trip rarely exceeds 45 minutes, and weaving between the emerald, mushroom-shaped Rock Islands, you will never think this tedious. Flying fish and dolphins accompany nearly every trip. One day a large

BILL BECKNER Mastigias papua Jellyfish Lake, Eil Malk, Palau

pod of pilot whales surfaced and played, within 25 meters of our boat. In the distance, an enormous waterspout reached down from the clouds and stirred the ocean like a cocktail. Palau is always magnificent.

While I firmly believe that every visitor must spend time with Palauans, whether in Koror, Babelthuap, Peleliu, or some other outpost of this far-flung island nation, I'm convinced that the best way to experience Palauan diving is on one of the three live-aboards operating here. Each has its own distinctive style, and I love all three.

Below is a sampling of Palau's most dramatic sites, but there are many, many others. Your operator will keep you apprised of what's particularly hot during your visit. The dive businesses try to coordinate their activities to avoid overcrowding and the resultant pressure on the reef system. Do try to keep your hands, fins, and gauges off the reef and do not leave the water with anything you didn't bring in. If

Palau is going to last, we're going to have to be careful.

If you are just starting out, and have trouble maintaining neutral buoyancy, Palau is probably not the best place to learn. The currents here can be merciless, and the depths are significant. If you have the experience to handle it, however, you are in for a real treat. The sites below are listed in roughly geographical order, beginning at Koror and working clockwise around the reef (see MAP 3.2, pages 96–97, for precise locations of the sites.)

SHORT DROP-OFF [1]

It's not that this wall is shorter than any of Palau's other drop-off reefs, it's just a "short" boat ride from shore (that should tell you a great deal about Palau). Off Uchelbeluu Reef, southeast of Koror, this is a thriving ocean community that is home to brilliant soft coral, fans, sponges, crinoids, and hard coral. Most divers have a fond re-

Snorkeling with the jellies in Eil Malk's Jellyfish Lake has long been one of the highlights of a dive trip to Palau. Unfortunately, the 1999 warming, which brought on several months of 32°C water temperatures, killed off the lake's main population of Mastigias, although the smaller population of the moon jelly Aurelia aurita survived.

It is hoped that not all the Mastigias have died, and the population will bounce back. If not, it has been suggested that the lake be restocked by transplanting jellies from one of the other anchialine lakes, where some are known to have survived. In either case, for the time being snorkeling in Jellyfish Lake has been banned to give the fragile ecosystem a chance to recover.

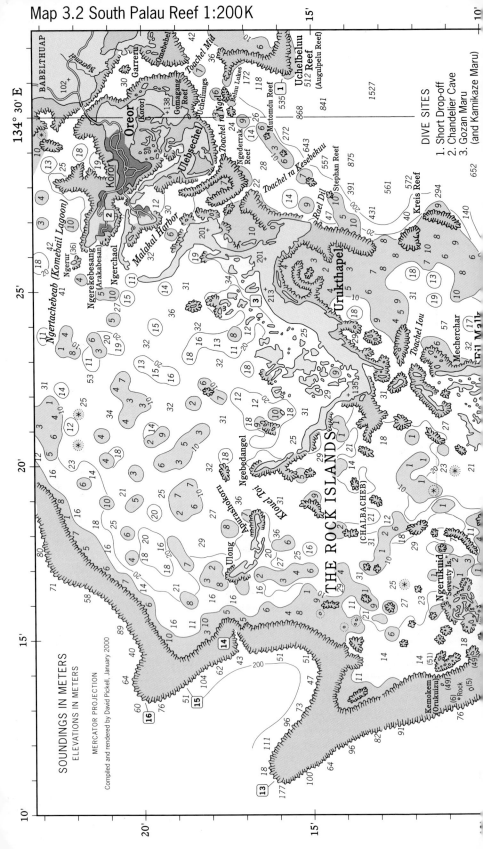

Map 3.2 South Palau Reef 1:200K

DIVE SITES
1. Short Drop-off
2. Chandelier Cave
3. Gozan Maru (and Kamikaze Maru)

SOUNDINGS IN METERS
ELEVATIONS IN METERS

MERCATOR PROJECTION

Compiled and rendered by David Pickell, January 2000

THE ROCK ISLANDS

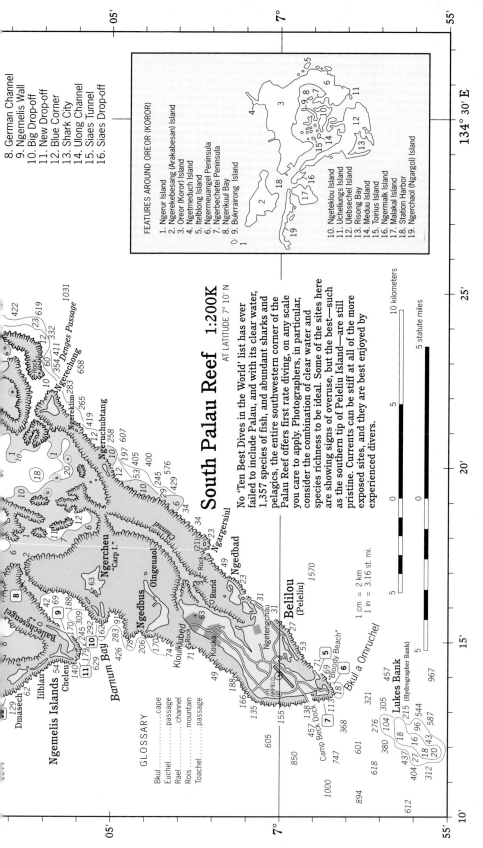

DAVID LEONARD   Nautilus belauensis   Palau

The nautilus is one of the most interesting of the cephalopod molluscs, and has fascinated scientists since at least Aristotle's time. The creatures spend their days resting at near abyssal depths (300–500 meters) and come up onto the deep reef (100–200 meters) at night to grub about for slow-moving crustaceans and, particularly, their molts. This daily migration was first confirmed in 1983 by researchers in Palau, who tagged specimens with transmitting depth sounders.

At least five different species of Nautilus have been identified, although different forms—and perhaps species—are still being discovered. Young nautilus do not disperse far, and populations around geographically isolated islands are genetically isolated as well. The population in Palau has been named N. belauensis.

membrance of this site for its magical wonderland quality.

This wall slopes gently from a beautiful and vital coral garden, lush with life: cleaner wrasse, parrotfish, butterflyfish; sponges, soft corals, crinoids, and tunicates. At seven meters, the slope drops off forever (or at least to 868 meters). This is where many divers make their introductory dive in Palau, and it is excellent for this purpose. There is a lot to see, yet you will also find time to make any last minute adjustments with your gear. You can dive it shallow or you can dive it deep, it's rich either way.

CHANDELIER CAVE [2]

Divers either love or hate this dive (I'm in the latter group). In the harbor near Koror is a tunnel that leads 130 meters into the limestone base of Ngerchaol Island. As you swim in here, you find yourself in a cavern filled with cool, crystalline water. At the halocline (where freshwater meets salt) the water has a smeared, dreamy appearance.

There are three main exits into sealed caves, through which you can emerge and remove your mask and regulator. If you like, in the last cave you may exit the water and sit or have a walk on the rocky shore of the pool (bring a camera in a waterproof bag). Large limestone formations adorn the vaulted ceilings, dripping groundwater.

There are no fish, nor any other life to see inside. As you leave the mouth of the cave, however, swim to the outer island wall just to the east of the opening. If you're very lucky, you can spot the elusive mandarinfish (*Synchiropus splendidus*) here. This little dragonet is one of the most beautiful and ornate fish in the sea. Bring a light on this dive, and make sure it works.

GOZAN MARU AND KAMIKAZE MARU [3]

The *Gozan Maru* is a beautiful wreck set right amongst and betwixt the Rock Islands. Seeking snug harbor during an American raid, this ship was nearly torn in half by a torpedo. The nearby *Kamikaze* sank from the secondary blast of the *Gozan*. The *Gozan* is by far the more interesting of the two. It's covered with coral interspersed with anemones, sponges and fans. An interesting gun rests on the rear deck, but the holds have been stripped of any ammo or cargo. The *Kamikaze Maru* has a bit of explosive materiel, but it really isn't worth the trip.

JELLYFISH LAKE [4]

Forty minutes by boat from Koror, this scientific curiosity is probably the most famous snorkel in the world. The lake is accessed by climbing a steep but manageable hill from the shore of Eil Malk into the interior. Arriving at the crest, you then descend to the edge of a mangrove. (There are said to be crocodiles here, but there has never been an incident.) Believe it or not, this is where you don your fins, mask and snorkel, and slowly—to avoid the rocks—paddle out of the shallows into what becomes a clear, restorative saltwater lake in a setting unlike anywhere else.

As large fruitbats flicker high above, you swim out of the shadows towards the sunlight where thousands of jellyfish congregate. Once there, you'll find yourself among white and rust-colored jellyfish, in such a dense grouping that there seems little room for water. A surreal experience, but you are not in danger. The absence of predators has caused the stinging ability of these creatures to atrophy, although sensitive skin will still feel a bit of a tingle.

This lake—and others like it in Palau and at Kakaban Lagoon, off the east coast of Indonesian Borneo—is one of the world's most interesting environments. Only a few small fish species live here (cardinals and gobies) and there is a unique anemone here that lives on jellyfish (*Entacmaea medusivora*).

Unfortunately, the 1999 La Niña warming event was tragic for

Jellyfish Lake, killing all of the rhizostome jelly *Mastigias papua* (previously the dominant species), although the moon jellies (*Aurelia aurita*) survived. At the time of this writing, there is talk of reintroducing *Mastigias* using stock from one of the several other anchialine lakes in the area. (This unfamiliar term means the lake is connected to the

DAVID LEONARD   Gui Garcia with nautilus trap   Palau

sea, but by limited and indirect means, such as an underground channel or percolation through the substrate.) In the meantime, Jellyfish Lake has been closed to visitors in order to give the environment a chance to recover.

PELELIU AREA

The southwest reef off the historic island of Peleliu offers some of

One-hundred-and-fifty-meter night dives are not routine among sport divers, so the live nautilus one sees in photographs are all specimens that have been caught in baited traps like this one. The traps are left at depth overnight, and then hauled up the next morning. Then the nautilus are released and photographed. Scientists studying the creatures have found that, if released quickly, adult specimens are rarely harmed by this process, but mortality for trapped and released juveniles can be high, reaching 100 percent for half-sized specimens.

CAMPING IN THE ROCK ISLANDS
Playing Robinson Crusoe

ON ONE TRIP TO PALAU, I DECIDED TO SPEND the days diving, and the nights camping. At the end of each day, I would be dropped off on a remote, uninhabited island in the Rock Islands to spend the night. It was usually around four in the afternoon that I carried my tent and belongings ashore, and my guide Maurice Tudong motored back to Koror.

I planned to camp for three days running, so I kept my meat and vegetables, which I bought the first morning, in the boat's cooler during the days. Since the market was in the same building as the hotel I stayed in, it was no problem to grab some steaks, fish, yams, bread, and greens.

ALONE IN THE PACIFIC

On the first night, suddenly alone in the Pacific, I first gathered wood and kindling, which at the same time cleared a site for my tent, just at the edge where the sand turns to jungle. The cry of unseen birds pierced the air as the sun set, and bats fluttered above as the sea casually lapped at the shore of the lagoon. Never did I see a boat or evidence of another human being while camping on these island jewels.

Fire started, I set up my free-standing tent (you wouldn't want to rely on stakes in either the sand or limestone ground) and gathered coconuts. I would often sit by the lagoon, husking enough coconuts to last the night and morning. The sweet water was invigorating, and when stored in the shade they remained cool and refreshing until morning. The meat of the younger nuts was tender and delicious, and made a good breakfast while I awaited Maurice.

Toward dusk, I would snorkel in the lagoon. Floating on my back I watched the lush canopy of stars storm the night, as large fruit bats criss-crossed in silhouette. Then, as the fire settled into glowing embers, I cooked my yams, meat, and fish. Then I warmed the bread, opened the Scotch, and toasted the generosity of land and sea.

When dinner was finished, I was careful to burn all remnants of the food to discourage any small animals and insects that might be anxious to freeload, and built up the fire to a crackling roar. In the orange glow, I often swam in the lagoon, excited, yet somehow calmed by my surroundings. Sleep came early these nights, hastened by the gentle splashing of the lagoon and the bizarre whistling of the "ghost birds." These creatures produce a soft whistle of random melody that islanders still insist comes from ghosts in the jungle as they wending their way through the afterlife. Whichever you choose to believe, the sound is haunting.

THE ELUSIVE COCONUT CRAB

For days I'd been asking where I could sample coconut crab—the most fabulous shellfish in the Pacific, and about which countless travelogues allude to only in reverent whispers. My reliable friend Jimmy suggested I split several old and rotting coconuts and place the halves at the foot of the limestone ridge that runs up from the shores of most Rock Islands. The crabs will gladly come out of their caves and crevices (where they hide from the rats that savor their meat with as much ardor as the rest of the world) and climb up to my bait. Then, he said, I'd be able to simply pick them up and save them for the next campfire.

One evening before bedtime, I cracked open a dozen old coconuts, and followed Jimmy's directions, set my travel alarm for three in the morning. When I rose the sky was saturated with starlight, and the ground was quite literally moving restlessly. There were no less than a million hermit crabs attending to their nocturnal business. Walking towards my bait, I saw a hundred pair of eyes shining in the dark, and briefly considered opening my own crab stand. Instead, I learned that rats also love coconuts. There wasn't a crab in sight, but I was standing ankle deep in an open call for the part of Mickey off-off-off-Broadway.

[Editor's note: The coconut or robber

TAMMY PELUSO Rock Islands, Palau

The Rock Islands offer many sites for an idyllic overnight camping trip.

crab (*Birgus latro*) is endangered throughout much of its range and in many areas is protected by law, so it is best that our author was unsuccessful. The Rock Islands are beautiful and fragile environments, and we strongly discourage collecting shellfish here. Some species (e.g. *Tridacna*) are even protected by Palauan law. When camping, you should bring all your food from the market.]

SHOWER AND A COLD BEER

Up with the persuasive sun, I struck my temporary lodging, diligently removing any sign that I had been there so the next traveler could enjoy the same isolated experience. The fire extinguished in a wisp of smoke, I was happy to see Maurice hadn't forgotten where he left me. Jimmy was duly informed of my crab hunt, as I muttered something about the direct relationship between rats and gratuities.

After a few days in the wild, I felt sufficiently tamed to crawl beseechingly to a comfortable hotel room where I could remove every grain of sand from my person and tune into CNN. There is no metaphor specific enough in scope and intensity to describe the cracking of the first cold beer as I lay on my bed, still wrapped in a towel after that hallowed shower.

In addition to water, food, and condiments, be sure to bring: snorkel gear, tent, machete, sheet to sleep on, travel alarm, toilet paper, matches or lighter, reliable flashlight, pressure lantern and fuel, mosquito coils, soap, towel, a good book, and a bottle of Scotch.

If I did this again, I would cave in to the 20th century and carry a small cooler, because if our lives were measured in satisfying beers, cracking a cold one out in the Rock Islands would have made the winner's circle.

I brought my tent from home, but you might be able to borrow one. The rest of the items on the list can be bought cheaply in Surangel's enormous department store (along with meat, CDs, fishing tackle and wedding dresses). Weather is never an issue and there aren't many black-tie affairs, so pack lightly.

the liveliest diving in the world. Anything can happen here (and usually does). A coral shelf, covered by just three meters of water, extends out from the island here for a couple hundred meters then, at the reef edge, drops suddenly to well over 100 meters. These are definitely advanced dives, but properly

TAMMY PELUSO   Ctenocella (Ellisella) sp. Palau

Whip corals, such as this specimen growing on one of Palau's steep walls, are a sign of a relatively current-swept reef. This common, widely distributed species seems to prefer clinging to a vertical or near vertical surface.

planned, are safe and certainly worth the effort.

All three dive sites are contiguous, and sometimes the whole site is called The Express, because of the fierce current that often rages along here. The drop-off reef is rich, and for some reason yellow seems to be the dominant color here. One "bluff" (Yellow Wall) is completely covered with thick, bright yellow soft coral.

This wall derives much of its character from the fact that it faces the wild, open sea. Head-spinning color and richness of life make this dive seem short, but a depth of three to 50 meters allows you ample latitude in your dive profiles. Sharks also enjoy this wall. We watched them splinter orderly schools of snapper into chaos, and often found ourselves surrounded by half a dozen reef white-tips. Huge barrel sponges cling to the wall here, their openings sheltering enormous sea cucumbers, fish, and other life. Black coral trees adorn the cuts and crevices that are filled with soft corals that bear colors so deep and bright they seem unnatural.

Lunch is taken at nearby Peleliu harbor, the site of so much fighting a half-century ago. It is still littered with half-tracks, planes, and tanks. During one lunch spent there, I looked around my group and realized that here were Americans, Japanese, and Germans making far better use of this installment now.

YELLOW WALL [5]

This site is offshore from windswept Orange Beach, where the Americans first landed on September 15, 1944. Yellow Wall is a bizarre underwater setting. The name is not really an exaggeration. It seems that everything here—coral, rocks, fish, gorgonians—is yellow. This golden vista is nothing short of captivating. The only trouble at this site is that sometimes the current will be so swift that you won't get to spend as much time here as you'd like. The only solution is to dive it again.

THE EXPRESS [6]

This site is well named. I've been catapulted, dragged, shoved, and tumbled along here. Sometimes it's all you can do to maintain buoyancy and depth, but it's a lot of fun, nonetheless. Clinging to this wall is every reef creature imaginable, and out in the blue water, pelagics abound. It was here that a five-meter tiger shark came in just a bit too close, and we quickly burned a thousand psi.

PELELIU WALL [7]

This is the southernmost of the three sites. The current here is fast and the fish action is crazy. Lots of sharks, tuna and schools of jacks, and large fans and sea whips. Sponges, soft corals, and hard corals adorn cuts and stone bluffs along this submerged ridge. This is definitely one of Palau's most attractive, exciting and enjoyable dive experiences.

GERMAN CHANNEL [8]

One of the most relaxing, yet satisfying dives I've ever experienced, was a 75-minute drift dive (alright, my tank *was* sucked dry) down the German Channel. The reef surrendered dozens of secrets as rain mottled the surface into an Impressionist painting fifteen meters overhead. This site is a channel at the inside of Barnum Bay, between the Ngemelis reef in the north, and the Ngercheu reef in the south. It was cut by the Germans during their occupation of Palau, hence the name.

My guide Maurice Tudong, who I will always remember, pointed out crocodile fish, interesting starfish, and neon reef lobsters. One thing you could spot from a satellite, though, was a giant *Tridacna* clam measuring a meter-and-a-half across.

The current can be swift here, but the site is safe, as you are ushered over a wide and sandy bottom. Huge coral heads dot this seascape; cuttlefish hide in the staghorn forests; enormous triggerfish guard their nests; garden eels and sand rays cover the bottom; turtles sleep beneath the table coral. Large mantas sometimes converge here to feed on the incoming tide. I love this dive.

NGEMELIS WALL [9]

This legendary wall dive offers something new each time the diver visits its sheer landscape. The ba-

TAMMY PELUSO Antipathes spp. and Cirrhipathes sp. Palau

thymetry here drops steeply to 309 meters, and the wall is home to sharks, turtles, and schooling snapper. I saw crimson sea fans three meters across, and sponges and giant clams abound. One member of our group spotted a blue marlin and a hammerhead shark on the same dive here.

Drifting over the deep blue

Black corals or antipatharians as a group prefer deeper, cooler, more poorly lit parts of the reef.

DAVID LEONARD Sepia latimanus Palau

DAVID LEONARD Triaenodon obesus (on bait) and Carcharhinus amblyrhynchos Blue Corner

The broad-armed cuttlefish is the only large cuttle found in this area, and the biggest specimens can reach a half-meter in length. If approached slowly, these animals will tolerate divers, and in some cases can seem even curious. This cuttlefish advertises its emotional state by dramatically altering the color, reflectivity, and even texture of its skin (or rather, 'mantle'— this is, after all, a mollusk).

At this feeding, the reef white-tips, despite their size disadvantage, seem to be doing a better job of getting at the bait than the grays. A Malabar grouper and a Napoleon wrasse join in the fun.

chasm, the diver is humbled by his surroundings. The abundance of life here, one senses, will go about its business with or without you.

BIG DROP-OFF [10]

This is a great dive in the sunlight. Everything is big here, even the nudibranchs. Reef white-tip sharks can often be seen herding huge schools of snapper. At fifteen meters, there is a stunning, bright red anemone filled with clownfish, of course. The drift usually leaves you in a beautiful coral garden at seven to ten meters; this is a perfect place to bleed off nitrogen while basking in a crystal-clear, sun-drenched pool.

NEW DROP-OFF [11]

From my logbook: "Visibility a zillion meters. Large shark at 20 me-

ters on this glorious sheer wall. Gazillions of reef juveniles swarming in the current. Kind of like a little Blue Corner in many ways. Sail along the steep wall; after two or three cuts, you will come to a lovely garden at 12 meters. Look in the sand gullies for resting sharks, huge grouper, and oversized, friendly Moorish idols."

The current can shift here, but if you hit it right, it will give you a lovely, gentle ride. Do keep an eye on your depth, as you can be easily distracted here. A great deal of pelagic life swims out of the blue—during my first visit to New Drop-off, I watched a two-and-a-half-meter tiger shark tear into a cloud of bluestripe snappers. I was only two meters away. Humbling.

BLUE CORNER [12]

Many diving areas around the world now have a "Blue Corner," but this is the granddaddy of them all, and is perhaps the world's most famous dive site. Starting at a depth of 12 meters, Blue Corner is an elbow in the western barrier reef north of the Ngemelis Islands that reaches out into the Philippine Sea. A sounding of 1,044 meters lies just offshore.

The wall continues south to meet the New Drop-off, and the length of this reef—which one typically drifts along at one to three knots—is home to an overwhelming variety and number of creatures.

On every dive here I saw sharks—silver-tip, mako, reef blacktip, gray reef—as well as sea turtles, grouper, schools of barracuda, large Napoleon wrasses, dozens of morays, crowds of reef fish, immense gorgonians, black coral trees, and bountiful multicolored coral. Marlin, whale sharks, and eagle rays are also sometimes seen. Mantas are not uncommon. The reef is covered with corals, soft corals, and anemones, some of these latter more than a meter across.

Bringing in food which attracts all these hungry feeders, a very strong tide runs through and around the corner, but your guide will know the best time to catch it. Blue Corner is, simply, among the finest dive sites in the world. One night, moored off this site on a live-aboard, I counted twelve boats, yet this site never seems crowded. By all means, do not miss it.

SIAES TUNNEL [15]

This is another wondrous wall dive, and one of the most exciting dives in Palau. It is located along the western barrier reef just north of the Ulong Channel, about 35 minutes from Koror. Like Blue Corner, it's an elbow, but the lure of Siaes is not its stark wall. This coral ridge is shot through with a hundred-meter tunnel running from a depth of 25 meters at the entrance to 50 at the exit, expanding to a width of almost 30 meters in some spots.

Several openings to the outer wall allow in just enough light to illuminate giant yellow and red gorgonians, three meters across. Without sounding alarmist, it should be noted that with depths averaging 35 meters, this tunnel is not to be dived casually. Strict attention must be paid to your equipment and air reserve. It's a long way up and out, should you have an emergency.

We were ready. Upon entering the tube, my guide didn't have to point out the massive whale shark gliding through ahead of us. Undisturbed were the leopard and white-tip sharks sleeping on the bottom. Bring a light to explore the endless crevices along the inside walls and "rooms"—home to shrimp gobies and sleeping sharks, both of which can be approached quite closely if you control your bubbles and movement. Above, black coral covers the ceiling.

Exiting, you're naturally ushered up the wall along the fans to a sun-lit coral field at seven meters, a perfect place to pass the time during a very essential safety stop.

The lionfish is a favorite with divers and photographers because of its sluggish and accommodating nature. This, of course, is because of its confidence that its venomous spines will deter any assault.

BILL BECKNER Pterois volitans Palau

A formation of mantas is one of the most exciting sights a diver can hope to witness. In the famed channels of Yap, such a vision is guaranteed.

TAMMY PELUSO Manta birostris Mi'il Channel, Yap

TAMMY PELUSO Yap

Many of the old ways are still followed in Yap. It is a place, for example, that a girl is still taught how to weave a basket from palm fronds, and where women, particularly outside of Colonia, are still comfortable wearing only a lava-lava. The state government takes cultural preservation seriously, and if you are interested in tradition, Yap Day, March 1, is a good time to visit.

Mantas put this diving area on the map little more than a decade ago, but there is much more to Yap than the famous channels. Some beautiful hard coral walls in the south, plenty of unexplored reef, and of course the place itself, the most traditional corner of Micronesia.

Yap

THE INTERNATIONAL DIVE COMMU-nity learned of Yap only quite re-cently, in 1989, when someone suggested to Bill Acker (now of Yap Divers) that people might come from all over the world to see the resident manta rays. Thus a star was born, and now these sleepy, tradi-tional islands are one of the most fa-mous dive destinations in the world. Once you're in Micronesia, it's very easy to get to Yap, since it is a mandatory stop on the Guam to Palau flight. Plan to get off here—this is a very interesting place, the mantas are wonderful, and the stopover is free.

Give Yap a shot, but to maintain a kind of dynamic escalation in your Micronesian diving experience, it's best to visit Yap before you go to Palau. Although unique (and in my opinion, fascinating), Yap does offer a somewhat more serene un-derwater experience than some of the other locales in Micronesia.

One thing you should not come here for is to party. Yap has quite ad-mirably resisted the onslaught of American cultural hegemony, which seems to have reached every other corner of the globe. Although all you ever hear about are the de-pendable mantas of Mi'il and Goofnuw Channels, these islands also offer peace, solitude, and some fine, virgin, seaward reefs.

The water is usually serene—clear and blue. Emerald jungle grows thick on the hillsides and in the valleys. There are few cars, and the streets are accessible for walk-ing—by both villagers and tourists. There aren't any public beaches to speak of, because all of the land is privately owned by clans and fami-lies, older forms of political organi-zation that are still powerful here. Thus all diving is from boats, which run continually between the main town of Colonia and the channels and walls of Yap's fringing coral terrace.

TRADITIONAL MICRONESIAN POWER

The 134 islands of Yap State, one of the Federated States of Micronesia, spread across 1,300 kilometers of the Western Pacific, and include most of the western Caroline Islands. The main islands of Yap, sometimes called Yap Proper, are called Wa'ab by the Yapese. The others, a scattered group of lightly populated atolls to the east, are called Remetau. In the past, the Yapese were among the finest seafarers in the Pacific, and the paramount chief of Yap Proper controlled a territory even bigger than today's Yap State, extending north to include the Mariana Islands, and west to include the Hall Islands north of Chuuk Lagoon.

An estimated 13,500 people live in Yap State, two-thirds of them on Wa'ab. The outer islands of Yap remain markedly traditional, and can be visited only with special permission, and only in the presence of a Yapese guide. Even on Yap Proper, in the capital of Colonia, many women wear a cloth or fiber wrap called the *lava-lava*, and it can be a bit of a shock for someone from Protestant America to see topless women blithely going about their business.

Outside of the capital, most of the middle and older generations (and even some of the younger citizens) dress in the traditional style, the women in *lava-lava* and the men in *thu*, fabric loincloths in one, two, or three layers, depending upon their age. The older men also affix strips of hibiscus bark on top of their *thu*.

Family clans are the source of political power on Yap, and property is communally held by the clans (watch where you leave your shoes). The Yapese social system is extremely complex, and even today the society is stratified by caste. Three traditional languages are spoken: Yapese on Wa'ab, and on the outer islands, Ulithian and Woleian.

The Yapese, when confronted by western tourists, are both shy and proud. If they and their culture are treated with respect, they can also be friendly and generous. This is not a good place for a noisy and oblivious traveler. Good manners, patience, and respect are necessary to appreciate Yap.

Organized tours offer visitors limited access to the villages, where tribal dances and songs are enacted, and handmade souvenirs sold. Controlling tourist access may help, but Yap's main struggle will be to get its younger generation to realize the importance of preserving the islands' traditions. Even here, it is becoming difficult to convince a 13-year-old that a tribal dance is more fun than dancing to American hip-hop. The pervasive influence of MTV and its genre are felt even here, and teens are often seen sporting Metallica and Beavis and Butthead T-shirts.

COLONY TO INDEPENDENCE

The first settlers are thought to have arrived on Yap around 3,500 years ago, but little is known of these people. In 1526, Dioga da Rocha became the first Western explorer to land here, stopping at Ulithi Atoll. The Spanish established a Catholic mission on Ulithi in 1731, but Jesuits were massacred after a disagreement with the island chiefs.

It is sometimes said that when the first Europeans to visit Yap pointed towards the island and asked what it was called, the Yapese, sitting their canoes, misunderstood and thought the visitors were inquiring about the name for their paddles. "Yap," is what they said. This, at least, is one story of how the islands got their name, al-

ROBERT RICKE and MARIA HULTS   Manta birostris Yap

though it is probably apocryphal. "Wa'ab" is close enough to European ears to "Yap" to be a sufficient explanation.

In the 1870s, an American sailor, David O'Keefe, survived a shipwreck and found himself on Yap. He developed a prosperous copra business, helping the Yapese mine and fashion stone money from basalt brought over from Palau in return for copra—which he then sold to European trading vessels operating in the Pacific. His was a rather odd tenure on these islands. He dubbed himself "His Majesty," and played the role to the hilt.

In 1899, Germany purchased Yap (and the rest of Micronesia) from Spain, and built hospitals, bridges, canals, radio towers and schools. They lost Yap to the Japanese, along with the rest of their Pacific holdings, in 1914. This began a period of virtual enslavement as Japan began to fortify Micronesia for empirical conquest.

Thankfully, Yap saw little action in World War II. The Americans, having already spent considerable lives, effort, and artillery on Palau and Chuuk, never invaded, although they did bomb the island daily for three years. Many elderly Yapese still speak Japanese.

The constitution of the Federated States of Micronesia, with Yap as the westernmost state, went into effect in 1979, and full independence came in 1986. In Yap State, the island chiefs are given wide berth in the decision-making process, and hold considerable political and social power.

REEF AND JUNGLE

Yap proper is a complex of five islands, of volcanic origin, surrounded by a wide fringing reef. With an average daily temperature of 27.4°C (81.4°F) and high humidity, days can be sweltering—although nights often are cool and comfortable. With a yearly average of 3,087 millimeters (121.5 in.) of rain, showers are frequent, but usually brief, and their cooling influence is welcome.

Mantas deploy their odd cephalic lobes and open their broad mouths only when they are actively straining plankton. Otherwise the lobes are tightly wrapped into streamlined points and the mouth sealed shut, as here.

Yap's Ubiquitous Quid

BETEL CHEWING IS A PASTIME THAT GREASES the wheels of every aspect of social intercourse in Micronesian society. "When you don't have the answer, chew betelnut," say the Yapese. "There is wisdom in betelnut." At least, I imagine, it gives you *time* to find the answer.

For visitors, the most notable manifestation of this habit are the "No Chewing" signs you will see posted in restaurants and businesses seeking the tourist trade. The average unsuspecting tourist is usually at least somewhat repulsed by the incessant and copious

SOHTE KENDIP EN **PWUH** BEATLE NUT SPIT NOT ALLOWED

DAVID LEONARD Pohnpei

spitting of the bright-red juice. Or shocked: more than one tourist has mistaken betel spit for blood (one early European visitor to Southeast Asia worried that the population was suffering from a massive outbreak of tuberculosis).

NUT, LEAF, AND LIME

Chewing betel is an ancient tradition, dating back at least two millennia. The quid has three traditional ingredients: areca nut (from the palm *Areca catechu*), betel pepper leaf (from the vine *Piper betle*), and slaked lime (usually from calcined sea shells). One takes a slice of areca nut, which looks like an acorn, though much bigger and without the seed cap, adds a bit of lime paste, wraps the lot in a de-veined pepper leaf, and chews.

The pharmacology of the quid is complex, including arecoline, arecaine, and five other less active alkaloids from the areca nut,

together with phenols—like eugenol, or clove oil—of varying strengths and types in the pepper leaf (the phenols present depend on the strain of leaf and where it was grown). Arecoline, like nicotine, is toxic in large enough doses, but unlike tobacco, betel is not physically addictive. The lime produces the proper alkaline environment to activate the other ingredients. The result is mild euphoria, and particularly at first, copious reddened saliva.

The betel habit is widespread throughout the Indo-Pacific region, stretching from Madagascar in the west, up the coast of Africa and into India (where it is currently becoming even more popular), throughout Southeast Asia, north along the coast of China, and east through Indonesia and the Western Pacific all the way to Fiji.

The palm and pepper vine are now so widely distributed that scientists find it difficult to determine where the plants originally evolved, but most evidence points to the Malaysian peninsula. The word "betel," in fact, is considered to have come from a Portuguese distortion of an old Malayan Sanskrit-derived word for leaf.

In addition to the three principal ingredients, many other materials are added to the quid, depending on local custom: cardamoms, nutmeg, cloves, camphor, gambier (a tanning agent, a popular addition in western Indonesia), dried ginger, black pepper, and tobacco.

Modern science has intervened as well. In Palau, betel chewers were using caustic unslaked lime powder, with hazardous results to the public health, until Dr. Victor Yano introduced the practice of using a paste of wetted lime (as is common elsewhere in the betel-chewing world).

The taste is bitter, but oddly pleasant. And our author feels obligated to note that, although not known for being obsessive or compulsive, he still finds it hard to explain why after a month in Micronesia he found himself chewing throughout the day.

Beautiful birds and bright green lizards fill the rain forests. The occasional domesticated pig or goat can be found tethered to a tree. As in much of the Pacific, fruitbats are prized as food on Yap, though there are increasing efforts to save them from local extinction.

Manta rays, of course, are Yap's main attraction, but there is a great deal of incredibly diverse hard coral, although there is little soft coral here. Outside the channels the water is especially clear in Yap, which makes it somewhat easier to spot pelagics in the blue water offshore. Keep your eyes open and you will be graced with visions of occasional sharks and all kinds of rays.

Lately, along with decreasing fish populations, I've noticed many areas where the hard coral was shattered. With the relatively small number of divers coming to Yap, I can only surmise that this is a result of fish-bombing, although I have not seen it first-hand. It is, however, considered a traditional right to harvest sea turtles, particularly on the outer islands. The impact of this practice on turtle populations is unknown.

A MODEST ECONOMY

Though tourism here is in an embryonic state, facilities, hotels, operators and visitors seem to double yearly. Almost half of the families in Yap, especially on the outer islands, exist at a subsistence level. Most of those who are employed work in the tourism and service industries. Clans work together to grow and manufacture needed food, clothing, and housing.

To compensate for the gradual reduction of U.S. aid, the government is initiating development of its fishing, tourism, and garment industries. The literacy rate is high, especially among the young. Many go on to study in the United States and Japan.

In Yap, the grease of civil society is often called "The Pacific Way," which includes decision-making by consensus, and living modestly. Herein lies the friction between Yap and modern global capitalism.

Yap has more than 13,000 stone 'coins,' if such a term can be used for items that reach four meters in diameter and can weigh five tons. The stone money, one of the most famous aspects of Yapese traditional culture, is called rai. The value of the stones is not based on size, but rather on a complicated formula that takes into account the age of the piece, as well as its history of ownership. The holes are so that the rai can be transported, by passing a log through, although as a practical matter they are rarely moved, even when ownership changes. It is disrespectful to stand or sit on stone money, and it is illegal to remove it from Yap, although one imagines that rai would be pretty impervious to theft.

TAMMY PELUSO rai Yap

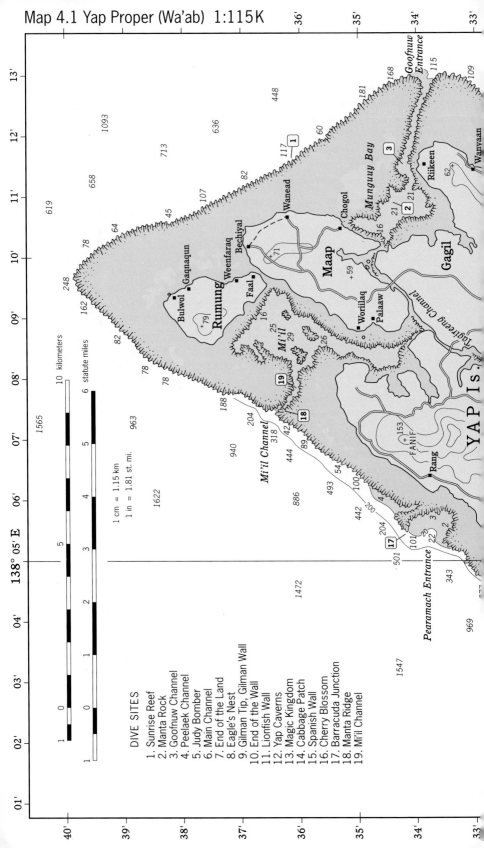

Map 4.1 Yap Proper (Wa'ab) 1:115K

138° 05' E

DIVE SITES

1. Sunrise Reef
2. Manta Rock
3. Goofnuw Channel
4. Peelaek Channel
5. Judy Bomber
6. Main Channel
7. End of the Land
8. Eagle's Nest
9. Gilman Tip, Gilman Wall
10. End of the Wall
11. Lionfish Wall
12. Yap Caverns
13. Magic Kingdom
14. Cabbage Patch
15. Spanish Wall
16. Cherry Blossom
17. Barracuda Junction
18. Manta Ridge
19. Mi'il Channel

kilometers

statute miles

1 cm = 1.15 km
1 in = 1.81 st. mi.

Goofnuw Entrance

Munguuy Bay

Rumung

Bulwol
Gaqnaqun
Weenfaraq
Bechiyal
Faal
Wanead
Chogol
Riikeen
Waryaan

Maap

Gagil

Mi'il

Woriilaq
Palaaw

Mi'il Channel

Tagreeng Channel

Rang

FANIF

YAP Is.

Pearamach Entrance

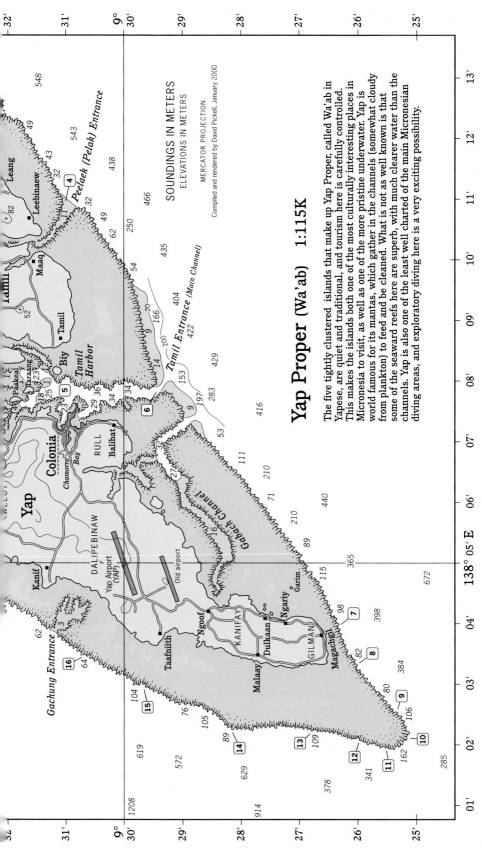

Yap Proper (Wa'ab) 1:115K

SOUNDINGS IN METERS
ELEVATIONS IN METERS

MERCATOR PROJECTION

Compiled and rendered by David Pickell, January 2000

The five tightly clustered islands that make up Yap Proper, called Wa'ab in Yapese, are quiet and traditional, and tourism here is carefully controlled. This makes the islands both one of the most culturally interesting places in Micronesia to visit, as well as one of the more pristine places underwater. Yap is world famous for its mantas, which gather in the channels (somewhat cloudy from plankton) to feed and be cleaned. What is not as well known is that some of the seaward reefs here are superb, with much clearer water than the channels. Yap is also one of the least well charted of the main Micronesian diving areas, and exploratory diving here is a very exciting possibility.

Yap

Colonia

Tamil Harbor

Peelaek (Pelak) Entrance

Tamil Entrance (Main Channel)

Gaabch Channel

Gachung Entrance

RULL

Balibat

Chamorro Bay

DALIPEBINAW

Yap Airport (YAP)

Old airport

KANIFAY

DALIPEBINAW

Kanif

Taafniith

Ngoof

Malaay

Dulkaan

Ngariy

Gilman

Magachgil

Garim

Tamil

Biy

Tamil

Maaq

Paakeal

Taraang

Leebinaew

Leang

Where Mantas have Names
and the Reef Walls are Stunning

YAP, OF COURSE, IS HOME TO A world-famous squad of cooperative manta rays, but there's much more to diving this still largely unexplored reef system.

"A lot of people are selling us this way: go to Palau, go to Chuuk, then spend two days in Yap to see the mantas and get out of there—but that's just wrong," says Yap Divers' Bill Acker. "The mantas are a great attraction, a great hook, but the southern tip—the Walls, Yap Cav-

By no means should you skip Yap's manta-filled channels, but some of the reef sites—Gilman Tip and Barracuda Junction come first to mind—are simply astounding.

erns—those are *great* dives. There's a pod of orca whales, carpets of soft corals, huge schools of pilot whales, hammerhead sharks, sawfish—and about half the reef has never been dived yet. We wish we had more time to explore.

"The only thing we're a little short on is wreck diving. Yap was only blockaded, not bombed. The whole Sixth Fleet was at Ulithi, a hundred-and-fifty miles from here, but outside of a couple of downed planes, there are no real World War II wrecks here to dive."

I have to agree with Bill. I have seen many vibrant hard coral reefs and wandering pelagics here. And,

what I consider to be Yap's most valuable asset, there is still a wealth of unexplored areas. I always try to get the dive operator to take me on exploratory dives. If you spend enough time diving here, I'll bet they'll agree to take you out for a look-see as well.

DIVING ON YAP

The islands' dive sites are clustered in three basic areas: the southern tip, the northeast channels, and the western reef and Mi'il Channel. Many of the sites in any one grouping are simply different stops along the same fringing reef.

The channels, in both the east and west, are dived to see the mantas. Goofnuw Channel is the most recently discovered, and Mi'il Channel is the most famous. You *will* see at least one manta on your dive, and probably more. (Yap Divers guarantees you will see a manta, or you can dive with them for free until you do.)

Mantas are clearly distinguishable by their markings, and those of Yap have been catalogued and named. There's Yoko, Stubby (named for the absence of his tail), and almost fifty more.

Divers wait for the mantas' arrival crouched behind a rock or outcropping on the bottom of the channel, which is 50 meters wide and 20 meters deep, bordered by vertical walls. Traversing the channels is a coral ridge that rises within a meter of the surface. The manta rays, which can grow to a span of almost five meters, glide along slowly as they feed on the

TAMMY PELUSO   Pterois volitans   Micronesia, unspecified

plankton brought in by the tide. No one knows exactly why the mantas come here—some say for feeding, others suggest the cleaning stations are more important. Bill Acker thinks Yap's channels serve as a mating ground.

The sites on the southern tip are drift dives along the reef wall, though there are some sites where you can get out of the current and explore at your own pace. After you've seen the mantas, you'll probably want to experience some of this lovely wall diving, but I know people who dive the channels twice a day for a week just to keep getting close to the mantas. They *are* otherworldly and very impressive.

The sites below are listed in geographical order, beginning in the north and working clockwise around Yap Proper, and keyed to Map 4.1, pages 114–115.

SUNRISE REEF [1]

Just offshore from the beach where the Maap Islanders watch the sunrise is this gem. It lies a mile northwest of Goofnuw Entrance, near the northeastern tip of Maap. The coral formations here are noticeably different from those on the other side of the island—they're bigger, and more colorful. Also, because this site is very little trafficked, the fields of lettuce coral, banquet-sized table corals, and thorny stretches of staghorn coral in blues and greens are all pristine and glowing.

Usually, the current here is negligible, and thus there is not as much big action here as at the southernmost sites. Nonetheless it's a lovely dive. Be on the lookout for a few large cuttlefish. You'll find the reef wall at ten meters, and follow this down to 30 meters, where you reach a flat bottom.

This is where most of the action is. The typically excellent visibility will allow you to see the occasional turtle or shark off in the blue water, but only on those days when the current is running.

For whatever reason, Yap's reef hosts an inordinate number of common lionfish, including a higher than normal percentage of melanistic forms. On some sites, such as 'Lionfish Wall,' you can encounter dozens of them.

Lionfish have been known to hunt in groups, using their broad pectoral fins to herd smaller fish into corners of the reef. Once pinned, the hapless victims are promptly inhaled.

The largest manta ray on record measured 6.7 meters (22 feet) from wingtip to wingtip, and there have been reports of specimens up to 9 meters (30 feet) across, although these latter should be approached with some skepticism. In any case, specimens of more than about five meters (16 feet) wingspan are rare.

Until relatively recently, scientists identified two species in the genus, but it has now been determined that there is a single, circumtropical species of manta. Thus Manta alfredi (Krefft 1868), the Pacific manta of the older texts, is now considered a junior and invalid synonym of Manta birostris (Donndorff 1798).

This channel—and Mi'il, on the opposite side—is the reason people come to Yap to dive. On the northeast side of the main island, the channel contains a stretch of cleaning stations sometimes known as "Valley of the Rays." The various sites in Goofnuw are called Manta Rock, the Car Wash, and Merry-Go-Round, and they are all frequented by a group of mantas that come here to feed, clean, or mate. The "season" for Goofnuw, when the mantas tend to stay on this side, runs from June through October. During the rest of the year, Mi'il is more productive.

Seeing the mantas here is a matter of waiting for them to come to you. Settle into the scenery, breathe calmly to thin your bubble stream, and wait for the mantas. They arrive with surprising dependability. By arriving early, you give the silt a chance to settle back to the bottom, improving the visibility. Between the current and the makeup of this chan-

nel, visibility rarely exceeds 20 meters, and is usually a bit less, so small groups of no more than six experienced divers is an optimum size.

The wait can be as long as 15 minutes, during which you'll have ample time to familiarize yourself with a square meter of underwater real estate. There is much to see living among the rocks—morays, shells, shrimp, lobsters, and interesting smaller fish—so this is not a hardship.

Suddenly, someone signals for you to look into the murky distance, and there they are. Very, very impressive, these ghostly black-and-white behemoths. The rays soar sometimes within inches of your head as they glide down the channel, so be ready for some serious excitement. It seems that their curiosity is also piqued, so the mantas will occasionally come very close and examine you.

Stay very still and observe. There is no "riding" on these majestic animals, so forget what you've read or seen in pictures from the

TAMMY PELUSO   Manta birostris   Mi'il Ridge

cowboy days of diving. First of all, the very idea of riding a manta is rude and dastardly, and second, if aggravated and bothered, they will likely leave the area, ruining one of the world's best dive sites. Go ride your buddy, if you have to.

PEELAEK CHANNEL [4]

This site is just around the corner, heading north, from the entrance to the main channel into Tamil Harbor. Turtles congregate here, and you're likely to see them on every dive. Thick schools of big red snapper dodge the sharks that are fairly common here. To witness the most action, stay calm and keep close to the channel walls.

MAIN CHANNEL [6]

There is a dive site at the mouth of the Main Channel, but with increased boat traffic, unpredictable currents, and questionable water quality, there are better sites to visit. A wreck called the *Laura Marie* lies here in 15 meters of water, but there is little of interest on her decks.

More interesting is a snorkel on the Japanese "Judy" bomber lying in five meters of water on the southern side of the channel mouth. It's a good site to visit during a surface interval between the northern and southern sites. Though much of the engine and exterior surface is overgrown with coral and encrusting sponge, the cockpit gauges and controls are still intact.

The Yokosuka D4Y or "Judy" bomber was expected to be the pride of the Japanese air force, though few did much damage to American hardware. They were certainly not as effective as the smaller, but deadly effective Mitsubishi A6M "Zero."

END OF THE LAND [7]

A pleasant half hour by boat, southwest of Colonia, takes you to the very southern tip of Yap Island.

TAMMY PELUSO Salarias fasciatus Micronesia, unspecified

Here, just offshore from Magachgil village in the Gilman district, is End of the Land. The site is an old river bed that continues out, carving a channel deep into the reef.

Swimming along this channel, perpendicular to the shore, you'll encounter fish and other creatures that prefer to live in an area out of the stronger current that sweeps laterally along the reef. Adjust your eyes to "macro," as many of the interesting animals living here are small and well camouflaged.

Look in the sand for the occasional sleeping shark, turtle, crocodile fish or sting-ray. Lobsters live in the crevices along the "river banks" and are best seen at night. In the open expanse in the middle of the channel, huge schools of jacks swirl in the tidal flow.

This combtoothed blenny is a large and common species, found from the Red Sea to Micronesia. As an algae feeder, this fish prefers areas of rubble and dead coral. This is a young specimen, and the strong red of its pectoral fins is a coloration some authors have associated with the Indian Ocean form of the species.

The Peaceful Devilfish

THE MANTA RAY (MANTA BIROSTRIS) is one of the ocean's largest and most spectacular creatures. The striking cephalic lobes earned this

DAVID LEONARD Colonia

A section of the manta board at Yap Divers. To date, they have done belly sketches of some fifty specimens.

only one species of manta, with a circumglobal range in tropical and warm temperate seas. Although there have been unconfirmed reports of specimens up to nine meters (30 ft.), the largest verified specimen, taken in the Bahamas, had a wingspan of 6.7 meters (22 ft.). Such giants—the animal weighed 1,400 kilograms (3,100 lbs.)—are rare, but mantas of four to five meters (13–16 ft.) across are common.

The rays gather in Yap's plankton-filled channels to feed, be cleaned, and, from December through April, to mate. Several similar sites have been discovered recently, including the offshore channels of Borneo's Berau Delta, and a site off North Flores. Recently, operators off the Kona coast of Hawai'i have identified a resident population (40 specimens have been named) in much clearer water.

SPIKE, STUBBY, AND JALAPEÑO

To date, Yap Divers has identified and named 50 mantas in the Yap population, 90 percent of them females. The program began in 1988, and at first the rays were named for physical characteristics, such as "Spike," who has only a short tail, or "Stubby" who has no tail at all (in both cases, probably from shark attacks). Then Bill Acker and the team realized that the markings on the white belly of the mantas were unique to each ray.

A fish with chili pepper–shaped markings is named "Jalapeño;" one that looks vaguely Asian, "Yoko." You get the idea. You'll recognize the mantas that you see, but if you spot and photograph a new one, Bill gives you the opportunity to name it yourself.

fish and the rest of its family (the nine smaller *Mobula* species) the name devilfish or devilray a long time ago, although this seems patently unfair for such graceful and inoffensive creatures. (The entire family is without stinging spines). "Manta," at least, has a more benign origin, coming from a Latino word for a rough blanket or cloak.

Currently there is believed to be

EAGLE'S NEST [8]

Just south from End of the Land is a sandy flat used as a refuge and cleaning station by many spotted eagle rays. I've seen them here on every dive and they're beautiful. Interesting and varied starfish and juvenile reef are numerous here, but the coral cover is poor.

If the current is running north, you will often (happily) end up here when you dive Gilman Tip or the End of the Wall. You'll know when you come to it because of the wide open plain of hard coral sloping out to sea. Also look for large schools of black barracuda.

GILMAN TIP / GILMAN WALL [9]

This is one of Yap's most famous dives. For millennia, new coral has been growing on top of old coral, forming huge bluffs of oddly shaped limestone on this ancient and very unusual reef wall. Before you descend, note how far the coral reef shelf extends out from the land here. Somewhere in this broad reef flat is a bottomless hole, in which the early people of Yap buried their dead. It is among the most sacred of Yap's ancient burial grounds and strictly off limits to tourists (and it's unlikely anyone would violate this taboo, since the dive boats wouldn't be able to navigate across the shallow, treacherous reef flat even if they wanted to).

This huge coral shelf dips gently into the sea for 20 meters, where storms of pyramid butterflyfish fall like confetti among lacy coral trees. Look among the rocks and corals here for a plethora of tunicates, shrimp, shells and sea cucumbers. There are dozens of big anemone clusters here. Then the wall drops almost vertically to 40 meters.

Here is where the current usually splits, and pelagics and schooling fish can be seen in the wash—schools of jacks circle near prowling

dog-tooth tuna, while reef white-tips and gray reef sharks patrol the margins. You will be drifting here, but in which direction will depend upon which side of the split you enter. Either way, your dive at Gilman Tip will take you to the adjacent site: Eagle's Nest or End of the Wall.

Visibility can exceed 50 meters

TAMMY PELUSO   Manta birostris   Mi'il Channel mouth

and it is not necessary to make deep dives here (or anywhere in Yap, for that matter). The coral cover tends to thin after about 25 meters anyway. Gilman has a particularly large number of what to me appear to be "exploded" brain corals.

END OF THE WALL [10]

This is the furthest reach of the reef, where the wall ends and the

The cleaning stations in Mi'il Channel are among the best places in the world to observe mantas. It looks to me like this particular specimen would love for a wrasse to come along and pluck that nasty looking tubercle from the tip of its right cephalic lobe.

TAMMY PELUSO   Manta birostris   Mi'il Channel mouth

For manta watching, Mi'il Channel is at its best from about October through June. During the summer and early autumn the mantas congregate in Goofnuw, on the opposite side of the island group, to take advantage of seasonal plankton flows.

reef is a kind of coral bluff from 20 meters to the 40-meter bottom. As you descend, watch the bottom, where you'll see sleeping sharks laid out like jet-fighters on a runway. Turtles, bumphead parrots and thousands of juveniles hover near the wall.

LIONFISH WALL [11]

Although Yap in general is home to an unusual number of lion-fish, this popular spot seems to have a spectacular abundance, including several of the more unusual black specimens (a melanistic form of the common lionfish, *Pterois volitans*). Spotting ten or twenty lionfish here a single dive is not unusual, and you will be surprised at their size—sometimes a foot long.

Sweepers cover the wall in many places, and jacks, butterflyfish and angelfish flourish. If the current is stronger, you'll see a fair amount of pelagic action, including tuna, rays, and turtles. Also scattered among the beautiful and large coral heads are an amazing amount of shells, both live and abandoned.

If you have good eyes, you can find the well-camouflaged leaf fish (*Taenianotus triacanthus*) here, which is rare in most of Micronesia. Look in the shallows at the top of the wall for this unusual scorpi-onfish. They often further the illu-sion of a blade of algae or sponge by waving gently in current. Lionfish Wall begins at five meters and drops straight down to 50. The vis-ibility is always remarkable—up to 60 meters. A very nice dive less than a kilometer north of End of the Wall.

YAP CAVERNS [12]

This site is a series of cuts in the reef slope that lead down to a sand bottom at 40 meters. The numerous large caverns and coral grottos are fascinating to explore, and the visi-bility here is always excellent. If you're good with air, and the current is running, you can do both Lionfish Wall and the Caverns on the same drift dive.

At ten meters, a shelf supports acres of huge hard corals among which swim a large, and quite im-pressive school of big bumphead parrotfish. When the current is up, a pack of gray reef and reef white-tip sharks can be found snooping around.

Huge brain corals and blanket-ing leather corals form the back-drop, and are home to the morays, parrotfish, and bronze sweepers, which comprise most of the action along with a smattering of small Napoleon wrasse, fairy basslets, lobsters, small fish of a hundred

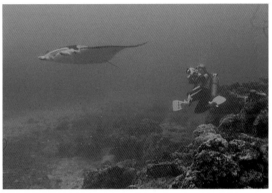

ROBERT RICKE and MARIA HULTS   Manta birostris   Yap

species, and big carpet anemones.

This is a marvelous drift dive during which you can break from the current to explore the cuts. As a night dive it is almost unsurpassed. The darkness brings out dozens of lobsters, lionfish and exotic shells.

MAGIC KINGDOM [13]

The coral here has formed sta-lagmites that peak high up into the surge zone. At the base of these strange forms, a sandy bottom reaches out into the deep water, dot-ted with fields of staghorn coral in electric blues and greens. Christmas tree coral and huge coral heads grow everywhere. Schools of jacks come

This videographer, completing his pan of a passing manta, is doing his job the right way. Whether shoot-ing still or moving media, you should do the following: stake out a position by the ridge, exhale calmly, and wait for the fish to come to you. Chas-ing these creatures will only let them know you are a rank amateur, and with a disdainful flick of their rays they will reward you with a brief view of their behinds, then disap-pear explosively into the gloom.

MIKE SEVERNS Epinephelus merra Majuro Atoll

The honeycomb grouper is a relatively small (less than 10 inches), and quite attractively patterned member of its genus. They like lagoons and other protected areas, and can be found lurking in thickets of branching Acropora or, as here, Seriatopora.

and go with the ebb and flow. There are few pelagics here, but there are big schools of red snapper.

CABBAGE PATCH [14]

At the edge of the main fringing reef, there's a short wall here. Ten meters down, it becomes an overhang, under which unicornfish, red snapper, and fusiliers peer out into the sun-filtered water. Sandy fingers comb the gullies between rocky cuts in the reef. At 20 meters, schools of large barracuda form. This is a great dive full of interesting landscapes against which you can frame your subjects.

SPANISH WALL [15]

Five meters drops to fifty, and then a sandy bottom slopes gently to the sea. Schools of red snapper, smaller sharks, and thousands of small reef fish swim amongst the coral outcroppings. This is one place in Yap where you will see some Nephtheid soft corals, mostly dark purple. It's a long and relaxing drift, and very pleasant.

BARRACUDA JUNCTION [17]

Outside the fringing reef, five kilometers south of the Mi'il Channel mouth, is one of the newer sites discovered in the past few years. It's a good example of how much better Yap is destined to become as more and more "treasures" are found. This vertical wall starts just below the surface and falls quickly to over 50 meters where it continues to drop into the sea. The hard coral is healthy and diverse. Large pelagics, including adult hawksbills seem to favor this spot. Every time I've dived the Junction I've been caught in a school of a thousand barracuda, which catch and juggle the filtered sunlight through their silver and black stripes.

South of Barracuda Junction is the rarely dived Cherry Blossom, a nice site with untouched coral.

MANTA RIDGE [18] and MI'IL CHANNEL [19]

Located northwest of Yap Island, Mi'il Channel winds its way from the open to form a large lagoon, bounded by Rumung, Maap and Yap Islands. This is Yap's original, and best-known manta channel.

Mi'il is best dived toward the end of an incoming tide, almost at slack high. The current can be very powerful here when the tide is running, and a dive here at these times should be attempted by an experienced diver only. The best season for seeing the mantas is late October through early June.

As you descend 20 meters into the 50-meter-wide natural channel, you descend you'll notice that both sides of the channel are lined with huge coral heads. You can gain temporary refuge from the fast current behind these, and also conceal yourself from the shy mantas. Large eagle rays also frequent this channel, and they are heading to Manta Ridge for cleaning as well. Always present are white-tip sharks (usually seen sleeping on the bottom) and schools of jacks. Among the rocks and coral heads are sea fans, crinoids, and large anemones.

Drifting through the channel, you will soon arrive at Manta Ridge, a coral and rock bridge across the channel which rises to within a few meters of the surface. This tidal backwater is filled with plankton and microscopic plant life which lures the mantas that can be seen here with practically every tidal shift. These suspended particles, however, also cloud the water, making a ghostly vista. The ridge has a lot of activity, as schooling snappers, jacks, rays and smaller sharks circle in the soup. There are lots of lobsters here. At 10–20 meters, it is not a deep dive.

To see the mantas, apply the same *modus operandi* as you did in Goofnuw Channel: stay close to the bottom and try to leave the sand undisturbed. The quieter you are, the closer the mantas will approach. The time of day when tide conditions are perfect for Mi'il will vary, of course, so to maximize your chances of seeing a memorable display of mantas, it would be best to set aside at least a few days for your visit to Yap.

This photograph makes it obvious how the hawksbill turtle got its name. Growing to a carapace length of less than a meter, this is one of the smaller of the sea turtles (only the two ridley sea turtles are smaller). Its range is circumtropical, and it and the green turtle are relatively common in Micronesia. Hawksbills tend to be found close to the reef, and they are omnivores, but favor invertebrates like jellyfish, hydroids, soft corals, sea urchins, and shellfish. The scutes of this animal's carapace provide the tortoise-shell of commerce. It has been suggested that with the proper technique, these can be removed without killing the animal, but this strikes me as questionable, and even grotesque. Plastic makes a perfectly fine material for a comb.

TAMMY PELUSO   Eretmochelys imbricata bissa   Micronesia, unspecified

An old truck on the San Francisco Maru. This 5,831-ton passenger/cargo ship is now one of the deepest, and most dangerous of Chuuk's wrecks—forty meters to the bow deck, and eighty to the bottom.

ROBERT RICKE and MARIA HULTS   San Francisco Maru   Chuuk Lagoon

The Yamagiri Maru, a 6,432-ton mixed passenger and freight ship, now lies portside down in forty meters of water, the bridge windows curtained with soft corals. The ship was carrying a deadly cargo—huge artillery shells, each half a meter in diameter and a meter and a half long, destined for experimental guns on the warships Musashi and Yamato. The guns were never fired.

This huge lagoon, the site of the Allies' single most damaging attack on Japanese naval power, now offers the world's finest wreck diving—some sixty beautifully encrusted ships litter the bottom here. "The sea tends her graves well," writes Sylvia Earle, one of the first divers to have explored Chuuk.

Chuuk

CHUUK LAGOON (UNTIL 1989 known as Truk) is one of the most famous dive sites in the world. Since it was first explored by sport divers in the late 1960s, this site has been known as the undisputed wreck diving capital of the world. Typically, a reputation like this makes promises a site cannot fulfill. This is not the case with Chuuk. No hype, no exaggeration: for wreck diving, on a world scale, Chuuk is truly in a class of one.

This wide, tropical lagoon, 64 kilometers across and 50–80 meters deep, conceals more than sixty shipwrecks and the remains of several hundred aircraft. Some forty of these, most of them clustered around the Nomoneas Islands, have been located and are diveable. In 1975 the entire lagoon was declared a living museum.

Most of the wrecks date from a single attack—Operation Hail-stone, one of the most devastating aerial bombardments in the history of warfare. Beginning February 17, 1944, for two days, thirty separate waves of aircraft from nine Allied carriers pummeled the Japanese fleet at Chuuk, then a heavily mined and guarded outpost called the "Gibraltar of the Pacific." The resulting losses totaled 250–275 Japanese aircraft and 220,000 metric tons of shipping, a record for the war. U.S. Task Force 50, which conducted the attack, lost just 41 aircraft.

The United States took control of Micronesia after the war, and the Japanese wreckage was unmolested. Jacques Cousteau, with the help of Kimiuo Aisek (as a 17-year-old, he witnessed Operation Hailstone) explored Chuuk Lagoon in 1967, identifying and photographing many of the ships, including the largest—the *Aikoko Maru*—as they

Map 5.1 Chuuk Lagoon (Truk) 1:300K

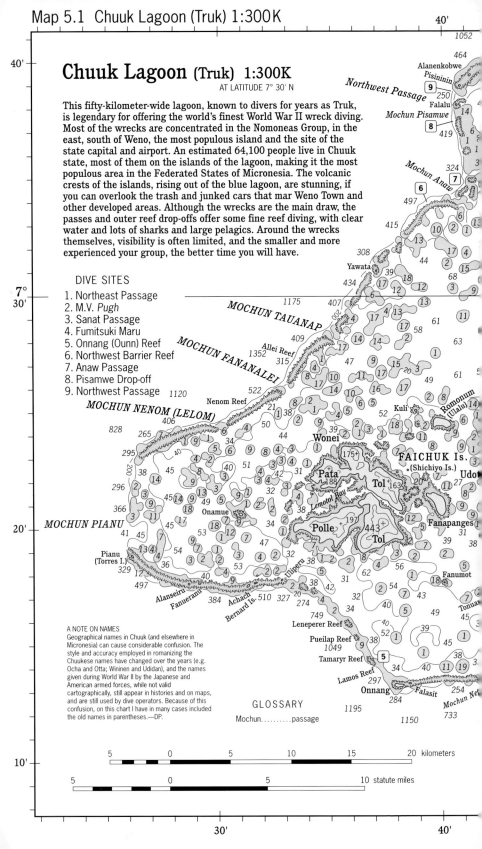

Chuuk Lagoon (Truk) 1:300K

AT LATITUDE 7° 30' N

This fifty-kilometer-wide lagoon, known to divers for years as Truk, is legendary for offering the world's finest World War II wreck diving. Most of the wrecks are concentrated in the Nomoneas Group, in the east, south of Weno, the most populous island and the site of the state capital and airport. An estimated 64,100 people live in Chuuk state, most of them on the islands of the lagoon, making it the most populous area in the Federated States of Micronesia. The volcanic crests of the islands, rising out of the blue lagoon, are stunning, if you can overlook the trash and junked cars that mar Weno Town and other developed areas. Although the wrecks are the main draw, the passes and outer reef drop-offs offer some fine reef diving, with clear water and lots of sharks and large pelagics. Around the wrecks themselves, visibility is often limited, and the smaller and more experienced your group, the better time you will have.

DIVE SITES

1. Northeast Passage
2. M.V. *Pugh*
3. Sanat Passage
4. Fumitsuki Maru
5. Onnang (Ounn) Reef
6. Northwest Barrier Reef
7. Anaw Passage
8. Pisamwe Drop-off
9. Northwest Passage

A NOTE ON NAMES

Geographical names in Chuuk (and elsewhere in Micronesia) can cause considerable confusion. The style and accuracy employed in romanizing the Chuukese names have changed over the years (e.g. Ocha and Otta; Wininen and Udidan), and the names given during World War II by the Japanese and American armed forces, while not valid cartographically, still appear in histories and on maps, and are still used by dive operators. Because of this confusion, on this chart I have in many cases included the old names in parentheses.—DP.

GLOSSARY

Mochun..........passage

Alanenkobwe
Pisininin
Falalu
Mochun Pisamwe
Northwest Passage
Mochun Anaw
Yawata
Mochun Tauanap
Mochun Fananalei
Allei Reef
Mochun Nenom (Lelom)
Nenom Reef
Mochun Pianu
Wonei
Pata
Polle
Onamue
Pianu (Torres I.)
Alanseiru
Fanuerami
Achach
Bernard Is.
Uligeru
Leneperer Reef
Pueilap Reef
Tamaryr Reef
Lamos Reef
Onnang
Falasit
Mochun Net
Faichuk Is.
(Shichiyo Is.)
Tol
Lemotol Bay
Fanapanges
Fanumot
Tonua
Udo
Kuli
Romonum (Ulalu)

Kilometers scale: 5 0 5 10 15 20 kilometers
Statute miles scale: 5 0 5 10 statute miles

40'
30'
7° 30'
7°
20'
10'

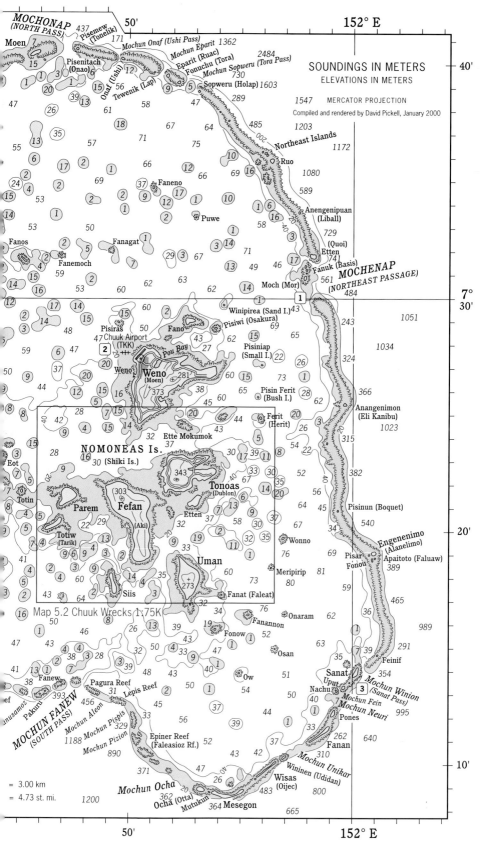

Map 5.2 Chuuk Wrecks 1:75K

DAVID LEONARD   The islands of Chuuk Lagoon, looking approximately south

Although some books mention the 'barrier reef' surrounding Chuuk Lagoon, more properly Chuuk is an 'almost atoll.' The original volcanic island has subsided, leaving only a few tips showing—the Faichuk and Nomoneas Island groups. The encircling reef is a palimpsest of the orginal coastline.

lay in their watery graves. American diving pioneer Dr. Sylvia Earle and photographer Al Giddings, also working with Aisek, evaluated the site again in the early 1970s. Today, thousands of divers a year visit this remarkable underwater museum.

Although known for depths that challenge most sport divers, many of Chuuk Lagoon's wrecks lie in a manageable 30–50 meters of water. Often, deck structures, masts and wheel houses start at a much more reasonable 12–35 meters.

Water clarity varies widely inside the lagoon, and it can be particularly cloudy during the rainy season, because of plankton blooms and jellyfish. The best time to dive Chuuk Lagoon is the dry monsoon, between November and May.

One of the best things about Chuuk is that most of the wrecks here are pristine, or near pristine. Some unauthorized "salvaging" means that some of the compasses, telegraphs, and smaller items are missing from some wrecks, but most ships still have their deck guns, engines, and screws. The Aisek family, among the first to have catalogued the sunken fleet, were also responsible for hiding sailors' remains deep inside the hulls so they would not end up in looters' collections.

Also unique to Chuuk is the unbelievable amount of coral growth

on every spar, mast and rail in the harbor. Dr. Earle and Giddings's survey of Chuuk, published in *National Geographic* in 1976, was one of the first to note the rapid growth rate of some corals and soft corals. Since nothing on the ships could be older than 31 years, Earle was able to establish accurate rates of annual growth. She found black coral trees three meters across, and hard coral colonies just as large.

Today, they are even bigger. Sometimes, the sheer number of fish—particularly pygmy sweepers—make photography difficult on many of the shallower sections of the downed ships.

A SUNKEN VOLCANO

The eleven islands in the center of the lagoon are the peaks of an extinct volcano, that has slowly subsided. In fact, the word "Chuuk" (pronounced "Chuke") derives from the Chuukese word for mountain, and most literally only applies to the Faichuk and Nomoneas groups. The other low cay islands on the barrier reef are *fanabi* or "sand islands," as are the other 290 atoll islands of Chuuk State.

Dense, impenetrable jungles cap each volcanic island, with coral banks and thickly rooted mangroves forming the circumferential breakwater. On the cay islands, eroded coral limestone creates dusty, infertile "soil." The reef circling Chuuk Lagoon is nearly continuous, and at 230 kilometers, one of the longest in the world.

Chuuk's annual rainfall averages 3,734 millimeters (147.0 in.), and from June through November, heavy rains, squalls and thunderstorms are fairly frequent. July and August are the wettest months, but even then the showers do not last long. Typhoons rarely strike here, and even in the rainy season, the weather can be perfect for weeks at a time.

Although the lagoon is calmest from June through October, visibility is not at its best during this period. September though April is the optimal time to dive. The yearly average temperature is 27.1°C (80.7°F), becoming cooler in the evening, and the humidity is consistently high, around 85 percent.

SHORT HISTORY OF CHUUK

Chuuk clan history begins in about the 14th century, when their ancestors arriving from what is believed to have been Kosrae. The Chuukese have a reputation even today for hot-headedness, and this served them quite well during the European age of exploration, when Chuuk was usually avoided because of the reputation of its inhabitants.

Spanish Captain Alonso de Arellano stopped in 1565, but after firing a few half-hearted shots at the hundreds of war canoes bearing down on him, he set the *San Lucas'* sails and departed. When Manuel Dublon entered the lagoon to collect sea cucumbers in 1814, he was the first European to stop at Chuuk in more than 200 years (his name, until recently, was attached to Tonoas Island).

The Spanish started the first copra plantations, but the Germans, who got the territory at the end of the 19th century, established a lasting peace among the island groups and convinced everyone to plant coconut trees.

When the Japanese began developing the Pacific territories they seized from Germany, they sent as many as 38,000 Japanese citizens to Chuuk, developing it as an important outpost of the Empire. As the war began, Chuuk was used by the Japanese as a repair facility, until in 1944 the United States decided it was too important not to attack.

The Japanese spotted the Allied reconnaissance planes, and moved their main battleships, carriers, destroyers and sub-chasers to the open sea and on to Palau. Seeing the ships leave, the Americans realized they had been spotted and threw out a red herring—using a code they

Like Vietnam War protesters in the United States, who placed flowers in the National Guardsmen's rifles, the warm Pacific Ocean has placed a beautiful Dendrophylliid coral on the bow gun of the Fujikawa Maru.

ROBERT RICKE and MARIA HULTS Fujikawa Maru Chuuk Lagoon

Chuuk

ROBERT RICKE and MARIA HULTS   Fujikawa Maru   Chuuk

ROBERT RICKE and MARIA HULTS   Kensho Maru   Chuuk

ROBERT RICKE and MARIA HULTS   Nippo Maru

THE GHOST FLEET

Diving Chuuk Lagoon is both fascinating and unsettling. When encountered on a dark sea bottom, layered with silt, even quotidian objects become otherworldly, like the basin and urinal (opposite, above) on the *Fujikawa Maru*. Tools of war, like a gas mask (right) and small tank (below) on the *Nippo Maru*, and a barrel of cartridge magazines (opposite, below) on the *Kensho Maru*, acquire poignancy as time, the sea, and the relentless activity of a quiet army of sponges, polyps, worms, and snails shroud them in living reef.

ROBERT RICKE and MARIA HULTS   Nippo Maru   Chuuk

ROBERT RICKE and MARIA HULTS Fujikawa Maru Chuuk

ROBERT RICKE and MARIA HULTS Shinokoku Maru Chuuk

The weight-saving holes in the spars and seats give away this Mitsubishi A6M fighter—the infamous 'Zero' (left)—now thirty meters underwater on the *Fujikawa Maru*. The apothocary of a ship's doctor (above) on the *Shinokoku Maru* has become a home for sponges and damselfish, but there are some relics, such as this one on the *Aikoku Maru* (right), that speak of a sorrow even the gentle efforts of the reef cannot erase . Please respect the remains of the men who died on these ships. The horror of their deaths was something we will never begin to understand.

ROBERT RICKE and MARIA HULTS Aikoku Maru Chuuk

knew had already been broken, they broadcast their "secret" plans to bypass Chuuk and head right to Saipan and Guam.

The Japanese cautiously relaxed, and as they did the U.S. Navy brought the largest armada ever assembled to within 45 miles of Chuuk. As Operation Hailstone began on February 17th, the Japan-

ROBERT RICKE and MARIA HULTS Yamagiri Maru Chuuk Lagoon

The Yamagiri Maru, north of Fefan Island, is one of the more accessible wrecks, with most of the interesting diving in fifteen to thirty meters.

ese were able to scramble 30 or 40 Zeros, and soon lost them all. In the first wave, 60 boats were sunk, and dozens of planes were destroyed on the runway.

In the second attack, in April, almost 600 of the 700 Japanese planes that made it into the air were downed over the lagoon. In the process, 81 American planes were destroyed. In June, a quick run to

Chuuk was planned to test the B-29s based in Tinian. Hundreds of Japanese were killed, and several islands were defoliated.

It took another 15 months before Tokyo surrendered, and in that time 15,000 people, including many Chuukese, starved to death on the battered islands.

STRUGGLING ECONOMY

An estimated 64,100 people, about half the population of the Federated States of Micronesia, live in Chuuk State. The state operates on a $20 million deficit, more than the rest of the Federation combined, and Chuuk is the target of considerable resentment by the rest of the federation.

In 2001, the Compact of Free Association with the United States will expire, causing many to wonder whether Chuuk will be able to manage without the $150 million annually in U.S. aid.

There have been continuing difficulties with the management of administrative funds intended for infrastructure, education, and social services on Chuuk. One of the biggest problems is reflected in the common saying, "Ke pach, ke fiber." Loosely translated, this means: "Stick by me, get a fiberglass boat."

Tourism is the only real industry here, and with only a couple of hundred hotel rooms, this is not enough to support an economy. The signs of poverty and dependency are more obvious on Chuuk than anywhere else in Micronesia.

Most Chuukese families get along through a combination of subsistence farming and occasional paid labor. A general lack of education here means that most management positions are held by outsiders. Historically these were Americans, but with the decreasing U.S. role here, they are increasingly coming to be held by Filipinos.

Deep, Beautiful, and Eerie
Exploring a World War II Graveyard

CHUUK LAGOON IS WORLD-renowned for its "Ghost Fleet," which attracts divers from every corner of the globe. Rusting hulls, some of which are still leaking fuel and oil, contribute heavily toward muddying the water with silt, so visibility is not as great here as at other Micronesian sites. "The smaller the group, the better the dive" is an important rule of thumb.

Experienced divers who can maintain neutral buoyancy and keep from scraping or in any way touching the wrecks will contribute toward a memorable dive for all. It is especially important here to *leave everything as you found it*. Future generations have a right to visit this memorial as well.

Most of the wrecks are quite deep (up to 80 meters), so make sure that your equipment is in top condition. The sunken fleet will not forgive faulty regulators, and dead batteries. Again, you must be responsible for yourself here. There is little margin for error at these depths.

Of the sixty or so ships that are known to have been sunk here, 38 have been charted, but the sites are not marked with buoys or any other visible signs (the Chuukese are wary of treasure hunters). Even finding the individual ships therefore demands a knowledgeable operator. Sometimes, the boat pilot will have to feel his way around for the exact location, especially in rougher weather. It all adds to the excitement, though, and be patient—you're in for a fascinating experience.

Chuuk also has some good wall diving on the blue water side of its fringing reef and reef cuts. Northeast Passage, Sanat Passage, Onnang (Ounn) Reef, Northwest Barrier Reef and Anaw Passage, Pisamwe Drop-off, and the Northwest Passage are some of the best reef dives (see MAP 5.1, pages 130–131, for the location of these sites). These

> For wreck diving, Chuuk is in a class of one. Many of the ships are deep, so be conservative here. And respect the artifacts and remains—this is a monument for future generations.

offer plenty of high-voltage, large pelagic fish action.

Wherever you dive in Chuuk, you will need to purchase a diving permit ($3); most operators take care of this for you. The numbers following the wreck names below, unless otherwise noted, are keyed to MAP 5.2, pages 142–143.

NIPPO MARU [1]

Off the eastern side of Tonoas Island, this is Chuuk's most impressive wreck. The *Nippo Maru* is a cargo vessel lying slightly to port in 50 meters of deep blue water. The bridge is at 30 meters, and her stern is pushed up against a wall. This boat, built in 1936, is filled with interesting artifacts: U.S. howitzers on the deck (35 meters) point to the sky in vain. There are light tanks, field artillery, and truck frames on the fore deck; empty shell casings and hemispherical mines in Hold #1 (45 meters) together with personal items including naval binoculars, shells, sake bottles, mess kits, boots, and pottery; in the bridge there is a ship's compass and a "working" throttle. It's interesting to swim along the railings and passageways, peering into the cabins. In the galley, a huge stove and cookware are still in place.

Discovered in 1979, the *Nippo* is 120 meters long with a 5-meter beam. She was able to do 16 knots. At one time she was a banana boat, but later became a water carrier. There are lots of fish here, including large schooling jacks and barracuda. Clouds of sweepers take the shape of structures. This is a deep dive, for early in the day.

AIKOKU MARU [2]

This is a large ship, lying just a mile south of the *Nippo*. A large gun graces the deck (55 meters), but the rear half of the ship is all that's left, starting from just aft of the rear stack. This fragment sits upright on a flat bottom (70 meters). There are large lounges with interesting artifacts (45 meters). The *Aikoku Maru* was 150 meters in length, with a 7-meter beam. Built in 1940, she was very fast, capable of 21 knots.

Unfortunately, the *Aikoku* has recently toppled over, while the *Palau Aggressor* live-aboard remained "moored" to its structure during a strong squall. There have been more than a dozen such incidents in the lagoon. Permanent, non-destructive moorings are long overdue in Chuuk.

M/V PUGH [2] Map 5.1 pp. 130–131

This is a cute little wreck that has nothing to do with World War II. The *Pugh* was sunk in 1965 by a group of presumed drug smugglers who then hopped a plane out of Chuuk. Today, the *Pugh* is filled with soft corals and reef fish—and is really quite beautiful. The vessel lies upright at 20 meters, and rises to within 6 meters of the surface. There are lots of clean passageways, and penetration is easy and safe.

FUMITSUKI MARU [4] Map 5.1 pp. 130–131

This destroyer, just found in 1987, surprised divers and historians alike. Japanese photographer Tomoyuki Yoshimura was able to locate it based on the recollections of sailors who survived the ship's sinking. Built in Japan in 1925 and launched in 1926, the *Fumitsuki* was in Chuuk undergoing repairs when her bridge was blown apart in the attack. The stern was uplifted by explosives, probably her own, detonated by Allied bombs. The *Fumitsuki* was capable of a remarkable 38 knots. She was 107 meters long, with a 10-meter beam.

Today, she rests upright, leaning slightly to port in 42 meters of water. What's left of her bridge lies at 30 meters, and her decks reach down to 40. There is an impressive torpedo launcher just aft of the machine gun deck mount. Large schools of batfish drift in and out of view. There is a great deal of black coral here, its branches forming delicate lace work against the blue water. Avoid deep penetration here, it's dark and confining.

There are human remains in some of the holds and in the engine room of the *Fumitsuki*, but respect the peace of those who died here. Can you imagine recreational divers penetrating the sunken ships in Pearl Harbor, arranging and photographing bones?

SAN FRANCISCO MARU [6]

This is the king of deep-water wrecks, and possibly one of the most awe-inspiring dives the lagoon has to offer. The *San Francisco* is

130 meters long, with a 17-meter beam. With 4,000 horsepower, the ship could reach a cruising speed of 14 knots. Unfortunately, not every dive guide will encourage—or, even allow—you to visit this site, since it is so deep.

The *San Francisco* is one of the oldest ships in the lagoon, having been built in 1919. She served as a cargo vessel in the war. The ship sits upright on a slope, bow down, in 80 meters of water, with her bow gun at 50 meters. Torpedoes and shells are scattered on the aft deck, and there is obvious bomb damage behind the wheel house. Starting at 40 meters, the bridge deck leads you down to the hull. You'll see light tanks at 55 meters and unusual hemi-mines on the fore deck. Penetration will afford you a glimpse of armored trucks in the forward second hold. Obviously, this dive is strictly for the early morning, if you're planning on doing another.

HOKI MARU [8]

Built in Scotland and used by New Zealand merchant marines, the *Hoki* was captured in 1942 on a voyage from Australia to Sri Lanka by the *Hokoku Maru* and the *Aikoku Maru*. (Today the *Aikoku* lies on the bottom just two kilometers away.) Though the bow is gone and the forecastle (at 23 meters) demolished, the *Hoki* rests upright in 50 meters of water. Her twin screws are at 45 meters; John Deere trucks, Caterpillar bulldozers, and tractors remain in the aft hold. Her engines are in place. The *Hoki* is 137 meters long with an 18-meter beam. She was powered by 3,550 horses and capable of 13 knots.

SEIKO MARU [9]

This 135-meter-long freighter is deep at 55 meters, but makes an interesting and thought-provoking dive. The top of the mast is at 10 meters, the bridge at 30 meters, and the deck at 40 meters, so you can choose your own profile. Unusual are the wooden wagon wheels, coral encrusted, that support an artillery gun. There is a spare prop

In the officers' washroom of the Fujikawa Maru, a tiled Japanese bath and even a stool remain preserved. This wreck is one of Chuuk's classic sites. It was an aircraft transport during the war, and contains Mitsubishi A6M 'Zero' fighters and parts. It is not particularly deep, and the masts remain above water, just south of Etten Island.

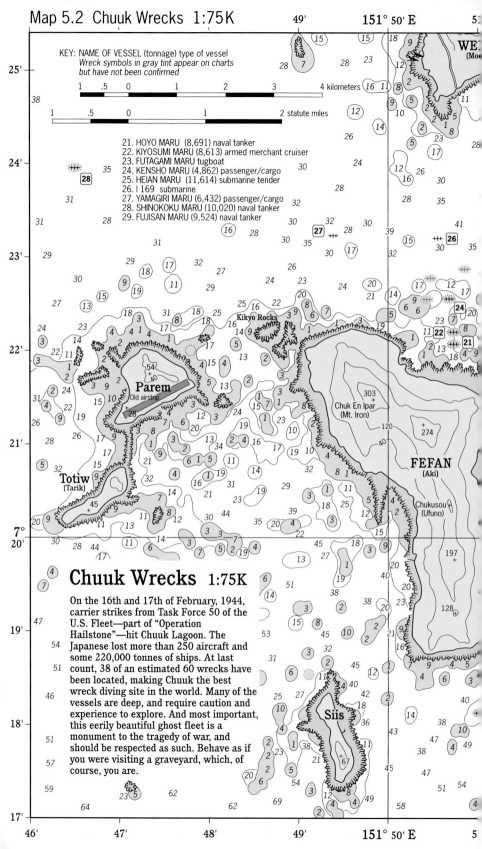

Map 5.2 Chuuk Wrecks 1:75K

KEY: NAME OF VESSEL (tonnage) type of vessel
Wreck symbols in gray tint appear on charts
but have not been confirmed

21. HOYO MARU (8,691) naval tanker
22. KIYOSUMI MARU (8,613) armed merchant cruiser
23. FUTAGAMI MARU tugboat
24. KENSHO MARU (4,862) passenger/cargo
25. HEIAN MARU (11,614) submarine tender
26. I 169 submarine
27. YAMAGIRI MARU (6,432) passenger/cargo
28. SHINOKOKU MARU (10,020) naval tanker
29. FUJISAN MARU (9,524) naval tanker

Chuuk Wrecks 1:75K

On the 16th and 17th of February, 1944,
carrier strikes from Task Force 50 of the
U.S. Fleet—part of "Operation
Hailstone"—hit Chuuk Lagoon. The
Japanese lost more than 250 aircraft and
some 220,000 tonnes of ships. At last
count, 38 of an estimated 60 wrecks have
been located, making Chuuk the best
wreck diving site in the world. Many of the
vessels are deep, and require caution and
experience to explore. And most important,
this eerily beautiful ghost fleet is a
monument to the tragedy of war, and
should be respected as such. Behave as if
you were visiting a graveyard, which, of
course, you are.

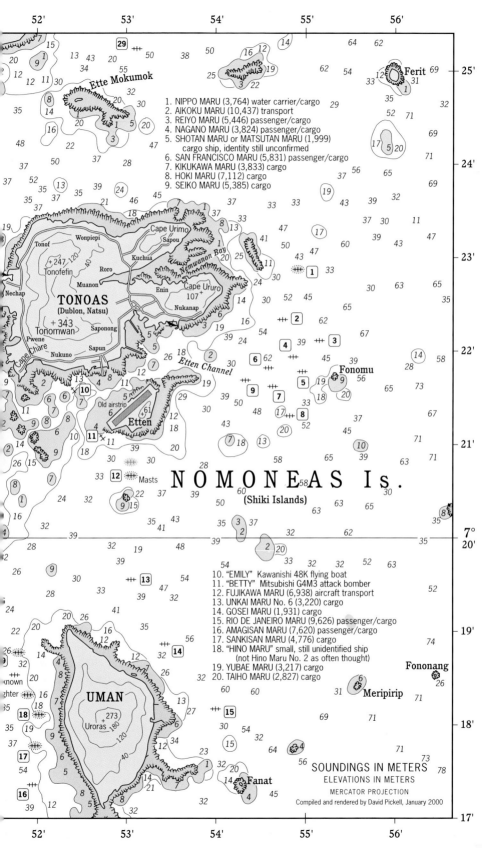

ROBERT RICKE and MARIA HULTS Fujikawa Maru Chuuk Lagoon

ROBERT RICKE and MARIA HULTS San Francisco Maru Chuuk Lagoon

Sinks in the Fujikawa Maru are well preserved. This is a rich site, and you could almost dive just here for a week.

Mines on the fore deck of the San Francisco Maru. This wreck is deep, and is only for experienced divers. Not all guides will even take clients here.

strapped to the deck house and two engine telegraphs are on the flying bridge. A ship's compass is still intact in the pilot cabin. Many personal effects—shoes, sake bottles, uniforms—litter the bridge compartments. Soft coral, encrusting sponges, and tree oysters grow on every crossbar and spar.

BETTY BOMBER [11]

This twin-engine, Mitsubishi G4M3 attack bomber ("Betty," to the Allies) lies in the sand, upright, in 15 meters of water near a big coral head. It seems as though it fell only a few meters short of the runway at Etten Island (where you'll often stop for lunch). The G4M3 had a 22-meter fuselage, and a 27-meter wingspan. The cockpit is twisted off on this one, but there are machine guns lying in the sand and cannon

on the tail. Look for the radio inside. It seems that both engines popped off on impact.

FUJIKAWA MARU [12]

This wreck is an all-time classic, perhaps the most famous of the sunken fleet. It is also very accessible in its relatively shallow grave. Originally damaged in an air raid over Kwajalein, the *Fujikawa* was anchored in Chuuk for repair work when Hailstone struck. The fatal torpedo hit can be seen towards the center of the starboard side.

She sits upright, with the prop at 40 meters and the main deck at 20 meters. Make a point of seeing the officers' bathrooms in the forecastle and the sinks along the far wall. There is still a tiled Japanese bath here. There's an impressive bow gun before the bridge house and a stern gun aft of the stack which rises to 10 meters. There is an interesting electrical shop which looks as though it was used yesterday. The conning radio tower is still fairly intact, but it was much better before one of the live-aboards tore off its bridge deck while setting anchor.

Though built as a 140-meter passenger liner, the *Fuji* was used in the war as an aircraft ferry and in the second of six holds are several Zeros, along with various spare parts—propellers, fuselages, wings, and guns. The mast, which reaches above water, is covered in hanging soft coral. There are numerous large-caliber bullets and gas masks lying on the deck. The passageway along each mid deck is fun to swim along and offers varied perspectives—here you'll see strange, long shafts, which are periscope parts. Sea whips and coral trees line the hand rails. You could spend weeks on the *Fuji*.

GOSEI MARU [14]

This is a coastal freighter that now lies on her port side at 70 meters. There is a huge torpedo hole in the midsection, and at 30 meters you can see fierce hull distortions and ripples incurred during the attack. The bomb drainage and bridge house are also partially destroyed. At 50 meters there is an intact stern gun. There are torpedo bodies in the midsection, and you can visit the aft engine room. The *Gosei*, launched in 1937, was 82 meters long with a 12-meter beam, and capable of 13 knots.

RIO DE JANEIRO MARU [15]

Now lying on her starboard decks, this wartime submarine tender was a luxurious passenger liner before being fitted with guns and armor for service in the Imperial Navy. She lies in 35 meters of water with the railing of her port deck at 20 meters. The superstructure and bridge is huge and a thrill to explore, although it can be dark and silty down there. The rest of the *Rio* is blessed with much better visibility than most of Chuuk's wrecks.

The large bow gun on the fore deck is still in recognizable condition, and the forward hold is filled with rockets and field artillery. A large aft gun rests on the rear deck. There are boxes and boxes of beer bottles, some of them still capped, and pottery and tableware are shattered against inside walls.

Sweepers fill many doorways and offer excellent photo opportunities. Lots of different corals and whips, though no great concentrations. Encrusting sponge grows more widely than soft corals on this wreck, possibly because of its silt-covered surfaces. There are often turtles here. The *Rio* was the sister ship to the *Heian Maru*.

AMAGISAN MARU [16]

This fascinating but rarely dived wreck lies aft up, 10 degrees to port, upright on a slope. Launched in 1933, she was big and wide: 150

meters with a 23-meter beam. With 8,500 horsepower, this hulk was able to make 19 knots. Look for the bow gun at 30 meters and the anti-aircraft gun platform on the stack. There is a tank truck and a minesweeper on the fore deck. In Hold #2 are torpedo holes and staff cars. I've always enjoyed visiting this wreck.

ROBERT RICKE and MARIA HULTS Fujikawa Maru Chuuk Lagoon

SANKISAN MARU [17]

The *Sankisan* was fully armed and loaded with ammo when an aerial torpedo neatly carved out her mid-section. But the ship sank so fast that the sea water extinguished the flames before her own volatile cargo exploded. Today she sits upright on the slope of a crater, with her stern at 50 meters and her bow at 40 meters.

Wing of a 'Zero' on the Fujikawa Maru. Conditions in the lagoon can be silty, a situation aggravated by large groups of divers, or those with imperfect buoyancy control. Watch yourself. On a wreck, one overenthusiastic kick can turn day into night, and make you very unpopular with your dive partners.

ROBERT RICKE and MARIA HULTS   Fujikawa Maru   Chuuk Lagoon

The cockpit of a 'Zero' fighter on the Fujikawa Maru. Note that not a single gauge remains. Please remove absolutely nothing from these wrecks.

This is one of my personal favorites. The forward mast and deck are completely overgrown with a rainbow of soft corals, oysters, tunicates, worms, anemones, and hydroids, and there are lots of fish. Several Toyota truck frames, their bodies rusted away, are lashed to the forward deck. There are aircraft parts on the deck aft of the bridge; on the deck is a perfectly intact machine gun; and in the mid-hold are trucks. There are wooden cases of machine gun and rifle bullets in the forward hold and scattered about on the decks. Do not touch or remove these—many are live and unstable.

Inner compartments have dishes, cups, and bottles, but it is dangerous to venture too far inside. Launched in 1942, the *Sankisan* was 120 meters long with a 15.8-meter beam, and capable of 16 knots.

"HINO MARU" [18]

This ship is most famous for its bow gun, which appears in many photographs of Chuuk Lagoon.

This is one of the better wrecks for a photographer utilizing available light, since it starts just below the surface and lies in 12 meters of water. The "Hino" is also a good dive for the inexperienced diver. Although the ship was largely destroyed in the attack, and later stripped by divers, there is a good deal of life aboard in the form of smaller reef fish and soft coral, fans, and whips. You can even snorkel here. Recently it was determined that this wreck is not the *Hino Maru No. 2* at all, and the ship remains unidentified.

HOYO MARU [21]

Nicknamed "The Gray Ghost," the *Hoyo* makes a wonderful night dive. Barely recognizable, the ship is cut into many pieces and covered in thick coral growth. The vessel's 156-meter length rests upside down on a sandy, easily stirred bottom. Millions of small fish cloud the hull which slopes from three to 40 meters. Because the wreck balances on its superstructure, you can swim underneath her, though it is a bit unsettling to pass under that weight. In the engine room are still many gauges, valves and switches. Black coral grows wildly.

Lance Higgs tells of a guest on his *Thorfinn* who was among the flyers who leveled this impressive ship. Flying in low, firing his machine guns, he remembers a Japanese admiral who was standing on the bow and waving his hands in defiance. When this airman returned to Chuuk Lagoon fifty years later, he dove the *Hoyo* many times. After one dive, he never surfaced. He was later found dead in a deep hold, no sign of having struggled.

KIYOSUMI MARU [22]

This troop ship sank quickly after a bomb hit her bridge and castle, and torpedoes hit her hull just fore of the midsection on the starboard bow. Today the *Kiyosumi* lies on her port side, in 30 meters of water against a slope. The *Kiyo* saw action in Midway, Saipan, and New Guinea before returning to Chuuk for repairs. This wreck is famous and oft photographed because of the coral-encrusted bicycles in Hold #5. Anti-aircraft guns are mounted on the fore deck and there are interesting torpedo launchers aft. The screw and rudder are still attached. She was 137 meters long with a 19-meter beam, and with 8,400 hp, could hit 19 knots. The *Kiyo* was launched in 1934.

FUTAGAMI MARU [23]

This fleet salvage tug of the Imperial Japanese Navy was 50 meters long with a 12-meter beam. A haunting wreck, the *Futagami* rests upright with a slight lean to port. She rests on a ridge wall with her stern in 10 meters of water and her bow at 35 meters. In the bridge, telegraphs and voice pipes are still in great condition. So are the boilers in the midsection, and the machine gun mounts behind the bridge. The aft deck holds extra props and rudders.

KENSHO MARU [24]

This is a relatively newly discovered wreck, found by Chuuk-ologist Klaus Lindemann and his wife, Mary. The *Kensho* is a comfortable dive, and it is nice to be able to explore without constantly having to watch your bottom time. The ship is covered with silt and mud, probably because she lies in a commuter shipping lane. This makes it critical for divers to use care while exploring the *Kensho,* to avoid stirring the sediments.

Part of the diesel engine and several gauges are intact. In one of the rear holds is a stack of Japanese bicycles, some completely swallowed up by encrusting coral—a great photo. She was hit by a torpedo just forward of the bridge, and is now bent in two. You will see binoculars, dinnerware, navigational tools, and a curious pair of antlers—which also crop up here and there on other ships. Radio equipment is still on the deck above the helm along with some personal effects. Among the heavy coral growth, there is a bow gun and ammo at 20 meters.

The *Kensho* sits upright in water ranging from 10 meters to 40 meters. She's in pretty good shape except for some bomb damage at the stern. Try to see the engine room. Though covered in silt and mud (be calm), there are gauges and engine cylinders that can be readily seen thanks to the open skylights. The *Kensho,* launched in 1938, was 116 meters long with a 16-meter beam. Her 3,450 hp pushed the ship along at 17 knots.

HEIAN MARU [25]

The name of this huge passenger ship is still visible on the bow, in both Japanese and English. Lying

ROBERT RICKE and MARIA HULTS   Unkai Maru No. 6   Chuuk Lagoon

A pile of shoes on the Unkai Maru No. 6. The Unkai, a cargo ship that displaced 3,220 tons before it went down, now sits upright on the lagoon bottom north of Uman Island.

on her port side, there is much to see on this wreck. Torpedoes and warheads on her decks, and periscopes and snorkels along the walkway amidships. There are staircases and walkways everywhere. Two large props rest in the sand below her, at 30 meters. Enter the bridge to see the telegraph and other instruments. Behind the bridge is a passageway that can be negotiated, if you are careful, leading past rows of cabins. At the end is the galley. If you aren't with an experienced guide, I wouldn't advise deeper penetration, though the engine room is well-preserved.

YAMAGIRI MARU [27]

This 150-meter freighter is lies on her port side in 40 meters of water. You reach the wreck at 15 meters, can descend along the hull to 30 meters. The bridge is accessible, and still contains the telegraph. The windows make interesting frames for photography if you shoot out into the blue. This is the ship containing a roomful of special

18-inch artillery shells. Each resembles a giant .38 caliber shell, 1.5 meters long and weighing a remarkable 1,500 kilograms.

This was the first batch of the potentially devastating ordnance headed for the *Musashi* and *Yamato*, great battleships specially equipped with the necessary "secret weapon" guns. Thankfully, the shells never left Hold #5 of the *Yamagiri*. Though they had passed the experimental stage, these huge guns were never used in battle.

SHINOKOKU MARU [28]

One of Chuuk's more popular dives, the *Shinokoku* sits virtually upright with her prop at 42 meters. The *Shinokoku*, as a fleet oiler, helped lead the attack on Pearl Harbor. In 1939, this 165-meter tanker was one of the few ships actually built in Japan. After being struck by an American torpedo she was anchored in Chuuk awaiting repairs when Hailstone hit.

Corals, shellfish, and sponges decorate the huge mast and cross

ROBERT RICKE and MARIA HULTS   San Francisco Maru   Chuuk Lagoon

spar on what might be the most beautiful wreck in the lagoon. The telegraph is in place in the wheel house at 15 meters. The interior is safe for moderate penetration, and contains many artifacts, including cookware, stoves, and a sick bay. I hope the bare light bulb is still hanging from its fixture when you arrive.

Lots of haunting angles, vibrant soft coral, and nocturnal fish life make this a wonderful night dive. You don't have to venture deep, since a great deal of the coral growth and sea life exists above 25 meters. There is a hole in the port engine room curtained by sweepers, and schooling fish cloud the decks. A stern gun is still attached and there is a bow gun at 13 meters. The bridge at 10 meters, is completely covered in rainbows of soft coral. Some human remains can be found on the deck.

OTHER WRECKS

There are so many wrecks in Chuuk Lagoon that it deserves its own book. In fact, I heartily recom-
mend Klaus Lindemann's *Hailstorm Over Truk Lagoon* and *Desecrate One, The Shipwrecks of Truk Lagoon*, for those interested in the full picture. Other good resources are Dan E. Bailey's *Wrecks of the Kwajalein and Truk Lagoons* and "Truk Lagoon Wreck Divers Map." Some other wrecks that make particularly good dives include the Emily flying boat [10], *Shotan Maru* or *Matsutan Maru* [6], and the *Unkai Maru No. 6* [13]. If you're persistent, your guide may also take you to some of the dives on the outer walls of the lagoon.

NORTHWEST PASS [9] Map 5.1 pp. 130–131

The outside of this reef is lovely and full of life. You can see reef white-tip sharks, large gray reef sharks, huge humphead wrasse, turtles, tuna, and even mantas. Visibility is excellent, approaching 50 meters. A sloping wall starts at about three meters and drops to about 40 before sloping off onto a pure white-sand plain that continues on down. Lots of reef fish school here.

The driver's seat of a truck on the San Francisco Maru. Built in 1919, she is one of the lagoon's older ships. In her prime, with four thousand horsepower on tap, she was capable of a fast fourteen knots.

The Indo-Pacific sergeant-major is a familiar species with a wide distribution, but it is not really common. Where the plucky species does occur, such as on this reef edge, one finds huge schools.

The hinge-beak shrimps are often found in large colonies on the reef. The name of this group comes from the hinge at the base of the long rostrum, an unusual feature which seems to make it easier for them to wiggle out of their old shells when they molt

This remarkable place is the Federated States of Micronesia's best-kept secret. The island is wet, green, and wild, the culture is fascinating, and the diving is excellent. Where else can you dive the coral-covered basalt columns of a ruined aquatic city?

Pohnpei

I DON'T REALLY EVEN WANT TO WRITE about this place. I'd much rather keep it to myself. So, I'll whisper: Pohnpei is one of the best places I've dived. To those who say Palau and Chuuk are the only places in Micronesia worth diving, I'd reply, "You're absolutely right. Go there." (And leave the pristine reefs of Pohnpei to me).

Whether you like walls or slope reefs, rich coral or blue water pelagics, macro subjects or sharks, Pohnpei has it. And this wonderful island also has history (both ancient and World War II), friendly people, good food, fun traditional "narcotics," modern hotels, and simple romantic getaways.

Chuuk can appear a bit too filthy at times, Palau can feel over-dived, Saipan might seem to have a few too many package tourists, Yap can impress one as overrated, Guam can be, well, too Guam-ish.

But Pohnpei is pristine, mysterious, and virtually unvisited. Sure, it's a quirky place for diving, you have to hit the tides and seasons right, and it's about the rainiest place on the planet, but this just adds to the fun. This is one of my favorite places in Micronesia.

A WET, GREEN, JEWEL

Pohnpei, spelled "Ponape" until 1984, is the largest and highest island in the Federated States of Micronesia. It is wet and beautiful. Nahnalaud's 778-meter peak is usually shrouded in mist, and waterfalls cascade down its glistening slopes. The island has more than forty rivers feeding its lush forest, and the waterfalls can be breathtaking, and well worth venturing inland to see. The famous Sokehs Rock, visible from the airport, is one of Micronesia's most recognizable natural features.

MIKE SEVERNS Cephalopholis argus Kosrae

The peacock grouper is common throughout Micronesia, except in areas that are heavily fished. It is considered a tasty fish, although larger specimens (a half meter or so) have been responsible for ciguatera poisoning in Hawai'i (not native to the islands, it was introduced there in 1956). Juveniles are particularly colorful.

There are no beaches to speak of here—the island is ringed with pristine mangrove forest, guarding the reef from run-off. Offshore, along its barrier reef, sharks glide above white sand, and bright sunlight reflects off of rich coral gardens. Visibility often reaches 65 meters—everything sparkles.

The state is comprised of nine scattered island groups, with some 165 separate islets, many of them unpopulated. Pohnpei State's Kapingamarangi Atoll is almost on the equator, and closer to New Ireland than to Pohnpei island itself. Fully 95 percent of the land area is on Pohnpei Island, as are most of the state's 44,100 people.

Pohnpeians in the capital village of Kolonia create a modest bustle as they go about their daily business. Government offices, gas stations, movie theaters, and retail shops line the street, offering anything you might need—groceries, beer, sundries, toiletries, souvenirs. Near the docks is a lesser "main" street lined with fisheries, warehouses, light industry, produce markets, and pepper and copra processors.

A few miles south of Kolonia past Sokehs Rock is Palikir, the capital of the Federated States of Micronesia. Construction to transform this sleepy fishing village into a "modern" capital town has largely being paid for by $15 million in U.S. aid. Just beyond Palikir is the national college campus, which stands next to a volcanic lump called Pwisehn Malek, literally "Chickenshit Mountain," left behind by a giant, legendary rooster.

The island receives 4,917 millimeters (193.6 in.) of rain a year, but this is measured at Kolonia. The mountainous inland probably receives twice this amount—perhaps 10 meters (33 ft.) of rain, about as high as anywhere on the planet. Rain falls nearly every day from March through November, although the sun may shine even while it is raining. It has been written that "Pohnpei drips, it never dries." Mid-summer is the heart of the wet monsoon, but light winds during this time ensure that the seas stay calm, and this can be the best time for diving. Typhoons are rare here. Daytime temperatures average 26.7°C (80.1°F), and humidity inland can be high.

VENICE OF THE PACIFIC

Although probably settled 2,500 years ago, little is known of Pohpei's earliest history. Island mythology says that the first settlers, directed to the island by an octopus, found only a tiny coral cay. With the help of magic, they built up the island, and planted mangrove around its border. The founders of Pohnpei then built an altar, on which they piled rocks until it reached great heights, hence the island's name: *pohn* ("atop") *pei* ("altar").

More is known from the age of the Saudeleurs, a royal family that ruled from Nan Madol, a stone fortress city that is today one of the most remarkable archaeological sites in the world. This "Venice of Micronesia" made of hard, black basalt, was built over three centuries, beginning around A.D. 1100. The ruthless Saudeleurs reached their peak in the 13th century, and wielded absolute power until the 17th century when Isokelekel, with a force of 333 warriors, rowed to Pohnpei from Kosrae and overthrew the Saudeleurs.

Isokelekel established a new system of district chiefs, with two lines: the *nahnmwarki* and (of secondary authority), the *nahnken*. The five districts of Pohnpei—Nett, Uh, Madolenihmw, Kitti, and Sokehs—date back to this period, and each still has a *nahnmwarki* and *nahnken* who are descendants of these chieftains. Many of the intricacies of Pohnpeian culture and traditional values can be traced back to this period.

The Spanish first sighted the island in 1528, and Pedro Fernandez

DAVID LEONARD   Peipapap   Pohnpei

DAVID LEONARD   Pohnpei

de Quiros, without landing, claimed it for the Spanish crown in 1595. The Russian sailor Fedor Lutke passed Pohnpei and the two nearby atolls in 1828, and named them after his ship, the *Senyavin*. This name still appears on older maps.

Contact between whaling boats and Pohnpei became common in the mid-19th century, when some fifty ships a year stopped at what they called Ascension Island to water and take on supplies. Even the American Civil War reached Pohnpei, when the Confederate frigate *Shenandoah* burned four Union whale ships to the waterline in Lohd Harbor. Smallpox and measles brought by the whalers cut the island's population from 10,000 in 1800 to 5,000 by 1900. The Americans signed a trading treaty with

Peipapap or Sokehs Rock is a great 200-meter outcrop of basalt just northwest of Kolonia. Climbing this, or just exploring Sokehs Island (it looks like a peninsula on the map) makes a nice way to spend a day out of the water.

A church on Pohnpei. Pohnpeians are approximately split between Catholics and Protestants, as are the Chuukese. Kosraeans are mostly Protestant, and Yapese are mostly Catholic.

SAKAU
Pohnpei's Traditional High

NIGHT HAD LONG SINCE FALLEN LIKE A DAMP TOWEL. A peppery, woodsy musk hung heavy in the breeze, thick and steamy, bearing the ghost of Magellan. The skinny dog lay sleeping on his side in the sand. Tin balls on a basalt slab ring hollow in the jungle midnight. White Christmas lights circle a bare green bulb. Half a hundred Pohnpeians converse animatedly.

Two masters, sitting cross-legged in the sand around four thick stones set on truck tires, pound roots into a wet pulp. They pack the mash into fibrous hibiscus bark and spin it like a locker-room towel until a thick, gummy effluent appears. This is *sakau*, legendary nectar of Nan Madol chieftains. The *sakau* is poured into half of a coconut shell and passed around the crowd. Everybody takes a sip. Only spitting and coughing interrupts the soft buzz of subdued banter.

THE PACIFIC'S FAMOUS KAVA ROOT

Sakau, known in most of the Pacific as kava, comes from the root of *Piper methysticum*, a pepper plant whose soporific, relaxant, and mildly narcotic properties have been enjoyed in this region for perhaps 3,000 years. The active principals of the plant, called kavalactones, are concentrated in the roots and rootstock. *P.* "methysticum" is now thought to be a sterile cultivar of *P. wichmannii*, a wild pepper native to New Guinea, the Solomon Islands, and Vanuatu.

In Fiji kava growing is a $47 million business, with $9 million in exports going to Europe and the United States, where it is becoming popular as a natural herbal remedy.

In Pohnpei, *sakau* is still a local market item. But consumption is increasing, and today 1.1 million kilograms a year are harvested, with a value of $3 million. In fact, so much *sakau* is now being grown on the island that environmentalists are worried—two-thirds of Pohnpei's inland forest has been cut in the last two decades, most of this for *sakau* plantations. The Nature Conservancy has started a "Grow Low" campaign here, to get the farmers to plant on less sensitive, low-elevation land.

Pohnpei in 1870, and the Spanish finally colonized the island in 1886.

Ruins of the Spanish fortress can still be seen on the outskirts of Kolonia, but the Spanish occupied the island for barely 13 years. During this time they faced a number of uprisings by the Pohnpeians, mostly in response to Catholic proselytizing. At this point, because of contact with the whalers, most of the island's population was Protestant.

Along with the rest of Micronesia, the Germans received Pohnpei in 1899. The Germans were interested in turning a profit, and used forced labor to build roads and develop the copra industry. This sparked a rebellion in 1910 in Sokehs, and four German officials were killed.

In retaliation, the colonial overlords brought troops from New Guinea, put down the rebellion, and executed 17 Pohnpeians. The entire population of Sokehs, 426, was banished to Ngeaur Island off Palau to work in the phosphate mines.

The German influence is still apparent here in family names and (perhaps unfortunately) on restaurant menus.

Pohnpei was not a strategic base for the Japanese during World War II, although they grew sugar cane here for alcohol production, and imported 14,000 citizens. The Allies bombed the airport and leveled Kolonia, but never invaded the island.

POST-COMPACT POHNPEI

The compact with the United States, and the aid it provides, runs out in 2001. Some observers expect Pohnpei to then secede from the Federated States of Micronesia and enter into a commonwealth with the United States. Tired of having to support problematic Chuuk, Pohnpeians see the quality of life in Saipan (which opted for commonwealth status rather than become

TAMMY PELUSO   Amphiprion chrysopterus in Heteractis crispa   Micronesia, unspecified

part of the FSM) and want it for themselves.

Despite these concerns, there is a sense of well-being in Pohnpei. Although more and more young elites venture to the United States for their education, many return to Pohnpei with their American diplomas, to help advance their homeland.

Pohnpei is in better shape economically than some of its partners in the FSM. The island has found a market for its copra, pepper, and fish, and tourism is growing slowly. The state president has called for "sustainable living," basing the economy on careful harvesting of renewable resources and non-damaging forms of tourism.

THREE-METER YAMS

Pohnpei's volcanic soil is rich and fertile. Coconuts, bananas, taro, breadfruit, manioc, and yams all grow very well here. Pohnpei's yams, like those of Melanesia, are huge, reaching three meters (10 ft.) in length, and weighing more than a person.

Fishing is common here, with a good deal of the family's time taken up by catching, preparing and preserving fish. Young boys can be seen paddling outriggers deep in the lagoons. On some dives, I've looked *down* to see boys free-diving at 20 meters to spear large parrotfish and other reef denizens.

Pohnpei's pepper is famous for its special, and very explosive, flavor. Grown by independent farmers, the pepper berries are hauled into town to the processing plant where they are packaged in various sized bags for sale, both locally to tourists and on the international market. Don't go home without some.

Coconut is processed at Pohnpei Coconut Products, Inc., and you can visit their plant on the main road into town from the airport. Pick up a few bottles of Kaselel Shampoo or a bar or two of their coconut soap. They make great gifts and you won't believe the suds. Next door is a *Trochus* shell button factory, Island Traders, where you can buy a bag of rock-hard shell buttons.

The orange-fin anemonefish can be seen throughout Micronesia, and is the most common species of anemonefish on the seaward side of reefs here (it is not as fond of the lagoons). This is one of the larger anemonefishes, reaching 12 centimeters in length.

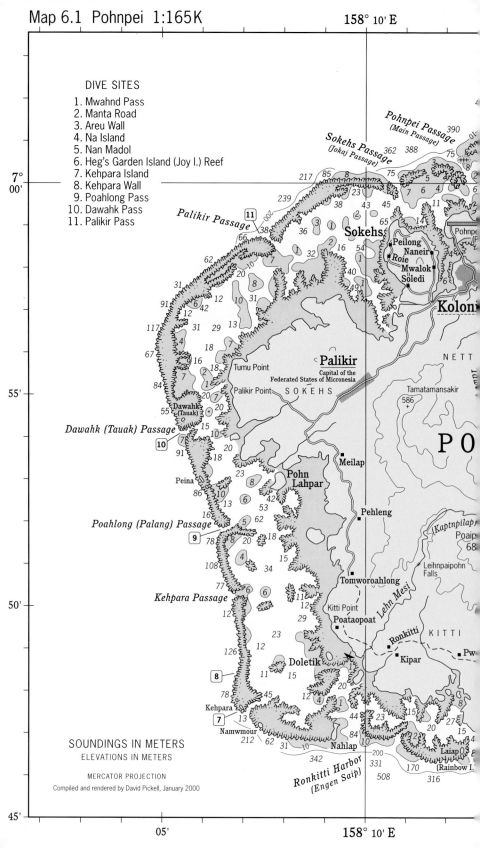

Map 6.1 Pohnpei 1:165K

158° 10' E

DIVE SITES
1. Mwahnd Pass
2. Manta Road
3. Areu Wall
4. Na Island
5. Nan Madol
6. Heg's Garden Island (Joy I.) Reef
7. Kehpara Island
8. Kehpara Wall
9. Poahlong Pass
10. Dawahk Pass
11. Palikir Pass

7° 00'

55'

50'

45'

Pohnpei Passage (Main Passage)   390

Sokehs Passage (Jokaj Passage)   362   388

217   85   8   75
239   23
002   38   38   43   45
11   38   36   3   1   65   14
   1   2   16   54   **Sokehs**
62   1   32   40   49   1
20   10   8   20   Peilong
31   6   42   12   10   31   Naneir
91   12   13   Roie
117   31   29   Mwalok
67   4   18   Soledi
   16   2   18   Tumu Point
84   7   1   20   Palikir Point   **Palikir**
55   **Dawahk** (Tauak)   20   Capital of the
   15   Federated States of Micronesia
91   10   S O K E H S
86   18   20
Peina   8   23   **Meilap**
   10   6   **Pohn   Lahpar**
16   13   42   53
   5   62   **Pehleng**
9   78   8   20   18
108   4   34   15
77   6   6   **Tomworoahlong**
12   11   12   Kitti Point
126   23   29   **Poataopoat**
8   12   **Doletik**   20   **Ronkitti**
78   11   15   **Kipar**
Kehpara   45   12   4
7   13   44   23   10
Namwmour   212   62   31   10   **Nahlap**
   342   84   10
   331   200
   508   170

Sokehs Passage (Jokaj Passage)

Palikir Passage

Dawahk (Tauak) Passage

Poahlong (Palang) Passage

Kehpara Passage

Ronkitti Harbor (Engen Saip)

Kolon

Pohnpe

N E T T

Tamatamansakir   586

P O

Kaptnpilap
Poaip   68
Leihnpaipohn Falls

K I T T I   Pw

Laiap   4
(Rainbow I.)
15   27
20

SOUNDINGS IN METERS
ELEVATIONS IN METERS

MERCATOR PROJECTION

Compiled and rendered by David Pickell, January 2000

05'   158° 10' E

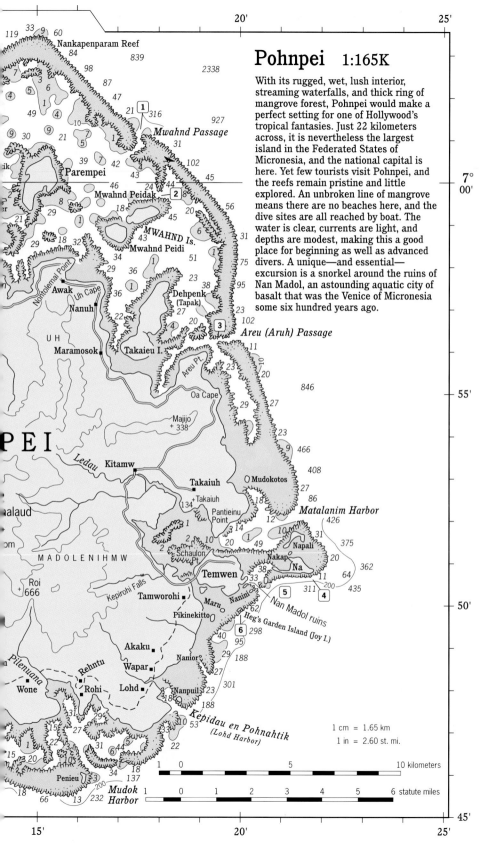

Pohnpei 1:165K

With its rugged, wet, lush interior, streaming waterfalls, and thick ring of mangrove forest, Pohnpei would make a perfect setting for one of Hollywood's tropical fantasies. Just 22 kilometers across, it is nevertheless the largest island in the Federated States of Micronesia, and the national capital is here. Yet few tourists visit Pohnpei, and the reefs remain pristine and little explored. An unbroken line of mangrove means there are no beaches here, and the dive sites are all reached by boat. The water is clear, currents are light, and depths are modest, making this a good place for beginning as well as advanced divers. A unique—and essential—excursion is a snorkel around the ruins of Nan Madol, an astounding aquatic city of basalt that was the Venice of Micronesia some six hundred years ago.

1 cm = 1.65 km
1 in = 2.60 st. mi.

10 kilometers

6 statute miles

DIVING POHNPEI

Great Reefs, No Crowds
and Two Beautiful Offshore Atolls

POHNPEI IS STILL LARGELY UNKNOWN as a dive destination, but if you are in Micronesia, it would be a mistake to pass it by. The reefs are very healthy on the main fringing reef that surrounds the island, and there are two perfect offshore atolls nearby, Ahnd and Pakein. Altogether, there are something like thirty known dive sites here, and among these are a dozen that are spectacular.

These reefs are still under-explored, so if you plan to spend some time here, doing some exploratory diving is a very real possibility. The exact locations of the Pohnpei sites

about 50 meters deep at mid-channel. Although the passage is almost two kilometers long, divers can choose their profile, drifting along the walls of the channel or exploring the reef inside the lagoon. When tidal conditions permit, the outside walls of the barrier reef can be dived, too, and the scenery here is pristine.

Visibility is usually very good in the pass, sometimes exceeding 50 meters. One can see sharks and pelagics here, and there are lots of reef fish and soft corals. This is a very rich stretch of reef, and a good place for macro-photography.

MANTA ROAD [2]

This is the site for spotting mantas at Pohnpei. Manta Road is a sandy, V-shaped channel running for about 800 meters along the north side of Mwand Peidak, or Upper Mwand Island. The channel is quite narrow, averaging 15 meters across, and shallow—15 meters deep. The sides of the channel are covered with lavish growths of hard and soft coral, and in some areas the hard coral has narrowed the channel to less than three meters.

The current here can be overpowering, and prudence should dictate whether or not to enter the water. You really do not want to be in here when the flood tide creates a 7-knot current through the narrows. Visibility here varies greatly, depending on the current.

Along with mantas, eagle rays and reef sharks, there is an unusual number of scorpionfish in this pass. As usual in a "manta channel," your best strategy to see the big rays

Exciting drifts through reef passages, steep, rich seaward walls, and two perfect little isolated atolls—all in one of the most exotic settings in the Pacific. What more could you ask for?

below, listed in geographical order around the island, can be found on MAP 6.1, pages 158–159. The numbers correspond to those used on the map.

MWAHND PASS [1]

This site, a break in the barrier reef, is only 25 minutes by boat northeast of Kolonia Harbor. Resembling an S-shaped funnel, with nearly vertical walls, the pass varies greatly in width and depth, typically a few hundred meters wide and

MIKE SEVERNS Nemateleotris magnifica Kosrae

is to lie low and close to cover, minimizing your movements, and wait for the soaring mantas to arrive for cleaning and feeding.

AREU WALL [3]

This site is inside the barrier reef, on the north side of the Areu Pass. Areu Wall is dived in a drift, along a wonderful, kilometer-long wall filled with grottoes, caverns, and caves. Its proximity to the open sea (through the pass) brings in sharks, barracuda, and mantas and other pelagic species. This vertical wall rises up from 43 meters, and the tidal currents here can reach 6–7 knots. Visibility is usually excellent, though at the height of the rainy season it can drop to as little as 15 meters. In the deep, there are huge gorgonians, and myriad reef fish inhabit the wall.

NA ISLAND [4]

An hour east of Kolonia, uninhabited Na Island makes an ideal day trip, offering gorgeous beaches, great snorkeling, and excellent diving. It is only minutes away from the Nan Madol ruins and Kepirohi Falls. The diving takes place along the fringing reef lining the south shore of Na. It is a slope, and covered by acres and acres of healthy staghorn *Acropora* and other hard corals. You will see an occasional shark or ray here, but it is the rich coral and the reef fish, rising in clouds, that are the highlights of this dive. Your guide will choose the best entry point from among dozens possible depending on the season and weather, but most dives will end up as drifts along the reef slope.

NAN MADOL [5]

Nan Madol, off Temwen Island in eastern Pohnpei, is one of the least known of the world's important archaeological sites. It also might be the only old city that is also a dive site. This impressive, aquatic city consists of 82 artificial islands built from huge rock "logs"—naturally formed hexagonal columns of basalt, some of them eight meters long. The ruins have been dated

The fire dartfish is a nervous little creature that can be found hovering over the sand, flicking its long dorsal spine up and down. If approached too closely or noisily, they will dive into their hiding places. The species is found throughout Micronesia.

Map 6.2 Ahnd Atoll and Pakein Atoll 1:100K

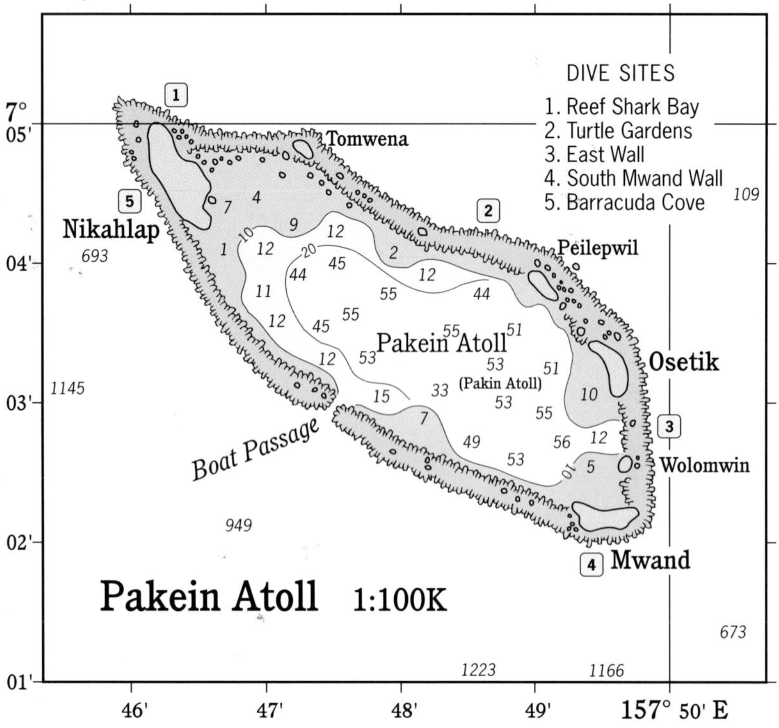

54'

DIVE SITES
1. Reef Shark Bay
2. Turtle Gardens
3. East Wall
4. South Mwand Wall
5. Barracuda Cove

7° 05'

[1]

Tomwena

109

[5]

Nikahlap

693

7

4

10

9

12

[2]

Peilepwil

1

12

20

2

04'

44

45

12

11

55

44

12

45

55

55

51

12

53

Pakein Atoll

55

53

51

Osetik

1145

(Pakin Atoll)

10

03'

15

33

53

[3]

7

55

Boat Passage

49

56

12

53

5

Wolomwin

1038

949

02'

[4] **Mwand**

Pakein Atoll 1:100K

673

01'

1223

1166

46'   47'   48'   49'   157° 50' E

48'

42

Ahnd Atoll 1:100K

47'

609

Ahnd and Pakein are two perfect little atolls, with low,
white-sand beaches and turquoise lagoons. Both lie about 35
kilometers from Kolonia—Ahnd (sometimes still rendered 'Ant')
to the southwest and Pakein ('Pakin') to the northwest. A single
family lives on Pakein, but Ahnd is home only to colonies of
seabirds. The diving here is excellent, but because of the isolation
of the atolls, current conditions on the outer walls are more
challenging than at other Micronesian locations, including
Pohnpei itself. Both atolls have but one passage, and on a
changing tide, drifts here can be very wild. The outer walls are
great places to see pelagics, including sharks and schooling
barracuda, and the lagoons of both atolls are rich in reef fish and
invertebrates and turtles. Diving here requires perfect weather,
and is impossible during the roughest season, approximately
December through February.

46'

620

45'

784

44'

905

43'

| 1 | .5 | 0 | 1 | 2 | 3 | 4 | 5 kilometers |

1 cm = 1 km
1 in = 1.58 st. mi.

| 1 | .5 | 0 | 1 | 2 | 3 statute miles |

42'

48'   49'   50'   51'   52'   53'   54'

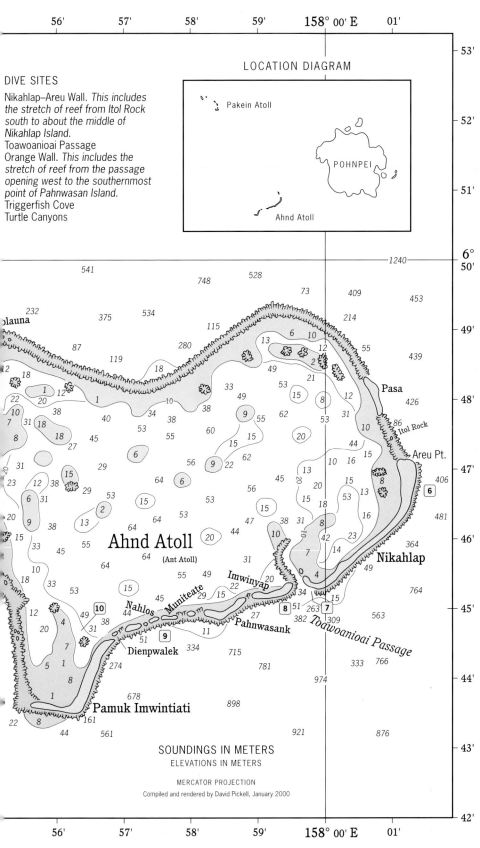

MIKE SEVERNS   Chaetodon ephippium   Majuro Atoll, Marshall Islands

MIKE SEVERNS   Chaetodon auriga   Kosrae

Butterflyfish are perennial favorites with divers, and there are at least forty species in Micronesia. The saddled butterflyfish (above) feeds on coral polyps and small invertebrates and is common in areas of good hard coral growth. The threadfin butterflyfish (below), is another common species.

A.D. 1285 to A.D. 1485.

The basalt was likely cut from Sokehs on the opposite side of Pohnpei, and floated to the site on rafts, which would be a difficult project with today's technology, not to mention the technology of 700 years ago (Pohnpeian legend says that two magicians used their powers to erect the city, which is almost easier to believe).

The Nan Madol ruins, one hour by boat from Kolonia Harbor, provide one of the most interesting dive experiences in the world. Current and surge are negligible, but visibility can be poor, depending upon run-off. Underwater, the basalt columns that have tumbled into the sea are covered in coral.

Most dives begin near a World War II Japanese barge and continue southwest along the tumbled columns. The seaward edge of the city is about 300 meters long, and the bottom here is no deeper than 25 meters. It is best to take your time on this dive, both to appreciate the site, and to avoid injury (the combination of limited visibility and rough surfaces demands care).

A tour of the ruins by boat is a must. Remember that Nan Madol is a sacred site to the Pohnpeians, and treat it accordingly. Remain seated in the boat as a sign of respect when passing within sight of the residence of the *nahnmwarki* of Madolenihmw.

HEG'S GARDEN ISLAND REEF [6]

Just south of Nan Madol on the eastern reef is a resort island called Heg's Garden Island (formerly Joy Island). You could dive here on a day trip from Kolonia, but an overnight stay on this enchanting island is a better alternative. There are sites right off the island, but the better ones—the operator has named about six of them—require a short boat ride.

Currents are usually light, and visibility exceeds 30 meters on the offshore sites. A fairly straight reef wall here runs for several kilometers, reaching depths of 45 meters as it slopes to a white sand sea bed. All sites offer similar encounters with the large pelagics that cruise the outside wall.

KEHPARA ISLAND [7]

About an hour southwest of Kolonia Harbor, at the southwestern corner of Pohnpei's barrier reef, is Kehpara, which like Heg's Garden is now a resort island called "Black Coral Resort." The outer reef here seems to run forever, and the area is marked by a great diversity of life. Kehpara has something for everyone, whether you're seeking macro subjects or wide angle, you'll find cowries and reef sharks, helmet conchs and mantas, cone shells and

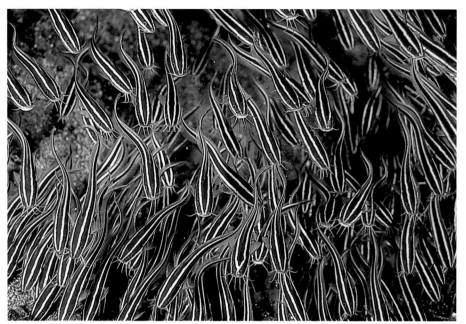

TAMMY PELUSO   Plotosus lineatus   Micronesia, unspecified

dogtooth tuna. The main attraction here are the huge gorgonians and black coral bushes.

Divers can choose between exploring the edge of the fringing reef (see next entry) or the channel and lagoon around Black Coral Isle. Dives in the channel have to be timed correctly for tidal current. Visibility is very high. At one point in the channel, huge pinnacles reach up from the white sand bottom at 20 meters.

KEHPARA WALL [8]

Perhaps the most attractive part of diving off the southwestern reef is this healthy and diverse wall that stretches for several kilometers north from the Black Coral Resort. Octopus, eels, and every reef fish imaginable mingle with sharks, eagle rays, mantas and turtles along a sloping reef that runs to a depth of more than 50 meters. Along the top of the reef are gardens that simply glow with color when the sun is high. Off the wall, in deeper water, you'll see dogtooth tuna, and sil-

vertip sharks. The sea has cut caves and grottoes into the lower parts of the wall. Kehpara Wall is one of Pohnpei's best dives. The visibility is usually excellent, and current is rarely a problem. There is also very good snorkeling on the reef top.

POAHLONG PASS [9]

This popular site is home to a wide array of corals—both hard and soft—as well as large schools of reef fish, tuna, barracuda, and sharks. Pelagic fish often cruise Poahlong Pass, as do occasional dolphins.

Depending on conditions, dives can be made in a number of areas along here, from the outer walls to the coral outcroppings inside the lagoon. In the channel here, the current is swift (but manageable) as you drift along a crescent-shaped reef wall that goes to nearly 40 meters.

DAWAHK PASS [10]

This is a nice drift that can be done along the outside barrier reef or in the reef channel, depending on your tastes and the tides. On the

Juvenile striped eel catfish gather in great, writhing balls over sandy or rubbly lagoon floors or seagrass beds. The adults, which reach about 30 centimeters in length, are shy and solitary, and almost never seen by divers.
You can sometimes play with a ball of juveniles, 'conducting' the school into various shapes using gentle movements of your hands. Be careful with this, however, and not just because it is rude to harass the little guys. Plotosids have a stiff spine on their dorsal fin and each of their pectoral fins that deliver a potent venom.
Adults make a good eating fish, as do all eel catfish, most of which are found in brackish and fresh water environments.

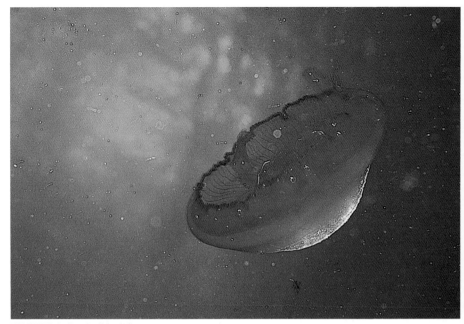

MIKE SEVERNS   Aurelia aurita   Majuro Atoll

The moon jelly is one of the most frequently encountered jellyfish, and has a world-wide distribution, in both warm and cold seas. At times, huge aggregations will appear on an incoming tide, and just as quickly disperse. It can reach a diameter of 60 centimeters, although most are smaller.

The population of these semaeostome jellies in jellyfish lake on Eil Malk in Palau survived the 1999 La Niña year warming, which the Mastigias (formerly more numerous) did not.

outside, current is usually light, but in the channel can reach 5 knots. The funnel-shaped pass runs between the open ocean and the lagoon in a northeasterly direction, offering vertical walls filled with fans and corals. Visibility is usually excellent, unless you've caught it on an outgoing tide after a heavy rain.

Most divers tour the south wall of the pass, about 1,200 meters in length, though the slightly longer north wall is also a fine dive. Conditions dictate your route. The walls slope to a sand bottom at 35 meters and are covered with good hard and soft coral growth. You can find lobsters and even seahorses here if your eyes are sharp, but don't forget to check the blue water for cruising pelagics.

PALIKIR PASS [11]

This is a great channel dive, and just a short boat trip from Kolonia Harbor. The bottom is more than 100 meters on the outside of the passage, and in the channel itself, about 45 meters. The pass runs for

nearly a kilometer, and is filled with marine life. I've seen reef sharks, big schools of barracuda and jacks, eagle rays, tuna, and Napoleon wrasse. Huge arrays of reef fish swarm over the hard and soft coral walls. Octopus, seahorses, and a large variety of shells live among the coral. Currents can be severe, but the visibility is usually outstanding. Keep an eye out for pelagics: I've seen wahoo here, and others have spotted an oceanic white-tip shark.

The Atolls

Some of the most exciting dives here are at two offshore atolls, Pakein and Ahnd. These isolated, empty sites—Pakein has a single family living on it, Ahnd is unpopulated except for seabirds—have an aura of paradise unspoiled. For dive site locations, see MAP 6.2, pages 162–163.

PAKEIN ATOLL

Pakein Atoll is one of my favorite areas. It is rife with interesting formations, and has lots of big fish and reef fish, some of them different species from those you'll see off Pohnpei proper. Pakein is a two-hour boat ride across open ocean from Kolonia, and really only accessible from June through mid-October. It is a classic atoll, consisting of a ring of coral with one channel.

Divers primarily explore REEF SHARK BAY [1], TURTLE GARDENS [2], the EAST WALL [3], SOUTH MWAHND WALL [4], and BARRACUDA COVE [5]. Visibility off the outer wall is spectacular at sixty-plus meters, but the swell at this exposed site can be appreciable. In and out of the tunnels, blue holes, caves, and walls, you will find sharks, rays, tuna and sometimes dolphin.

AHND ATOLL

Here is perhaps the best of Pohnpei diving. The outside reef, pass and lagoon walls simply overflow with marine life. Lying an hour-and-a-half by boat from Kolonia Harbor, Ahnd—like Pakein—is a bit of a trek, but well worth the ride. Most dives are drifts, in relatively deep water. Since this is an exposed site, the swell can reach two meters, and currents can be severe, but these are not the norm. Visibility can reach 50 meters, but on an outgoing tide, runoff from the atoll can decrease the visibility somewhat.

NIKAHLAP–AREU WALL [6] is a lovely dive, although there are a few more current anomalies here than at the other sites, due to the unusual topography here. TOAWOANIOAI PASS [7] is the atoll's only opening. It is an excellent place to see turtles, sharks, rays, large schools of barracuda, and visitors such as billfish and dolphins. Above 20 meters, the channel sides are characterized by caves, cuts, caverns and swim-throughs.

ORANGE WALL [8] is named after the giant orange elephant ear sponges here. The reef wall runs west from the mouth of the passage. The direction of your dive will depend upon the tidal flow, and if you are starting near the passage mouth, dive in the morning to take advantage of the angle of the sun.

Aniculus is one of the largest and most distinctive hermit crabs, and eventually has to find a fist-sized shell in which to live.

TAMMY PELUSO Aniculus maximus Micronesia, unspecified

This view of Kosrae shows why it is called "The Islands of the Sleeping Lady" (she is supine, with her head on the left edge). It is a quiet, beautiful island, that sees very few visitors.

TAMMY PELUSO   Kosrae

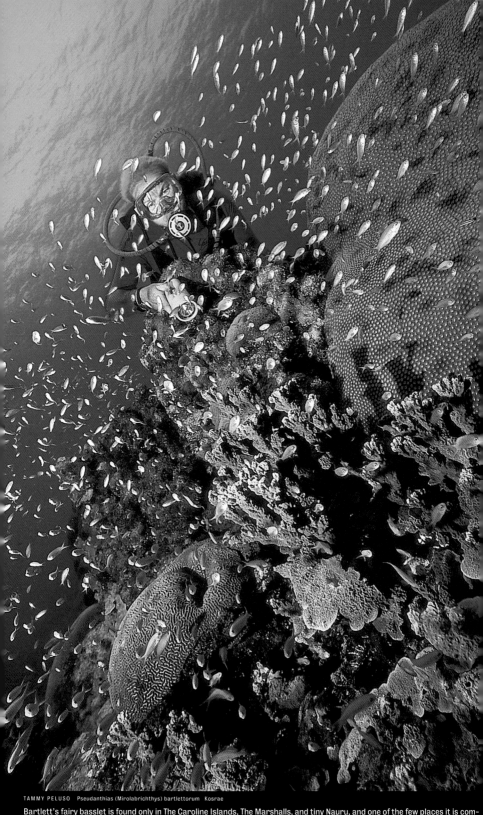

Bartlett's fairy basslet is found only in The Caroline Islands, The Marshalls, and tiny Nauru, and one of the few places it is common is Kosrae. In general, fairy basslets love clear, plankton- and coral-rich outer reef slopes, the steeper the better.

While not as immediately awe-inspiring as the more famous sites to the west, the 'Sleeping Lady,' as this island is affectionately called, offers many charms of her own: a quiet pace on shore, beautiful beaches, and pristine, well-cared-for reefs.

Kosrae

ACCORDING TO LEGEND, THE GODS became angry with a woman and laid her in the sea, asleep on her back. She became an island: Kosrae, the "Island of the Sleeping Lady." Her pointed breasts, some 600 meters tall, are easy to spot, although the rest is a bit of a stretch. It is said that she was menstruating at the time, and the Kosraeans traditionally sought ocherous red clays with which to paint their canoes from the area formed by her loins.

Kosrae, pronounced "Ko-shrye," is a green, lush, and peaceful place. It is one of the least developed parts of Micronesia, and a visit here can be a welcome break from more crowded places like Chuuk or the Marshall Islands. High mountains form the island's spine, and a wide coral shelf surrounds the island, especially on the eastern shore. The sheer drop-off at the end of this shelf presents some beautiful diving.

Vast, empty, white-sand beaches line the shoreline. All are easy to get to, and pristine. In the evenings, women and children, their pants rolled up, wade out onto the shallow coral shelf to net small fish. The skies are deep blue, and the clouds are always tall, white and puffy. When the moon is new, the stars here are as thick and close as they get anywhere on earth. When the moon is full, everything turns silvery, and your shadow lies long and black against the white beaches.

Kosrae, formerly spelled "Kusaie," is slightly smaller than Pohnpei, and the easternmost of the Caroline Islands. Kosrae State is the only one in the Federation with a single island. Mountains account for more than two-thirds of the total land area, so virtually the entire population of 9,600 lives in five coastal villages. A single partially paved road on the east side of the island links Okat to Utwe and Tafunsak municipality. The capital is Tofol, in the east, with about one-third of the island's population.

The reef flats that surround Kosrae are considered to be among the most pristine remaining in the world. During the December mating season, large numbers of sea turtles congregate here. Kosrae receives 4,466 millimeters (175.9 in.) of rain a year—in Micronesia, only Pohnpei is wetter. The air is humid and the island is covered in thick jungle growth. Temperatures are warm and very consistent—27.2°C (81.0°F)—but the air is freshened by the northeast trade winds.

INSARU AND THE WHALERS

The first Kosraeans remembered in history were a feudal aristocracy that ruled from Insaru, a fortress city on Lelu Island, from about A.D. 1400 to A.D. 1800. It was from here that Isokelekel and his 333 warriors left to liberate Pohnpei, 560 kilometers away, from the Saudeleurs. The ruins of this city are still visible, and after Nan Madol the most important archaeological sight in Micronesia.

In the 19th century, Kosrae was known as "Strong's Island," named in 1804 by a Nantucket whaling captain after the governor of Massachusetts. The island became a regular stopping point for whale boats, both for her fine timber and for dalliances with the island women. In the mid-19th century, Kosrae was governed by Awane Lapalik I, who had a good relationship with the whalers and by whom he was called "Good King George." Contact with the whalers proved devastating to the Kosraeans, however, and influenza and venereal disease reduced the population from 10,000 to a mere 300 in two decades.

The notorious American pirate and opium trader Bully Hayes visited Kosrae in 1874, where his ship *Leonora* sank during a storm in Utwe Harbor. Being wooden, there's not much left of the brigantine, but the corals that have replaced the wood are thick, beautiful and worth the trip. (You literally have to beg to be taken to this site, so be persistent.) It is said that he rescued the treasure and buried it nearby on Kosrae, but was killed in a fight before he came back to get it. Many have looked, but no one has found it yet.

Life on Kosrae under the Japanese was harsh, and at the height of World War II the Kosraeans had to hide in the hills. The Americans bombed the isolated island, but never invaded. Starting out in the Trust Territory as part of Pohnpei district, Kosrae became its own entity in 1977—a status it has maintained since independence.

In 1852, Congregational missionaries arrived from Hawai'i to convert a population decimated by disease, and today Kosrae is the most religious island in Micronesia. The people are devoted Congregationalist Christians (although there are a few Baptists and Mormons), and churches are packed on Sundays. Liquor is strongly discouraged (tourists have to buy a $3 permit to drink). The Kosraeans credit the early evangelical Christians with saving their lives and culture. Conservative dress is expected here (women bathe in knee-length dresses) and the Sabbath is respected (no diving on Sundays).

A FERTILE ISLAND

Because of the heavy rainfall, Kosrae is completely blanketed with thick vegetation. Colorful birds burst from the forest. Five main rivers flow from the mountains, generously irrigating and replenishing the volcanic soil. Yams, taro, and manioc swell underground, while banana, pandanus, coconut, and breadfruit trees provide shade and food. Limes, oranges, and tangerines are also cultivated. This is one of the few Micronesian islands where you can enjoy good produce. (You can find a fresh lime for that sunset gin and tonic, but you better bring your own gin—customs will allow you to enter with two bottles).

The farmer's market on the Lelu causeway sells produce as well as fresh crabs, lobsters, and yellowfin tuna. Pigs are raised everywhere on Kosrae, and pork is a vital part of the diet. Fish, especially smaller reef fish, are consumed in great numbers. Everyone fishes and everyone catches—since the reef is healthy and not over-exploited, fishing is better here than on other Micronesian islands.

HALF A SMILE

Today Kosrae finds itself caught halfway between tradition and the modern world. The paved road from Okat goes three-quarters of the way around the island, but stops before Walung, where the people value their traditions and privacy more than progress.

"It used to be 'your problem is my problem; what affects you affects me; when you cry, I cry, too,'" said Luey K. Luey, special assistant to the Kosrae state president. "But now, we are confused. We have lost something and there is nothing yet to replace it. We used to walk around with real smiles; now we have only a half smile."

I believe in Kosrae. I think the Kosraeans will be successful in salvaging what is important from the past, and in building what is necessary for the future. Can Chuuk restock its wrecks with the artifacts that have been stripped? Can Yap keep MTV at arm's length and preserve its heritage? Kosrae has the advantage in this of being able to learn from the mistakes made by its

neighbors in the Federated States.

The Kosrae government, suddenly aware that tourism can be a valuable resource, is taking steps to prevent what is happening in other parts of Micronesia (Chuuk, for example) from happening to the Sleeping Lady. Fishing limits are being considered for the Taiwanese

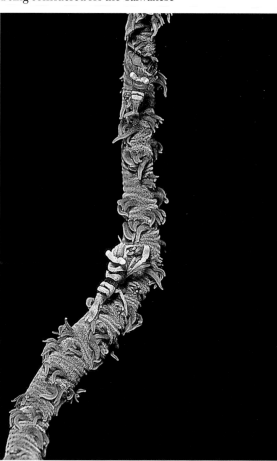

TAMMY PELUSO   Dasycaris zanzibarica (female at bottom)   Micronesia, unspecified

trawlers in the harbor, despite that the fees from these trawlers make up the island's largest source of income after U.S. aid. A nickel-a-can bounty has almost single-handedly turned this once heavily littered island into a pristine tropical paradise. Why can't the rest of Micronesia put some common sense to work?

This little shrimp lives only on the black coral Cirrhipathes. Under natural light, the resemblance between shrimp and host is even greater than the photograph (lit by flash) suggests.

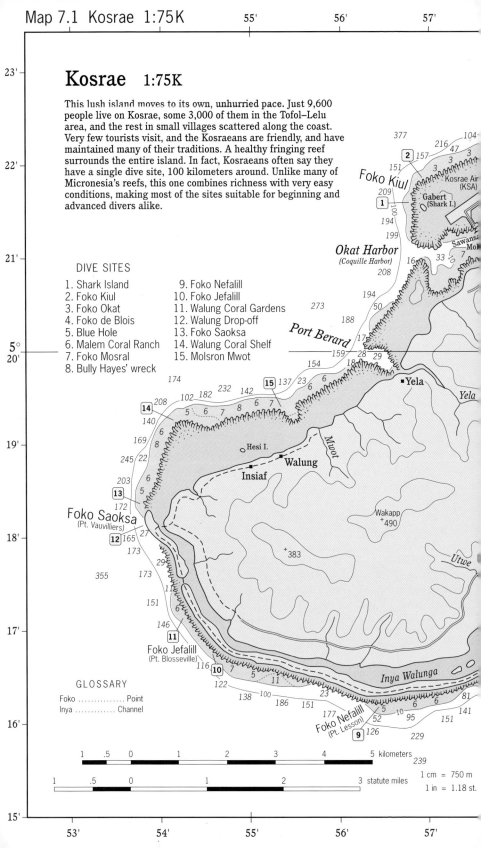

Map 7.1 Kosrae 1:75K

Kosrae 1:75K

This lush island moves to its own, unhurried pace. Just 9,600 people live on Kosrae, some 3,000 of them in the Tofol–Lelu area, and the rest in small villages scattered along the coast. Very few tourists visit, and the Kosraeans are friendly, and have maintained many of their traditions. A healthy fringing reef surrounds the entire island. In fact, Kosraeans often say they have a single dive site, 100 kilometers around. Unlike many of Micronesia's reefs, this one combines richness with very easy conditions, making most of the sites suitable for beginning and advanced divers alike.

DIVE SITES

1. Shark Island
2. Foko Kiul
3. Foko Okat
4. Foko de Blois
5. Blue Hole
6. Malem Coral Ranch
7. Foko Mosral
8. Bully Hayes' wreck
9. Foko Nefalill
10. Foko Jefalill
11. Walung Coral Gardens
12. Walung Drop-off
13. Foko Saoksa
14. Walung Coral Shelf
15. Molsron Mwot

GLOSSARY

Foko .... Point
Inya .... Channel

1 cm = 750 m
1 in = 1.18 st.

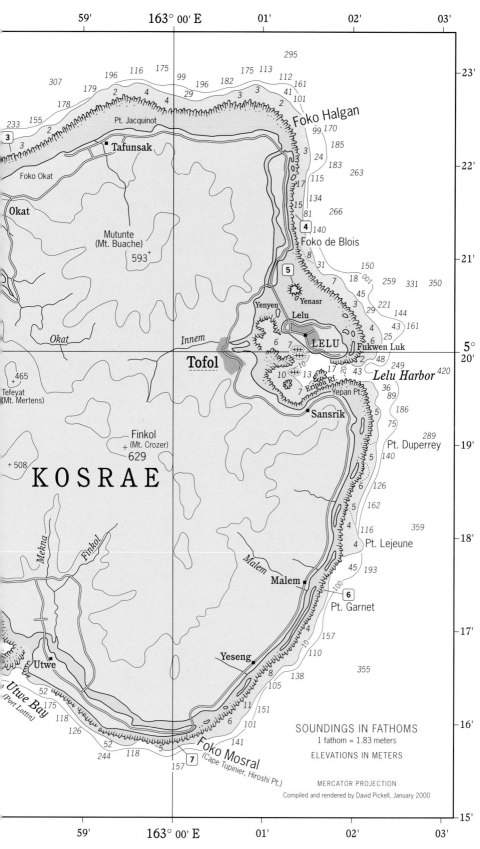

DIVING KOSRAE

Just One Dive Site
(But It's a Hundred Kilometers Long)

KOSRAE IS PRISTINE AND SELDOM VIS-
ited by divers because she lies in the
long shadow of Micronesian hot
spots such as Palau, Chuuk, and
Yap. Diving in Kosrae can be fun, although ultimately not as challenging
or rewarding as at these more famous sites. If you are a beginning
diver, you will find more good
dives with easy conditions at Kosrae. There are merits to a stop in
Kosrae, but if you're expecting the
kind of experience offered in Kwa-

**From the wreck of Bully Hayes'
wooden pirate ship to sheer, current-
swept drop-offs to calm, colorful,
reef flats—Kosrae gets better the
more time you spend here.**

jalein, Palau, or Pohnpei, you will be
disappointed.

This is a gorgeous, lush, and
friendly island and while I do not
believe that Kosrae offers world-
class diving, it is an excellent place
to spend a week diving in a more relaxed and relatively unchallenging
atmosphere. The reefs are pristine,
and the hard coral in particular has
grown large and impressive.

Much of the diving is accessible
from shore, but there are several operators who will be happy to take
you by boat to the best sites. And
there are some nice sites: Pirate
Bully Hayes' ship, the *Leonora*, still
rests at the bottom of Utwe Harbor,

and a few World War II wrecks have
been found. Just offshore from the
new airport, Shark Island and Foko
Kiul, though not "guaranteed"
shark dives, offer a good chance to
see pelagics as they swim close to
the reef. To the west, Walung Drop-
off , Walung Coral Gardens and the
Walung Coral Shelf offer colorful
diving in gin-clear water.

Two coral monitoring programs
have been set up by Marine Resources, following AIMS proto-
cols. The Kosrae Village Resort is
responsible for setting up volunteer
groups using the Reef Check methods. If you're interested in partici-
pating in these programs, contact
Katrina Brandt at the resort. Hard
coral spawning has been observed
to take place on Kosrae six days following the July full moon.

All boats leave from the dock
(just offshore from the new airport)
built by the U.S. Army Civil Action
Team based here, and trips to the
dive sites, especially in the south and
east, can be long. Try to arrange a
trip where you can lunch at one of
the many smaller islands surrounding the main island so you'll be able
to continue your dive day without
the long trip back to the dock.

Kosrae has pioneered the installation of 56 mooring buoys which
surround the island. This is the result of a model of cooperation between public and private entities,
not to mention fishermen and
divers, and it is something the
other more highly trafficked islands would do well to duplicate.
The sites below, listed geographically beginning at the airport, are

176   KOSRAE

DAVID LEONARD Kosrae

both keyed to MAP 7.1, pages 174–175, and the local buoy numbering system.

SHARK ISLAND [1] AND FOKO KIUL [2]

These sites are on the reef just offshore from the airport. At the seaward edge of the reef, the coral drops in a steep wall from 15 meters below the surface down to several hundred meters.

The potentially strong current along this wall makes this a dive for experienced divers who like a good roller coaster, and may also present challenges for underwater still photography.

Common sightings at these sites include sharks, barracuda, eagle rays, Napoleon wrasse, dogtooth tunas, rainbow runners, turtles, as well as lots of smaller reef fish. This location is also home to many crinoids, lobsters, and other invertebrates. If there are mantas exploring Kosrae, this is where they'll be. Don't bother diving here at low tide or during the full moon, as it is usu-

ally deserted. (Buoys 39, 40, 41.)

FOKO OKAT [3]

This site, also called Parrotfish Canyon, is near the Okat channel mouth. Foko Okat usually hosts lots of wave action and fast, unpredictable currents, which bring great schools of fish. Healthy table and smaller boulder type corals are everywhere. Check the crevices here for octopus, which can sometimes be quite large. (Buoy 42.)

FOKO DE BLOIS [4]

This site is also called Clownfish Drop-off, and many large anemones, with their colorful commensal damselfish, cling to the coral here. Unfortunately, there is little else to recommend this dive, and your time could be better spent elsewhere. (Buoy 40.)

BLUE HOLE [5]

This is not a true, karstic blue hole, but rather a great, 150-meter-wide opening on the shallow Lelu

Dive boats at Kosrae. All boats leave from this dock, near the airport in the north. The sites on the windward side and in the south—twenty to twenty-five kilometers away—can make for a rather long trip.

reef flat. It acts like a huge tide pool, and many of the small sharks, stingrays, turtles, and other animals who had been exploring the reef flat during high tide wait out the tidal change in this whole. The maximum depth is about 20 meters. Watch for potentially dangerous surge during tidal changes.

This is an interesting dive, and there are lots of small fish, especially puffers, and many, many lionfish. Visibility is usually comparatively low, maybe 10 meters, and it drops to almost nothing at times. This is a protected site, and a good dive if you absolutely have to get wet and salty and the island is blown out by bad weather. (Near Buoys 52 and 53.)

MALEM CORAL RANCH [6]

The reef top here starts at 15 meters and gently slopes down to a wide coral shelf. Table and staghorn corals are common and there are some giant coral heads. There is a great deal of fish life here, including sharks and other large visitors. The Ranch is on the wind-ward side of the island, and therefore not always accessible. A juvenile whale shark has been recently seen at this interesting site. (Buoy 9.)

FOKO MOSRAL [7]

Also called Hiroshi Point, this site is at the southernmost tip of Kosrae off Utwe. The easy beach entry makes this an excellent dive for all levels. It is also a good spot if you are with a non-diving partner, as the snorkeling is excellent. The top of the reef, 7 meters from the surface, is mixed sand and coral patches. Groups of parrotfish, eagle rays, and many smaller reef fish frequent the point. This makes an excellent night dive. Over the edge of the wall, sharks and other cruising pelagics can be seen. As it is on the weather side of the island, Foko Mosral can only be dived in good conditions. (Buoy 15.)

BULLY HAYES' WRECK [8]

Still bearing her cannons, the *Leonora* has somehow survived, though barely. Inside the natural

The broad-armed cuttlefish is a striking and otherworldly creature. Note also the 'comet' clinging to the coral rock just under the cuttle's belly. This is a regenerating arm of the sea star Linkia multiflora.

TAMMY PELUSO Sepia latimanus Micronesia, unspecified

harbor in the mouth of a river's silty bottom, here you can find garden eels, juvenile reef fish, and dark-phase lionfish. Sometimes, turtles sleep in the sand. There is not much left of the ship other than a few timbers and spars poking through a hundred years of silt. The wreck lies from 12 to 23 meters. (Buoy 19.)

FOKO NEFALILL [9]

Newly discovered, fast currents sweep you along with many large fish, including giant jacks, immense schools of barracuda, rays, and sharks. An excellent, if sometimes challenging, dive. (Buoy 21.)

WALUNG CORAL GARDENS [11]

Here, off the southwestern shore of Kosrae, steep, sloping walls lead you to a photographer's paradise. There's usually little to no current, and the wall is very manageable. Over the edge, you can spot sharks and other large pelagics, but the magic on this dive is on the top of the reef at the 15–20 meter zone. Being on the leeward side of the island, there's a marvelous collection of unbroken hard corals and vast arrays of smaller reef fish, as well as octopuses and many other interesting invertebrates. A good novice dive. (Buoys 25 and 26.)

WALUNG DROP-OFF [12]

This is a rich, sheer wall, near the island's westernmost point. Currents here are often strong. Resident schools of barracuda, large jacks, and rainbow runners are often joined by spotted eagle rays, Napoleon wrasse, turtles and occasional pelagic species. The reef top here is just as magical as at Walung Coral Gardens. Look carefully under the coral heads, you may be rewarded with the sight of very enormous, very shy puffer. You can also see huge barracuda or Napoleon wrasse being groomed in cleaning stations.

MIKE SEVERNS   Chaetodon punctatofasciatus   Kosrae

MIKE SEVERNS   Centropyge flavissimus   Kosrae

Mantas lately have been spotted here. Just south of the drop-off is a resident school of spinner dolphins that entertain passing dive boats. Watch for hammerhead sharks, which have been seen near Buoy 29. (Buoys 29 and 30.)

FOKO SAOKSA [13]

Ripping currents can make this point un-diveable, but if conditions allow, this is a great place to see large schools of barracuda, rainbow runners, and sharks. Water temperatures can be a little cool here. (Buoy 30N.)

MOLSRON MWOT [15]

A sandy bottom marks this newly discovered site, where a large group of resident stingrays sweep along at 30 meters. (Buoys 34 and 35.)

Kosrae is not the best place in Micronesia to see sharks and pelagics, but the reefs, dominated by hard corals, are rich in colorful inshore species like the spot-banded butterflyfish (above) and the lemon peel angelfish (below).

If you are willing to look, every diving area has its particular charms. For example, although most divers would consider Palau to be a better diving area than Kosrae overall, the beautiful little lemon peel angelfish shown above is not found in Palau.

The Prinz Eugen is the most famous wreck in Kwajalein Lagoon. Built as a sister ship to the Bismark, it is some 200 meters long, and after World War II passed first to the British, and then the Americans.

MIKE SEVERNS Prinz Eugen wreck Kwajalein Atoll

As part of the atomic test fleet deployed in Bikini Atoll, the Prinz Eugen survived blasts Able and Baker. It was to be scuttled in the open ocean, but developed leaks, and made it no further than Kwajalein, where it now rests, just off Enubuj Island.

This is the undomesticated frontier of Micronesian diving. The islands themselves are low, sandy cays, but inside these huge atolls are some of the best wrecks found anywhere in the world, as well as warm, clear water, and lots of sharks.

Marshall Islands

FORGET EVERYTHING YOU'VE EVER heard about Kwajalein Atoll—that is, assuming you ever did hear anything about "Kwaj"—and pack your gear and go. Kwajalein, the capital of the Ralik Chain of the Marshall Islands and the world's largest atoll, has what every diver wants: unexplored reefs, loaded wrecks, millions of unafraid reef fish, curious sharks, and even an occasional sperm whale. White sand beaches, with the requisite palm trees, crest every low coral island. Fresh fish is grilled on the dock. Crisp blue skies light a gin-clear lagoon. And the place is full of friendly, helpful people.

The Marshall Islands are the untamed frontier of the Micronesian region. This independent republic consists of 870 reefs, 29 atolls, and 5 separate islands (1,225 islands altogether), all scattered across 1,500 kilometers of the west-central Pacific. The Marshall Islands atolls are classic formations, with a ring of reef and coral islands surrounding a central lagoon. Despite the huge number of islands, the land area here is tiny—all 1,225 islands, taken together, would fit on Guam three times over.

The islands are narrow scraps of coral sand, supporting coconut palms, pandanus, breadfruit trees, and shoreline tangles of beach morning glory, but little else. These are among the lowest islands in the world. The highest elevation in the entire nation, on Likiap, is a mere 10.4 meters, less than the height of a full-grown coconut tree. The rise in sea level expected to accompany global warming is of only passing interest in most parts of the world, but in the Marshalls a mere one-foot increase would be catastrophic, drowning much of the country.

The Marshalls run in two parallel chains, the Ratak or "sunrise" chain in the east, and the Ralik or "sunset" chain in the west. The Ratak Chain is the more populous, containing about 39,000 of the nation's estimated population of 65,000, and is the site of the capital—Darrit–Uliga–Delap (usually abbreviated "D-U-D") on Majuro Atoll. Most of the population in the

MIKE SEVERNS Priolepis cincta Majuro Atoll

The Pacific convict goby is a tiny creature that hides in rock crevices or, as here, furrows of coral.

Ralik Chain is on Ebeye, the nation's second-largest "city," on Kwajalein Atoll. Some 95 percent of the population is Marshallese.

FAMOUS NAVIGATORS

Marshallese legend states that the first man was Uelip, who lived on the island of Ep with his wife. One day a tree began growing from his head, splitting his skull. Through

the crack emerged two sons, Etau and Djemelut. Following an argument with his father, Etau took a basket of soil and set out on his own, flying through the air. Along the way the soil spilled, in the process forming the Marshall Islands.

Anthropologists consider that the first people reached the Marshalls perhaps 4,000 years ago. The original Marshallese were among the world's best canoe builders and navigators. By necessity, perhaps, since these low islands are so hard to spot from a distance, the Marshallese learned to navigate by sensing through the hulls of their canoes the reflected swell from islands still far too distant to see.

Instruction in this art took place by means of constructing "stick charts," diagrams made from bent twigs (representing swell patterns) and cowrie shells (islands). This information was memorized before the sailors left for distant islands. Stick charts are still made today (they make popular souvenirs), and stick chart patterns are often seen as decoration in the islands, but few Marshallese can actually still read them.

Two Spanish sailors passed the Marshalls in the early 16th century, but Spain never attempted to colonize these islands, which lay outside the most important Pacific trade routes. The islands get their name from Captain John Marshall of the HMS *Scarborough,* who, in 1788, charted the southern half of the Ratak Chain and landed briefly on Mili Atoll. The Russian explorer Otto von Kotzebue investigated these islands on two trips, in 1817 and 1825, and his journal provides the first detailed description of the Marshallese and these islands.

Whereas the Caroline Islanders, for the most part, welcomed the increasing number of Yankee whalers and European traders who began visiting in the 19th century, these en-

MIKE SEVERNS Nebrius ferrugineus Kwajalein Atoll

counters in the Marshalls led almost always to violence—in mid-century, the entire crews of three whaling ships were murdered on the southern atolls of the Ralik Chain. (In retrospect, the Marshallese strategy may have been the best one, since diseases brought ashore by whalers decimated the populations of Pohnpei and Kosrae.)

Protestant missionaries arrived in Ebon Atoll, the closest to the Pacific trade routes, in 1857. In 1878 the Germans signed a treated with Chief Kabua of Jaluit Atoll, and in 1885, annexed the Marshalls. The Germans set up coconut plantations and copra processing facilities, with sales handled through local Marshallese chiefs, but the government didn't formally take control of the islands until a typhoon wiped out the plantations in 1905.

In 1914 the Japanese took the Marshalls along with the rest of the region, fortifying bases as well as expanding the copra trade. In February 1944, Majuro Atoll fell to the Americans in the heaviest barrage of World War II—some 36,000 shells were fired at the Japanese fortifications. Majuro became the first prewar Japanese possession captured in World War II.

After the war, the Marshall Islands became part of the Trust Territories of the Pacific Islands, administered by the United States. With the passage of its own constitution, the Marshall Islands became a self-governing republic in 1979. A popularly elected 33-member legislature now chooses the country's president.

THE ATOM BOMB TESTS

From 1946 through 1958, the United States used the Marshalls for its nuclear testing program, over this period detonating 66 nuclear devices in Bikini Atoll and Enewetok Atoll. Both these atolls, despite several hundred millions of dollars in clean-up, retain radioactive residue, as do Rongelap and Utrik, which received fallout from a 1954 blast on Bikini.

Bikini, best known in the West as

Nurse sharks are most active at night, and during the day tend to rest in caves or under overhangs. Their favorite food seems to be octopus, which explains the nocturnal hunting schedule. Although many sources say these sharks are harmless, do not take this to mean they can be touched or otherwise pestered. They grow quite large and are tough animals. If cornered or bothered, they can get ornery, and are quite willing to chomp down and hold on—in some cases, even after the victim is pulled from the water.

MIKE SEVERNS   Carcharinus amblyrhynchos   Rongelap Atoll

Gray reef sharks are graceful, curious, territorial, and sometimes irritable—everything you could ask for in a shark. The
it feels that you have encroached on its territory, will perform an interesting threat display: it arches its back, pectoral

lagoons, and particularly, lagoon passes and steep seaward drop-offs. They are chiefly fish eaters. The gray reef, when
, and snaps its tail and head back and forth. If you ever see this, you know instinctively what the shark is trying to say.

the nickname of a risqué French bathing suit invented in 1947 (and originally called the "atome"), was known to the Marshallese as the most beautiful of their atolls, and the favorite of the creator Loa. After 23 bomb blasts, including the massive hydrogen bomb "Bravo" of 1954, several of the atoll's islands are gone and Bikini Island itself remains irradiated. The saga of the Bikinians, moved from their island in 1946, then returned, then moved, then returned again, is one of the saddest chapters of the Cold War.

The Enewetok islanders, whose atoll received 43 blasts, have been returned to Enewetok. Because of a huge underground blast in 1958, this atoll now has a 1.5-kilometer-wide, 60-meter deep crater in the middle, and one island has been filled with irradiated waste and capped with concrete.

In 1961, Kwajalein Atoll became a target site for Inter-Continental Ballistic Missiles fired from California. Radar dishes surround the lagoon.

A CHARMING SHANTY TOWN

Although there is diving available in Majuro, savvy divers will head right for Kwajalein, currently the best (and best-organized) diving in the Marshalls. Everyone I have met who has visited this place comes away from it was a love of the entire experience, which is somewhat strange. It is easy to understand the appeal of Kwajalein's diving, but the island city of Ebeye—pronounced "*EE*-bye"—is not what most people would think of as a charming destination.

Ebeye is a wind-swept, forlorn bit of coral gravel covered shore-to-shore with tin, cardboard, mesh, and plywood sheds painted in drab institutional blues and grays. This Pacific "Tobacco Road" stretches the length of the island, little over a mile, and is home to 14,000 people, making this one of the most densely populated places on the planet. (And 70 percent of the population is under the age of fourteen.)

Although to a middle-class

This stick chart pattern, etched into a concrete wall on Majuro, is a reminder of the Marshall Islanders' history as some of the world's greatest open ocean navigators.

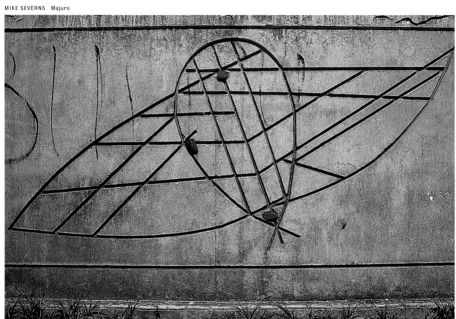

American it looks like squalor, the Ebeyeans will note that things have improved considerably since the 1980s, and now most of these houses, despite their appearance, have electricity and running water, the latter from a new desalination plant. The streets are paved, and at nights high-pressure lamps light your way—one of the very few places in the Pacific you will see such amenities.

A leisurely walk all the way around the island takes a half-hour or so, or a taxi will take you anywhere you want to go for a dollar. Extending north from Ebeye are many more islets, now connected by a coral road.

If you walk around this island, you will find out The Marshallese are genuinely kind and generous people, anxious to show you their way and share a Bud Light with you. This is why visitors come away so charmed. The smiles make the gray shacks beautiful.

DAVID LEONARD Ipomoea pes-caprae Ebeye

MIKE SEVERNS Kwajalein Island

JUST SCRAPING BY

The economy of the Marshall Islands is dependent on $40 million a year in grants from the United States, which make up some two-thirds of the government's income. Further income comes from payments on a $240 million, thirty-year lease for the use of Kwajalein.

The Japanese remove 11,000 metric tons (24 million pounds) of fish from these waters every year, mostly tuna, but also 600 metric tons of billfish. For the privilege of netting and long-lining these fish (worth nearly $200 million) the Japanese pay the Marshall Islands a mere $1 million.

After this, there isn't a whole lot of business here. Small merchants and traders, limited tourist facilities, a copra mill on Majuro, and similar small-scale operations make up the rest. The Marshalls have the lowest per capita gross national product in the region, just $1,680.

All levels of foreign investment require approval by the Foreign Investment Board, and while no specific investment incentives are offered, the Marshall Islands remain a low tax jurisdiction. In addition, it has negotiated preferred trade status with the United States and certain other industrial countries. The Republic imposes no income taxes. There is a severe trade imbalance with imports outweighing exports 3:1.

Approximately 1,000 of the Marshallese living on Ebeye find work on the Kwajalein Island base, mostly in construction, janitorial, electrical, and other trades to support the operation of the $4 billion Kwajalein Missile Range, now officially called the United States Army Kwajalein Atoll (USAKA).

Kwajalein is almost relentlessly drab above water. Beach morning glory vines and a scruffy strand forest of coconut, pandanus, and other pioneer species cover the islands linked by the causeway north of Ebeye Island (above), and Kwajalein Island itself is a monument of institutional concrete (below).

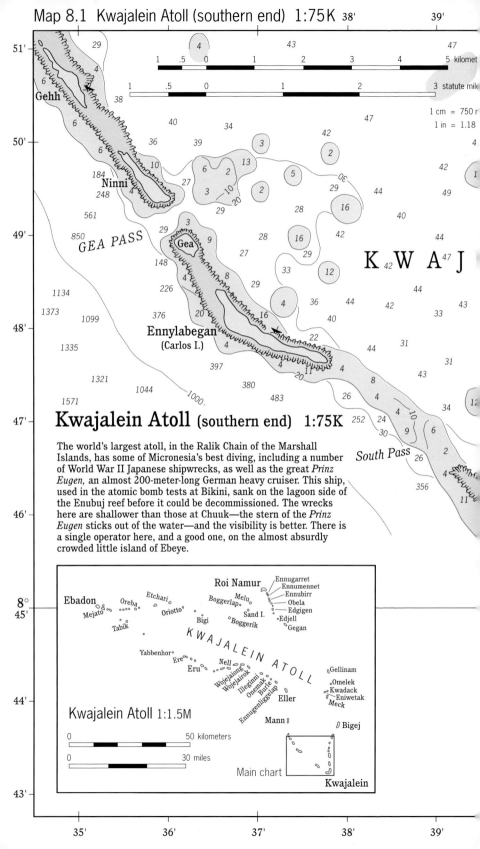

Map 8.1 Kwajalein Atoll (southern end) 1:75K

1 kilomet

statute mile

1 cm = 750 r
1 in = 1.18

Gehh

Ninni

GEA PASS

Gea

Ennylabegan
(Carlos I.)

K W A J

South Pass

Kwajalein Atoll (southern end) 1:75K

The world's largest atoll, in the Ralik Chain of the Marshall
Islands, has some of Micronesia's best diving, including a number
of World War II Japanese shipwrecks, as well as the great *Prinz
Eugen*, an almost 200-meter-long German heavy cruiser. This ship,
used in the atomic bomb tests at Bikini, sank on the lagoon side of
the Enubuj reef before it could be decommissioned. The wrecks
here are shallower than those at Chuuk—the stern of the *Prinz
Eugen* sticks out of the water—and the visibility is better. There is
a single operator here, and a good one, on the almost absurdly
crowded little island of Ebeye.

Roi Namur
Ennugarret
Ennummennet
Ennubirr
Obela
Edgigen
Ebadon
Oreba   Etchari
Mejato   Oriotto   Melu   Sand I.
Boggerlap   Edjell
Tabik   Bigi   Boggerik   Gegan

KWAJALEIN ATOLL

Yabbenhor
Ere   Nell   Gellinam
Eru   Wojejatong   Omelek
Wojejairok   Kwadack
Illeginni   Eniwetak
Onemak   Eller   Meck
Bure
Ennugenliggelap
Mann   Bigej

Kwajalein Atoll 1:1.5M

0   50 kilometers
0   30 miles

Main chart

Kwajalein

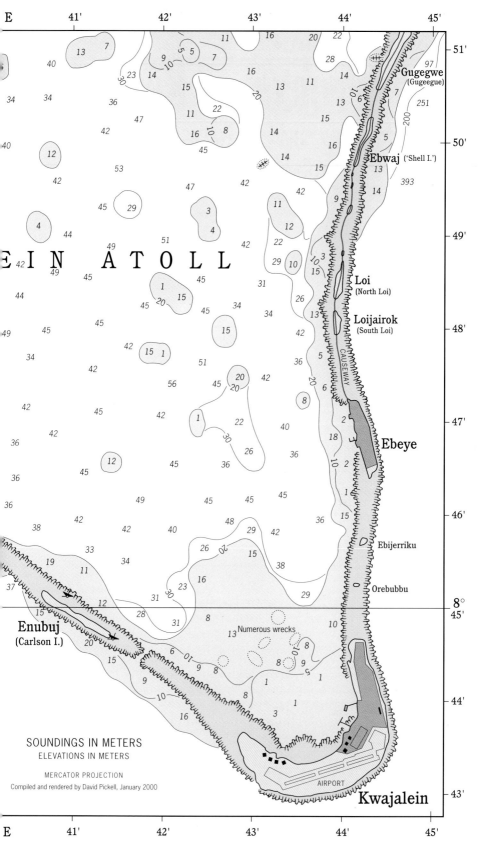

SOUNDINGS IN METERS
ELEVATIONS IN METERS

MERCATOR PROJECTION

Compiled and rendered by David Pickell, January 2000

The Wrecks of Kwajalein
Rich, Interesting, and Easy to Reach

THE MARSHALL ISLANDS ARE THE frontier of Micronesian diving. Here is a great, 1,500-kilometer long swath of the Pacific Ocean, with two chains of huge, pristine atolls. Conditions are excellent. The water is warm—29°C (84°F) — year round, and visibility at the best sites reaches 70 meters. Organized diving is still only available in a few areas, and these are far from being fully explored. Marshall Islands diving is an adventure.

Bikini and Mili are exciting sites for the experienced and well-heeled diver, but Kwajalein Atoll has the best and most convenient diving in the region, with excellent wrecks and marine life.

Because the Marshalls lie so far from Indonesia and the southern Philippines, which is the center of biodiversity for Indo-Pacific reefs, the number of fish and coral species on these reefs is lower than at, say, Palau or the Western Caroline Islands sites. In species richness, the Marshalls lie somewhere between Palau and Hawai'i, which is what you would expect from their location, with the southern atolls being better in this regard than northern ones.

But a somewhat bland coral and reef fish population is a small price to pay for stunning water clarity, and turtles, rays, sharks, and some in-comparable World War II wrecks. The Marshalls, in particular, are one of the best places in the world to see sharks—reef black-tips, reef white-tips, and gray reefs in particular. On some dives you will see dozens of them, and at sites where divers are rare, they can be almost too curious.

The Marshalls are tropical, but cooled by the northeast trade winds. The temperature at Majuro, the capital, averages 26.8°C (80.4°F) year-round. An average 3,444 millimeters (135.6 in.) of rain falls each year, and the driest months are January, February, and March. The northern atolls are slightly cooler and drier than Majuro. Typhoons are uncommon, but storms can brew in the spring and fall. The summer months generally bring the calmest seas and winds, and are the best for diving.

Dive operations here are still new and relatively low-key. At the time of this writing, there was organized diving at five atolls: Majuro, Arno, Mili, Bikini, and Kwajalein.

Diving in Majuro is only fair, due to the extensive commercial activity, but nearby Arno Atoll, and Mili Atoll, the southernmost of the Ratak Chain, can be spectacular. The visibility is excellent at these pristine spots, and Mili's North Point, in particular, is an exceptional shark dive. It is quite expensive and time-consuming to reach Arno and Mili, however, and each of these trips is a one-off adventure, so we have not covered these sites at length in this edition. The Practicalities section lists operators who can take you here.

In 1996, Bikini Atoll, the victim of 23 atomic explosions, was opened to dive tourism, and it is now one of the world's hottest dive destinations. This warm lagoon contains the wreck of the aircraft carrier USS *Saratoga*, which at some 270 meters (880 ft.) is the largest wreck in the world at sport diving depths, as well as numerous others, all of them victims of U.S. bomb testing. Because of the more isolated location of Bikini, the depths, and perhaps irradiation from the blasts, these wrecks are not heavily encrusted like those at Chuuk, and the ships' structure, guns, and other accouterments are perfectly visible. While spectacular, Bikini diving is very deep—60 meter (190 ft.) decompression dives are the norm—and quite expensive. Bikini is a specialty area for a very experienced, very interested diver, so we have not covered it at length (see Practicalities section for operator).

The best developed part of the Marshalls for diving is Kwajalein Atoll, which offers a number of excellent World War II wrecks, both shallow and deep, as well as some reef sites. There is also a lot of virgin territory here, and plenty of places left to explore. There is only one operator here (but a good one) located on Ebeye Island. The sites listed below are in the southern part of the lagoon, shown in MAP 8.1, pages 190–191.

GEA ISLAND WALL

The inside of Gea Island and the reef connecting it to Ennylabegan Island is a rich slope and wall covered with hard and soft corals. Near Gea immense coral heads rise up from the sand, and further south the reef goes to a drop-off. There are lots of reef fish here, and the occasional shark, turtle, eagle ray or manta ray.

SOUTH PASS REEF

Due west across the lagoon from Ebeye is a cut in the reef called South Pass. This is a major thoroughfare for plankton and

The fairy wrasses are skittish, beautiful little creatures and, it must be said, a nightmare to photograph. Ichthyologists still have some work to do on the genus and there are several in the Micronesian region, including this one, that remain unnamed.

MIKE SEVERNS   Cirrhilabrus sp.   Kwajalein Atoll

MIKE SEVERNS   Butterflyfish: Heniochus acuminatus; Sponge: Cribrochalina olemda

This butterflyfish has claimed the only landmark in a great field of Porites coral.

nutrients—and, therefore, for hungry fish—and makes an exciting dive during the right tidal conditions. Turtles, sharks, and tuna are a few of the animals you can see here.

PRINZ EUGEN

The most famous wreck in Kwajalein is the 199-meter (654 ft.) *Prinz Eugen*, a German heavy cruiser with quite a rich past. The *Prinz Eugen* made its greatest impact on history in May 1941, when together with her sister ship, the *Bismarck*, it sank the HMS *Hood*.

At the end of World War II, the *Prinz Eugen* was surrendered to the Allies, and in 1946, the ship was among the fleet taken to Bikini Atoll to serve as targets in early atomic bomb tests. The *Prinz Eugen* survived two blasts. First "Able," the world's third atomic explosion, which detonated 158 meters above the water on July 1, 1946, then "Baker," the world's fourth atomic explosion, which detonated 27 meters below the lagoon on July 25, 1946. After the tests, the *Prinz Eugen* was towed with the rest of the test fleet to Kwajalein Lagoon.

Slow leaks had developed in the ship, and by the time it reached the lagoon, tugs towed it to Enubuj Island to get it out of the shipping lanes. Winds then blew it onto the reef, where it sank.

The ship's stern lies on the reef with the rudder and the starboard propeller near the surface (in 1978 the port prop was removed and taken to Bremerhaven, Germany, to serve as a memorial). The bow is relatively deep, about 35 meters, and hangs in mid-water, suspended above the lagoon bottom.

You can easily visit the Admiral's Bridge, high on the main mast, and the crew quarters, at 12 meters. The *Prinz Eugen* had four main gun turrets, each with two eight-inch guns, as well as many smaller guns mounted along both gunwales.

There is a torpedo locker on the port side main deck, and the ship carried a dozen deck-mounted torpedo tubes, two sets of three tubes on each side of the ship. You can still see artillery shells, furniture, chairs, beds, and gauges without much penetration. Much of the ship is within easy reach for snorkelers.

The Japanese Shipwrecks

A two-month-long series of bombing raids, beginning in December 1943, preceded the Allied invasion of Kwajalein. When the smoke cleared on February 5, 1944, more than 30 Japanese ships lay silent in the depths of the lagoon. Most of the wrecks are in the southern end of the atoll, within 15 kilometers of Kwajalein Island.

The end of World War II was followed by the Cold War, and many of the islands of Kwajalein Atoll became part of the U.S. Army's Kwajalein Missile Range. Most of the wrecks were discovered by military divers in the mid-sixties, but the secret Inter-Continental Ballistic Missile experiments conducted here kept Kwajalein Lagoon closed to civilian visitors and tourists until just a few years ago.

ASAKAZE MARU

Also known as "K4-Upright," for the buoy near which she lies and her resting position, this 129-meter ship is the largest wreck in the lagoon. After serving the Japanese Navy in numerous sea battles, The *Asakaze Maru* was sunk on December 4, 1943 by U.S. bombers. The ship rests upright on a 49-meter bottom. Her superstructure towers four stories above the main deck, and turtles and fish swim through the rigging.

There is a three-inch cannon on the bow; an identical gun on the stern was blown from its mount by one of the explosions that sank the *Asakaze*, and it lies at the bottom of

MIKE SEVERNS Sphyraena forsteri Dalap Point, Majuro Atoll

Most of the smaller species of barracuda school during the day and feed by night. The blackspot barracuda is no exception.

the No. 6 hold. Inside the No. 4 hold is a Japanese car. The ship's huge anchor rests in the sand, now a maze of coral.

The engine room was destroyed by a half-ton bomb that fell straight down through the skylights. Below the wreckage of steel walkways and bulkheads you will spot gauges, levers and other mechanical equipment.

TATEYAMA MARU

The *Tateyama,* also known as "K4-Side," is a 104-meter merchant freighter sunk by U.S. Navy bombers on December 4, 1943. She now lies on her starboard site on a 43-meter bottom.

Although not a warship per se, the *Tateyama Maru* was still armed with a three-inch bow gun and a wide-barreled machine gun on the starboard side of the wheel house (now at 32 meters). The cargo hold near the stern is filled with artillery shells, some of which have spilled out alongside the ship, and the forward cargo holds have large

water tanks. Thousands of empty beer bottles are strewn against a starboard bulkhead.

Human remains have been found in the engine room, and more are probably buried in the deep silt that has accumulated here.

The odd-looking "K4 Barge" sits upright, near the *Tateyama Maru,* on a 43-meter bottom. As the barge sank it dragged down with it the large mooring buoy to which it had been chained.

AKIBASAN MARU

Also known as "P-Buoy Wreck," the *Akibasan Maru* is probably Kwajalein's most popular site. This 114-meter freighter was sunk in an American skip-bomb strike on January 31, 1944. The *Akibasan* was at anchor at the time, and the ship is now the closest major wreck to the Kwajalein dock. The force of the explosions split the hull at one of the aft cargo holds, and the ship settled upright on a 50-meter bottom. Since the Akibasan rests on two coral mounts, it is

MIKE SEVERNS Apogon cyanosoma Majuro Atoll

possible to swim under the hull amidships. The main deck is at 30 meters or a little deeper.

Because of the relatively shallow depths, the *Akibasan* has attracted more coral growth than the other Kwajalein wrecks, and it is the most beautiful one in the atoll. The superstructure was gutted by fire, and the wooden upper decks have collapsed, so the sunlight streams into the holds, which are richly overgrown with sponges and soft and hard corals. Large schools of jacks sweep around the superstructure.

Although the upper sections are spacious and brightly illuminated, deeper inside the wreck things quickly turn cloudy and dark. Some of the cargo holds are empty, but in the forward holds you will find pontoons and airplane parts. In the spacious stern castle, huge gears and steering mechanisms are still relatively intact.

IKUTA MARU

Also known as "P-North," because it is a few hundred meters north of P buoy, this 92-meter freighter was sunk January 12, 1944. Her stern was almost completely shorn by a torpedo hit, and lies on the bottom away from the rest of the ship. The *Ikuta Maru* is the deepest of the wrecks at Kwajalein, and rests on her port side at about 60 meters. The starboard side is more accessible at 40–45 meters. These depths limit bottom time, but there is much to see here. I recommend visiting this wreck more than once.

The *Ikuta Maru* was the most heavily armed of all the Japanese wrecks in the lagoon, bearing a five-inch gun on the bow and another on each side ahead of the bridge. Rounds for these guns (still live) are scattered in racks near the gun mounts. The *Ikuta* was also equipped with several machine guns on the superstructure, and heavily fortified with sliding armor panels to protect the large windows from incoming artillery.

You can still spot electronic and mechanical equipment resting in the silt. Crates of gas masks and blue

This fish can be found from the Red Sea to the Marshall Islands, but only in Micronesia and the Marshalls is it called the orange cardinalfish. In the Indian Ocean and western Pacific, the longitudinal stripes hinted at in the specimens above are very noticeable, and in that region it is called the orange-striped cardinalfish.

Cardinalfish are mouth brooders, and their fry do not disperse very far. Thus the populations are genetically isolated, which can lead to the development of different coloration and even behavioral and morphological characteristics.

MIKE SEVERNS   Prinz Eugen wreck   Kwajalein Lagoon

These cables on the Prinz Eugen wreck are so encrusted with sponges and coralline algae that at first one takes them for whip corals.

ammunition which spilled out onto the sand. The bottom of the lagoon here is littered with mines, bombs, and torpedoes.

"MYSTERY MARU"

Also known as "O-Buoy Sub Chaser," this ship's origin and name are unknown. Small, at 85 feet, her four-hold, steel-covered wooden hull rests in 45 meters of water. Her bow was destroyed in the attack on Kwajalein, and since then, the wood has largely decayed, and the Mystery Maru's steel hull has collapsed. Today, the rubble rises only a few feet above the sand, and bears little resemblance to the fast ship she once was.

She must have gone down fighting, since the area is strewn with spent machine gun cartridges. There are more than a dozen skulls and hundreds of human bones in and around this wreck.

CHOKO MARU

The *Choko Maru* is a 104-meter freighter sunk on December 4, 1943 by U.S. bombers. The ship lies on her port side on a 44-meter bottom. The ship was lightly armed, and the only gun she carried was a three-inch deck cannon, still affixed to its wheel on the bow.

The engine room, at 40–44 meters, is the deepest and darkest section. Here small, jagged tears in the rusted skylights allow faint streams of filtered sunlight into the hold. Amazingly, though much of the ship was gutted by fire, the bridge superstructure is still largely intact.

The *Choko Maru* was filled to capacity—barrels and pipes in the forward holds, and many sets of small-gauge railroad wheels, axles, and fittings in an aft hold. Huge spare propellers are bolted tight against the bulkhead in the No. 4 hold. There are gun mounts at the bow and stern.

The biggest attraction on this

sake bottles can be found in the forward cargo holds, which were converted into troop quarters, and there are also personal effects scattered in these compartments.

SHOEI MARU

Also known as "O-Buoy Wreck," this four-hold freighter lies upside down at 45 meters near the extreme southern end of the lagoon. Her stern was destroyed by the explosion that sent her to the lagoon floor. The superstructure, derricks, and rigging are crushed under the inverted hull. There is a car under the deck in a forward cargo hold. Look for hemispherical mines on top of the car, under its running board, and inside, on the driver's seat. Nearby, a biplane fuselage lies in the sand. The *Shoei Maru* carried wreck are the barracuda—huge schools of them—which are not seen elsewhere in the lagoon, and this wreck is sometimes called "Barracuda Junction." Gray reef sharks, spotted eagle rays, and lionfish are also here in numbers.

SHELL ISLAND WRECKS

These are two small, schooner-class Japanese freighters that sank near some small coral heads, just inside the lagoon from Ebwaj, or "Shell Island." They are within 70 meters of one another, in 33 meters of water, and an easy swim from the island. The ships are covered in coral and other stationary sea life, yet still retain their ship shape. This is a beautiful site, well-endowed with fish life.

SKI BOAT AREA WRECK

This is the wreck of a short distance freighter that lies just off the western shore of Kwajalein Island. Shallow (15 meters), she has several cargo holds, and engine room and superstructure that are still inter-esting to view. This makes a good end of the day dive.

EOKO MARU

This wreck is also known as "First Ship," because it was the closest shipwreck to the marina at Roi Namur Island, at the northernmost extent of Kwajalein Atoll. The 104-meter *Eoko Maru* was sunk on January 29, 1944 by the USS *North Carolina*. This wreck is about 100 kilometers away from Ebeye, a little too far for a day trip. The *Eoko Maru* lies on a 35-meter bottom, near Roi Namur.

During the attack, a large shell sailed through the bulkhead into the radio room, which is strewn with the crumbling remains of electronic equipment. Many areas of the ship, however, are in relatively good shape. The portholes admit a fair amount of sunlight, which streams into the cabins and holds. This is an interesting dive, and it is possible to spend quite a bit of time here, because of the relatively shallow depths.

The stern of the Prinz Eugen rests on the reef, supporting the vessel. The bow sticks out into open water, seeming to hang there of its own accord, at about thirty-five meters.

MIKE SEVERNS   Prinz Eugen wreck   Kwajalein Lagoon

Although the island group contains the world's largest atoll (Kwajalein) and spans fifteen hundred kilometers, the highest elevation in the Marshalls is just a few meters above sea level.

MIKE SEVERNS Rongelap Atoll

Nautilus belauensis
Palau

David Leonard

Try these other titles in Periplus Editions' line of Surfing Guides

ISBN 962-593-313-1

Leonard and Lorca Lueras' *Surfing Indonesia* is probably the most comprehensive guide ever written on the Indonesian island chain . . . Whether you are traveling to the Mantawais in a luxury yacht or slumming it in Kuta, this book is a must.

Surfer magazine, January 1998

I've had *Surfing Indonesia* on my desk the last two years and in that time I've picked it up again and again, sometimes to glance at it for a moment, sometimes to pore over it for an hour. I always take it with me when I leave Bali to go surfing again, and always get it out when friends on holiday in Bali visit me. The great amount of research that has obviously gone into *Surfing Indonesia* and its wide range of contributors means it offers a wealth of information and a variety of writing styles and perspectives on surf breaks and surfing.

Surf Time magazine, September 2000

ISBN 962-593-322-0

Five Stars
The classy layout and glossy action photos [*Surfing Indonesia* and *Surfing Australia*] would make these titles ideal for a coffee table, but these guidebooks are small enough to fit in a backpack or the glove box of a Sandman panel van. They even have waterproof covers.
Both have comprehensive maps to each country's surfing spots, with guides to local conditions, the best surf season, special gear you'll need, and what's going to hurt you—"watch out for great white sharks." The books are also dotted with feature articles that are more interesting and down-to-earth than the stuff that fills the pages of most surfing magazines.
If you're planning a surfing trek through either country, they're worth every cent.

Ralph magazine, July 2000

ISBN 962-593-593-8

ISBN 962-593-541-X

Periplus Diving Guides

Diving Indonesia(Third Edition)
ISBN 962-593-314-X

"*Diving Indonesia* has to be the most fascinating book published in the last year."

BBC World

"*Diving Indonesia* comes described as "A guide to the world's greatest diving," and lives up to its promise. This guide features 120 color photographs, up-to-date travel information, maps of all major dive sites, essays on reef life and ecology, charts of site conditions, plus information on local geography, history, and lore."

Ocean Realm

Diving Southeast Asia(Second Edition)
ISBN 962-593-312-3

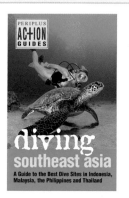

"Perhaps no other region in the world presents such clear waters and abundant undersea life as Southeast Asia. The azure seas, a bounty of reefs, submerged wrecks and fabulous coral gardens should get even the most hardened land lover into a wetsuit and mask.

This guide to the best dive sites in Malaysia, Indonesia, the Philippines and Thailand maps out the watery worlds that await the enthusiastic diver. The detailed information—whether it's a walk-in dive, a night dive, diving in remote locations or from live-aboard boats—provides everything you need to take the plunge: the visibility, the current, the type of fish, the quality of the coral, the choicest spots."

Going Places

Diving Australia(Second Edition)
ISBN 962-593-311-5

"An unbelievable collection of dive sites and information brought from renowned dive authors, Neville Coleman and Nigel Marsh. This handy book covers every state with detailed information on the sites. Every site has a map and an icon-based guide to tell you what you can expect to see, the reef life, the visibility, reef and pelagic fish, drop-offs and pinnacles. It has over 200 lovely colour photographs and most importantly, is easy to follow.

Basically, there is an awesome amount of information in this book. As a general guide to diving in Australia—this is the business."

Scuba Diver

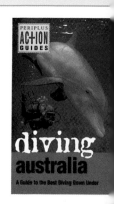

NEW

ISBN 962-593-323-9

Available in 2001

ISBN 962-593-064-7

Periplus Diving Guides available at bookshops travel stores around the wo If you cannot find them wh you live, please write to us the name of a distributor o est to you:

**Periplus Editions c/o Berke
Books Pte. Ltd., 5 Little Ro
#08-01, Singapore 536983.
tel: 65-280-1330,
fax: 65-280-6290**

PRACTICALITIES

Contents

Travel Advisory

Perhaps 1.5 million people a year visit Micronesia, but the vast majority are package tourists to Guam and Saipan. Some 40,000 a year visit Palau, and the rest of these beautiful islands see just a few thousand people a year. They are uncrowded, restful, and isolated—perfect for a dive holiday.

In Micronesia, sometimes the simplest things can seem absurdly difficult. Making telephone calls, changing money, reserving hotels and the like can turn into a frustrating experience, especially if you're in a rush. While people are accessible and will do their best to help, it is not always within their power. Relax. You are in the islands, and the pace here is not the same as back home. (Which is why, after all, you came here.)

General

VISAS AND DOCUMENTS

U.S. citizens do not need a visa to visit Micronesia. In fact, U.S. citizens don't even need a passport (a birth certificate and valid driver's license will suffice) although we recommend you bring one. Visitors of other nationalities will need a valid passport. If visiting Guam, non-U.S. citizens will need to obtain a U.S. visa ahead of time, and if visiting the Marshall Islands, they will need to purchase a 30-day visa upon arrival. The other islands do not require visas for tourist visits up to 30 days. Tourist visas can be extended (usually up to two additional months) at the immigration desk of the relevant country, sometimes with a fee ($25–$50). All visitors are required to have onward tickets.

Entry to the outer islands of Micronesia are often controlled, or even prohibited. These tend to be the most traditional parts of the country, and permission to visit these areas must be negotiated with traditional cultural leaders. Many of the outer islanders are not interested in being photographed, studied, or even visited by curious tourists.

Every country in Micronesia has instituted a departure tax ranging from $5 to $10. (Sometimes you'll be handing your cash to a shady-looking character in sunglasses who simply tosses it into a briefcase near the check-in counter at the airport.)

CUSTOMS

I have never experienced any problems or delays at customs desks in Micronesia, but baggage searches are sometimes carried out. Palau is considered more of a stickler for customs searches than the other countries. Forget any importation/exportation of narcotics, firearms, ammunition, endangered species, live plants, war relics (especially war relics—you *will* spend time in jail), fresh fruits and vegetables and meats. Wine, liquor, and cigarettes are also monitored, although quantities for personal consumption are allowed.

Drugs

Drug use is absolutely forbidden everywhere in Micronesia. You won't see it going on, and you will be thoroughly searched if there is any suspicion that you are "holding." Do not make the foolish mistake of attempting to import any illicit substances. You do not want to experience the business end of the Micronesian legal system.

EMBASSIES

The United States, Japan, Australia, the Philippines, the People's Republic of China, and Korea have embassies in Micronesia. See regional listings for contacts.

WHAT TO BRING

Micronesia makes few demands on your wardrobe, so go ahead and pack light. Light slacks, shorts, some T-shirts and a least one nice button-down shirt, comfortable walking shoes, and sunscreen and a good hat to protect you from the glare of the tropical sun are the only essentials. Women should dress modestly in Micronesia, and skimpy bikinis and halters are definitely frowned upon. This is especially true on the more traditional outer islands. In the evening the temperature can drop a bit, but rarely will you want to don anything more than a sweater or a light windbreaker. Pack several bathing suits so you'll never have to don a wet one. A collapsible umbrella is not a bad idea, and make sure you have a good small flashlight. Batteries, film, dive equipment, spare parts and the like are expensive or unavailable here, so bring what you will need.

CLIMATE

The weather here is incredibly consistent, with both water and land temperatures hovering around 28° C (82°F). Rainfall is variable, as noted in the text, but the showers usually end quickly.

TIME ZONES

Guam +10 GMT, The Northern Marianas +10 GMT, Palau +9 GMT, Yap +10 GMT, Chuuk +10 GMT, Pohnpei +11 GMT, Kosrae +12 GMT, The Marshall Islands +12 GMT.

ELECTRICITY

Power is 110 VAC at 60 Hz almost everywhere in Micronesia. Some live-aboards offer 220 VAC, but it is advisable to bring a converter if you require other than 110 volt AC power. Current here is unreliable, and a surge suppresser is a good idea for electronic equipment such as laptops.

Heat and humidity can also wreak havoc with your equipment, particularly sudden changes, such as between air-conditioned interior environments and the hot, moist outdoors, which can cause condensation. When moving between environments, allow your computer ample time to adjust to the change before operating it (this is important for camera equipment as well.) Internet connections are available in many venues to check your e-mail.

Money

The U.S. dollar is the currency of choice throughout Micronesia, and the best one for a traveler to carry. Australian dollars and Japanese Yen are accepted in some areas, but not all. It is best to change other currencies into U.S. dollars upon arrival on Guam, at the Bank of Hawaii or Bank of Guam (they offer the best rates). Major credit cards are accepted, but again, not everywhere. Be aware of your credit balances and limits as many establishments do not have credit authorization machines and will therefore automatically honor your charges. Traveler's checks in U.S. dollars are usually accepted at larger establishments. ATM machines are scarce outside of Guam and Saipan.

Commodities such as batteries, film, electronics, and dive gear are very pricey in Micronesia. Food, beer, and soft drinks, on the other hand, are inexpensive. Hotels can be found in every price range (except in Guam), but none are give-aways, and often the mid-range accommodations are not really worth the price.

TAX AND TIPPING

Tipping is expected in restaurants in Guam and the Northern Marianas (10–15 percent), but in the rest of Micronesia, gratuities are not generally expected (it is starting a bit in Palau and Pohnpei). I usually leave modest gratuities in most restaurants and bars. Taxi drivers rarely seem to expect tips. The best bet is to regard tipping as a nice gesture when good service warrants an extra measure of consideration.

Palau has recently instituted a $15 per diver tax, good for a month of diving in their waters, and it is rumored that Palau also has instituted a $35 per week bed tax, but I haven't run across it. Tipping live-aboard staff is traditional, and operators suggest 5–10 percent of the package cost.

BARGAINING

Prices are sometimes negotiable on souvenir items, taxis, certain hotels, roadside vendors and (occasionally) diving but, usually, bargaining is not customary and can be considered rude. Since there is not an overwhelming choice nor supply of handicrafts, there is not much to negotiate. In Palau, you can knock a few dollars off the price of a story board, but the artists know someone else will soon come along and pay the original price, so good luck.

Some dive operators might negotiate the price of diving if you are planning to spend a week or so with their operation. I've experienced some flexibility here, but not much. Diving is relatively expensive in Micronesia and the operators do not seem inclined to bend much in this regard.

Some of the smaller hotels will give you a slight break (10–20 percent) if you ask for a corporate discount, but this is not common. Keep in mind that any flexibility in price will be directly proportionate to your attitude and behavior.

Communications

LANGUAGE

English is the lingua franca of the islands, and all but the oldest Micronesians are fluent in it. There are also a number of traditional languages spoken here, including Chamorro and Palauan (both Malay-based); Ulithian, Chuukese, Yapese, Pohnpeian, Kosraean, Nauruan, Gilbertese, Marshallese (all Micronesian); and Kapingamarangi (Polynesian). Japanese is spoken in some areas, and Micronesians can speak Filipino, Korean, Vietnamese, or Spanish.

TELEPHONE

International telephone service is extraordinarily expensive ($3–$4 per minute), no matter which system you use. Connections are often inaudible and difficult to achieve. Each island has a telecommunications office, often open 24 hours. Though still expensive, the rates can be a bit softer at these facilities, and the lines are better. They offer a variety of services, including faxing, telegram, telephone and messaging. There are local pay phones here and there that use phone cards, but I've never had much luck using them.

Telephone codes

Guam	671
Northern Marianas	670
Palau	680
Federated States of Micronesia	691
Marshall Islands	692

THE POST

Micronesia's international post is handled by the United States Postal Service, and U.S. rates apply. Delivery times can be disappointing (a postcard can take six weeks to arrive back home). Even DHL and Federal Express fall down here. I have had experience with all means of postal and courier service here, and cannot name a single one that hasn't let me down.

Health

Medical care is spotty in Micronesia, and it is best to be very careful here. On Guam and Saipan, you will find dependable, modern medical facilities. In Ebeye, the U.S. Army will not let you die (although you are not really on

their watch). The hospital in Chuuk, on the other hand, is where you go to die, and in Yap, you are virtually on your own. Palau has a brand new hospital, but I've not personally seen it yet. Decompression chambers are available on Guam and Palau; the U.S. Army base on Kwajalein has one, and though they're not allowed to advertise, they will not turn your bent body away (see page 210 under "Hyperbaric Medicine.")

On land, none of the species of fauna and very little of the flora is dangerous. Malaria is not a problem here (though dengue fever can be), and immunizations are not required, unless you have come from an area with cholera and yellow fever.

Your biggest enemy is the sun. Do not underestimate its power in the tropics: if you can throw a shadow, you can be severely burnt. Two years ago, I was careless enough to receive a critical dose of sun poisoning, which was one of the most long-lasting and painful things I have ever gone through (I'll spare you the rather disgusting details, but trust me, you don't want to get it!). Wear a T-shirt and use waterproof sun block with an SPF of at least 15, whether it's cloudy or not. Don't worry, you'll still come home with a tan.

Although mosquitoes are not a major irritation, in the summer, while fruit is ripening on the trees, black flies can drive you absolutely mad, so bring repellent.

The Marshalls have an enormous AIDS problem, but it is not limited to this island group. Micronesia is not know for wild sexual freedom, but even if you are not having sex this devastating disease can be acquired if you receive transfusions, vaccines,

acupuncture, or decide to get a tattoo. Again, be careful, be smart, and be cool.

DRINKING WATER

Tap water is not a problem in many of the urban areas, notably Guam and Koror, however, bottled water is always a safer bet. Ask locally. On certain islands, such as Chuuk and Yap, you must be extremely careful. Ebeye, which is the most Third World looking town in Micronesia, has very good tap water, thanks to a huge new desalination plant. Even here be careful, though, as that nice clean water may sit in an old dirty cistern or run through old pipes before it ends up in your glass.

Remember, if you're going to avoid tap water, that includes ice, unpeeled fruits, and raw vegetables. This is a precaution that is often overlooked, and has ruined many vacations. This warning applies to any fruit or vegetable *washed* in tap water—"if you can't peel it, don't eat it" is the standard rule of thumb.

EATING HABITS

Not enough is said about the dietary needs and proper nutrition of scuba divers while engaged in intensive and repetitive diving. Some live-aboards continue to serve heavy, greasy, difficult-to-digest meats, starches, and fried foods three times a day. Do yourself a favor: eat light, healthy foods, including salads, fruits, pastas, toast, fish, and, if you must, lean meats. Avoid anything that will cause you to develop gas or which wastes valuable energy in digesting.

Healthy food can be difficult to find in Micronesia, as the people here often subsist on fatty, high cholesterol items, but it will be worth the effort. Diving is not an aerobic sport, and you do not need to consume massive quantities of calories and carbs to get along. Just remember that cramps, exhaustion, gas and indigestion can be dangerous at the wrong time and inconvenient at best. Avoid alcoholic beverages, especially if you are scheduling four or five dives daily. Your chances of getting bent dramatically increase as your blood is thinned and your senses dulled from the effects of alcohol. I do not suggest you become a monk, just use your common sense. I love an ice-cold beer at the end of the day, but during the dive day, I abstain completely. Don't forget that most dive days begin at seven or eight in the morning (not very pleasant if you are hung over.)

Raw meats and fish must be treated with respect; unless you're absolutely comfortable with a restaurant's hygiene, save the sashimi dinner for when you get home. Mayonnaise is frequently used, and, with an average temperature of 28°C and unreliable refrigeration, it can spoil easily.

CIGUATERA

In some areas of Micronesia the fish can be ciguatoxic. Ciguatera is a toxin (not a bacterium) which derives ultimately from an algae, and concentrates most dramatically in predatory fish higher up on the food chain. It can be painful and even life-threatening. Barracuda, moray eels, various snappers, some groupers, and other similar species are often ciguatoxic, but other reef species can acquire the poison as well. Ciguatera is a localized phenomenon, and seems to be particularly associated with areas that have been disturbed, such as by dredging, which brings on a bloom of

the ciguatoxic algae. Open-water species (like tuna) are safe. It is probably best to avoid all reef fish if ciguatera warnings are in effect.

Transportation

Continental Micronesia ("Air Mike") services every island we cover here, as well as some we don't. It is my sincere feeling that this airline is in dire need of competition, as service can often be spotty, with connections frequently missed. However, the cost benefits of one airline servicing the region can be readily seen as you begin to add stops to your itinerary. Add-ons are far more inexpensive than initiating a new schedule with a different airline.

With the occasionally unreliable service, it's good to know that if you are inconvenienced, bumped or delayed by the airline, they will usually offer (or, at least, grant on demand) anything from a meal voucher to a free night or two in a hotel (my biggest score was a week in a decent hotel including meals).

CONTINENTAL MICRONESIA

I have tried every which way to save on Air Mike fares—juggling islands and direction and the order of stopovers, and have rarely gained at all for the trouble. It is advantageous, however, to repeatedly ask for the lowest fare, as I've found it to be somewhat flexible. If your ticket is complicated, including many stopovers, Continental will refer your call to their international rate desk, which is staffed by experienced and very helpful representatives. They tend to advocate in your favor when computing rates and itinerary, and will often offer sugges-

tions as to how to more easily and/or more inexpensively configure your flights. In general, look for off-peak fares, which are often reduced to about half price.

There are some special fares originating out of the United States which give you the flexibility of making several different and varied stops along the island route. Check on the "Circle Micronesia" package. Depending on where you want to go, these can be a better deal than adding all the legs individually, but they can also come out to the same price, with more restrictions. The "Circle Micronesia" package, leaving from San Francisco or Los Angeles, costs $1,300–$1,700 (depending on where you turn around from) including four stops. Extra stops are $50.

Since airfares are capricious, changing from season to season (sometimes week to week) and since restrictions vary from passenger to passenger, it is not practical to list a full schedule of fares for each possible itinerary. However, expect a round-trip ticket allowing you to visit the full complement of destinations covered in this book—Guam, Saipan, Yap, Palau, Chuuk, Pohnpei, Kosrae and Kwajalein—to cost approximately $2,000 departing from California, Hong Kong, Tokyo or Seoul (service is also available from Australia and New Zealand).

Most international visitors will enter the region at Guam. From there, some inter-island flights cost as little as $60, others are $500 or more. Schedules are complex, with each island served on different days depending whether you are heading east or west through the chains. It is a real challenge to arrange your itinerary to follow the different departure days during the week.

There are four flights a week Guam–Chuuk–Pohnpei; six flights Guam–Kosrae; seven flights Pohnpei–Guam and Chuuk–Guam; three flights Kosrae–Kwajalein–Pohnpei and there are many more permutations. It's a bit maddening. You will have to do some work putting together an itinerary here, and I recommend using a good agent rather than trying to do it yourself.

Inter-island fares do vary a great deal depending upon which days and times you fly. Somehow, the more questions you ask of the ticket agent, the cheaper your fare becomes, so don't be shy. Try to strategize your island-hopping in order to save yourself money and downtime. Guam-Yap-Palau, with a layover in Yap runs in the neighborhood of $350; Guam–Chuuk–Ponape, $600. Continental Micronesia also offers a four-island pass, starting and ending in Guam, for about $650. Some tips:

1. Watching to see that your checked baggage is correctly tagged—Continental Micronesia must have a huge warehouse full of lost luggage and they sure aren't saying where it is.

2. Continental Micronesia is notorious for over-booking flights. Always re-confirm your departure two to three days before you are scheduled to leave.

3. If you request a seat number when either originally booking your trip, or when reconfirming, you are almost virtually guaranteed not to be bumped (use this advice!)

Continental Micronesia Guam (✆ 671 647-6453), United States and Canada (✆ 800 231-0856), Japan (✆ 03 3592-1631), Hong Kong (✆ 852 525-7759), Taiwan (✆ 2 719-5947).

Other airlines

Japan Airlines and others serve Guam from many various points in Asia, and should be checked against Continental Micronesia when evaluating schedules and fares. Once in Guam, however, you will most likely be flying on an Air Mike itinerary.

Air Nauru also serves the islands, but it's not nearly as flexible or convenient as Continental; they also service Australia and New Zealand. Their rates are similar to Continental's, so you might as well stick with the full-service airline. Air Marshall Islands offers service within the Marshalls, as well as to points in the South Pacific.

Baggage

If you're cutting it close as you plan your dive vacation, you may want to consider packing your dive gear, or at least the vital components (regulator, computer) in a carry-on bag. In the event your baggage is lost or delayed, you won't miss your dive.

LOCAL TRANSPORTATION

Islands and the main towns and villages where you'll most likely be lodged are small enough so that you can stroll from store to hotel to restaurant. Bicycles are usually available either from the hotel or from a local rental company. (With the dicey roads and sparse medical care available here, wear a helmet.)

Taxis are by far the most convenient and reasonably-priced mode of transportation in Micronesia. A taxi will take you exactly where you want to go, the driver will offer a bit of advice on where you *can* go, and leave you with nothing to worry about. The fare to any-where in Ebeye, for example, is $1. In Pohnpei and Chuuk, it's not much more. The drivers are conservative and almost always obey speed limits and traffic signals (no doubt exactly like the taxis in *your* city).

The only place in Micronesia where a car rental makes sense is Guam, with its easy and convenient shore diving.

SEA TRANSPORTATION

Though packet ships and light freighters do occasionally offer field trips that carry passengers between the islands (for a few cents per kilometer traveled), it is really not practical for the dive traveler. If you desire information on this mode of travel, visit the commercial docks in Chuuk, Yap, Pohnpei or Kwajalein and inquire. Schedules are imprecise, and arrival times vague.

Certain islands, it should be noted, do have ferries servicing *outer* islands within the various atolls. Usually, there are many restrictions barring tourism on these traditional islands.

Accommodations

The hotel experience varies widely from island to island. Again, you need to decide what's right for you in selecting the appropriate accommodations. In Guam, all the major international chains have properties, though they seem to be have been designed primarily for the Japanese tourist trade (and the 1980s Japanese boom economy). Very expensive hotels are easy to find, but it requires some investigation to yield more affordable, and sometimes more charming, alternatives. Note: while there is often a surcharge, air conditioning has real value everywhere you venture in Micronesia.

International chain hotels on some of the islands average $150–$200 per night, and are often sold out. At more rustic hotels, especially on Yap, Pohnpei, Palau, Kosrae, and in the Marshalls, rooms can be had for well under $100 per night. There are no real bargains here, however. If you are on a real tight budget, you can spend in the neighborhood of $45 per night, but the rooms will often be dingy, water pressure non-existent, and security dicey.

Strange, and yet typical of the upside-down priorities here, of all the mechanical and electrical items in the whole of Micronesia, the only thing you can consistently depend on is the crystal-clear reception of the cable TV. I usually recommend the thatch bungalow accommodations when available for their charm, comfort and more reasonable cost. Insects are not an overwhelming problem, and the gentle trade winds crossing your bedroom will ease you into a most comfortable rest.

Food and Drink

As you would expect in a region as diverse as Micronesia, you can find both good, and not so good food as you travel from island to island. Coconut crab, lobster, tuna sashimi, fresh reef fish, local pork, fresh fruits, vegetables and interesting starches (taro, tapioca, breadfruit, etc.) are the best of the lot. The beef is almost always frozen and ought to be overlooked. Japanese, Chinese, Filipino, and Vietnamese food can be found almost anywhere, as can the American burger and fries.

Restaurants tend to be either very good or very bad, with little middle ground. Prices are the same either way, and usually very reasonable. Jimmy, the chef at Ebeye's otherwise untenable Anrohasa Hotel, prepares authentic Chinese cuisine using the freshest ingredients. At another restaurant, you might be offered Spam sushi by a waiter with a straight face.

Spam deserves special mention, as this potted meat product is nowhere more popular than in the Pacific Islands. The taste was acquired from American GIs, and to this day, Spam is what you are served when your Micronesian host wants to show you he or she really cares.

Diving

I cannot overemphasize how important it is to be responsible, alert and aware while diving in Micronesia. There is little here that can hurt you except your own negligence. You don't have to be bitten, stung or cut to get hurt—the currents here are very strong and agonizingly unpredictable. While dive operators are fighting to renounce their reputation as cavalier, it is not difficult to end up miles away in three-meter seas when you surface from your five-knot drift dive. Any kind of signal device—Dive-Alert, safety sausage, whistle, strobe—is a good investment here.

Micronesia is famous for its fantastic variety of mind-boggling, twisting, back-eddying currents, and can teach you a thing or two about the power of water. These currents are vital to the food chain, and bring the reef-bound fish and plants vital nutrients on which they feed while helping to churn oxygen back into the sea. Used wisely and treated with caution, these same currents can carry you along vast stretches of undersea real estate, giving you an effortless and exciting diving experience. And in the current is where the electrifying fish action takes place.

Most dive guides will test the currents before they give you the okay to enter the water, and often a dive briefing will be changed to accommodate the unpredictable current. Sometimes, you will encounter eddies and reversals of the current you were previously riding. If after a few seconds you feel the water is too strong to swim against, simply go with the flow. Exhaustion can lead to more trouble than a change of course. Remember that everyone in your group is usually subject to the same currents, so you will alter your course together. The chase boats are fast, and will pick you up wherever you surface. The boat operator will most likely be aware of your "revised" dive plan, moving along with you, anticipating the spot where you will surface.

There are decompression chambers located on Guam, Palau (try to avoid this one), Kwajalein (they don't advertise it, but the U.S. Army will not turn you away, should you need it). I strongly urge you to acquire DAN's reasonable diving insurance, which will cover the expensive helicopter ride to a distant facility and the medical care you will need in the unlikely event you are injured while on your dive vacation.

Divers Alert Network (DAN) Peter B. Bennett Center, 8

West Colony Place, Durham NC 27705 USA. Membership services: ☎(800) 446-2671. Web: www.dan.ycg.org This well-known U.S.-based non-profit has been providing medical advice in the case of diving injuries, researching diving medicine, and promoting diving safety for a long time. They are often the first organization called by local emergency personnel in the case of a diving accident.

The organization publishes the bimonthly *Alert Diver,* which is distributed to members. DAN offers yearly membership for US$29, and three different insurance packages for an additional US$25 to US$35 a year. We highly recommend DAN membership and insurance.

The organization maintains a medical information line for questions about diving health and problems (☎[919] 684-2948; 9am–5pm U.S. Eastern Time) and a 24-hour-a-day hotline for dive emergencies: ☎(919) 684-8111.

DIVE EQUIPMENT

It is always best to bring your own basic equipment—BC, regulator, gauges, computer, mask, snorkel and fins, dive light—and equipment that you are familiar with is best (Micronesia is not the place to try out new gear). If you forget something, or something malfunctions, you can get rental gear from the major operators (but you will pay a premium).

Though the water and air are both warm, most divers wear at least a Lycra skin or a 3 mm or eighth-inch wetsuit to serve as protection from coral. Some, myself included, simply wear swimsuits, though I must admit I have gotten cut when currents swept me up against a wall, or two. If you're on a live-aboard, making multiple dives a day, a wetsuit is recommended.

Dive computers are especially handy here, if not mandatory, as multi-level drift dives are frequent. A good repair kit will also be useful, since repair and equipment shops are in short supply. Bring lots of sunscreen.

DIVE INSTRUCTION

Some areas offer instruction, some do not; check the islands you intend to visit. Resort courses (or introductory courses) are usually available, but this is not really the place to learn to dive. A full glossary of dive operators and available services can be found in the regional sections that follow.

Photography

Photo opportunities are everywhere, so bring plenty of film. If you run out of film or batteries, you will pay dearly. Slide film is very, very hard to find, so bring an ample supply. Some of the larger towns and cities (especially on Guam and Saipan) will have everything you need, but it will be more expensive than what you're used to paying.

Given the heat, there is no point to buying professional emulsions. I always pack my film in my carry-ons which allows me a visual inspection instead of having to subject them to the constant barrage of old, leaky x-ray equipment in the many airports through which you'll pass.

Getting your film processed in Micronesia is not a good idea. I've had many rolls ruined by bad, old, or warm chemical baths. Unless you really need to see your results immediately, wait until you return home.

Especially beware of processing with live-aboard dive operations. I have had rolls of E-6 ruined in live-aboard processors, and seen all kinds of outrages, including outdated film (baked in the tropical sun) passed off as new.

If you shoot black and white you can all but forget about any kind of sales or service here. There is a Quick Photo in Guam at the newer mall that processes B/W, but I can't speak for the results.

Shopping

Handicrafts in Micronesia vary in quality and availability depending upon where you are, but some charming and unique items can be found. Coconut products, spices and other natural resources can and should be bought. The Marianas are filled with strip malls and department stores catering to Japanese tourists, and bargains are rare; other regions are virtually devoid of all but small food shops.

While many of the handicrafts sold in Micronesia are machine-made in the Philippines, certain islands do have trademark souvenirs that you may want to take home. In Palau, you will hunt for the perfect storyboard. From Yap, you will bring your sweetheart a *lava-lava.* Pohnpei offers flavorful black pepper and excellent coconut products (writer Gene Arthur notes of Pohnpei's coconut shampoo that the only thing in the world that produces more suds is Budweiser). Kosrae woodcarvers fashion sharks and other fish from local hardwoods, fitting real sharks' teeth into the mouths. In Chuuk you will find the charming love-stick.

Though the waters of Micronesia are filled with beautiful shells and coral, remember to leave them there for our children to see.

Guam

Guam is like a little piece of the United States in the middle of the Pacific. There are many services here, and a lively restaurant and bar scene. Here is a place to stay in a nice hotel, eat well, and do some convenient shore dives—from your own rented car, if you like.

My Way To dive Guam, I would build a few more days into my schedule, either on the way in or on the way out of Micronesia, book a hotel and rent a car. Then I would get a map, visit Micronesian Divers Association (MDA) and rent some tanks, and head off to take advantage of Guam's accessible reef system. There aren't many places in the world where you can experience such a wide range of underwater environments without boarding a boat.

If you are traveling alone, or just don't feel like exploring yourself, just book a few days with MDA and let them do all the work. Guam also has great beaches that are always fairly empty. It's a real fun scene, with lots of beachfront music, bars, night life and, of course, wonderful snorkeling and swimming.

General

GETTING THERE

Many international airlines stop in Guam. From here, Air Micronesia will supply you with the necessary connections to fulfill the balance of your itinerary. Continental Air Micronesia connects in Guam with flights to all the islands in Micronesia. The flights operate in a leapfrog pattern, stopping at particular islands on particular days of the week. A little pre-planning will serve you well.

Continental Air Micronesia ✆646-0220
Japan Air Lines ✆646-9195
Korean Airlines ✆649-9683

LOCAL TRANSPORTATION

From the airport to the main towns of Agana, Tamuning, Dededo and so on, taxis cost less than $15. Buses cover most of the downtown area and make good connections with the rest of the island, although waiting time can be onerous.

If you are availing yourself of the many hotel packages that include diving, you can get by without renting a car, but the only trouble is that you will be dependent upon taxis and hotel shuttles, and this is one island where a bit of freedom can go a long way.

Car Rental

I highly recommend renting a car during your stay on Guam. Many major chains operate here, and there are some local concerns, too. Prices begin at less than $40 per day, but average around $75.

TOURIST INFORMATION

Guam Visitors Bureau 1270 N. Marine Drive, Suite 202, Harmon, ✆646-5278. The visitors bureau offers some great maps and tourist guides at no charge. If you write them ahead of time, they'll send them to you in the mail.

SEASON

I've dived here all through the year, however, in the rainy season the surf can be a bit dangerous. In the summer, the water is calmer, the visibility is at its highest and the eastern coast settles down a bit, offering access to some unusual reef systems there.

MEDICAL SERVICES

Health and emergency services on Guam are much like those in the rest of the United States: well-run and expensive. The Coast Guard air and sea rescue division handles emergencies, and there is a chamber on the island. The water is fine on Guam, although if you have any doubt or are particularly sensitive, drink bottled water.

Emergencies

Air Sea Rescue (Coast Guard) ✆477-8742, ✆339-6100, ✆339-7100. The U.S. Coast Guard acts as a single emergency contact for all island water rescues. One call to them and they will contact all other parties required to affect a rescue.

SRF Guam Recompression Chamber ✆339-7143, ✆339-6246.

Guam Memorial Hospital in Tamuning ✆646-5801

Dive Operators

Guam's dive operators are all quite good. Prices are relatively moderate, with two-tank boat diving running $70–$100 a day, depending on location. Tank rentals are $4–$5.

Aquatic Tours P.O. Box 24849, Tamuning 96933. ℂ646-1696, Fax: 646-1620. Two boats; resort open water course; equipment sales; packages to Palau, Yap, and Chuuk.

Fish Eye Diving Guam 900 North Marine Drive, Piti 96925. ℂ475-7000, Fax: 477-2550. One boat; resort open water course; equipment sales; southern Guam specialist; Japanese language.

Gently Blue Holiday Plaza Hotel #2103, Tumon 96925. ℂ/Fax: 646-0838. E-mail: aki@ite.net Web: www.pluto.dti One boat; PADI instruction; equipment sales and rental.

Guam Tropical Dive Station P.O. Box 1649, Agana, Guam 96932. ℂ477-2774; Fax: 477-2775. E-mail: gtds@ite.net Web: www.gtds.com Three boats; PADI instruction; nitrox, mixed gas and oxygen available; equipment sales and rental, including cameras.

Micronesian Divers Association (MDA) 856 North Marine Drive, Piti, Guam, 96925. ℂ472-6321 and ℂ472-6322; Fax: 471-6329. E-mail: mda@mdaguam.com Web: www.mdaguam.com Contact: Pete Peterson The granddaddy of Guam diving, Pete Peterson runs a no-nonsense store in Piti, where you can buy or rent just about anything you need. Soon to celebrate 25 years in business. Pete's passion is the monthly one-hour television show he produces with Tim Rock and John Ryan. Nominated for a prestigious Cable Ace Award, the show features dive excursions in Micronesia, marine life, and diving safety in a video magazine format. Two boats; PADI instruction; nitrox and oxygen available; equipment sales, repair, and rental.

Papalagi Dive Shop 901-C Pale San Vitores Rd., Tumon 96911. ℂ649-3483, Fax: 649-3498. PADI, Japanese client specialists.

Professional Sports Divers P.O. Box 8630, Agat, 96928. ℂ565-3488, Fax: 565-3633. E-mail: psdivers@kuentos. guam.net Web: www.psdguam.com Two boats; PADI, NAUI, and IANTD instruction; nitrox, mixed gas and oxygen available; equipment sales and rental.

Rainbow Dolphin & Diving P.O. Box 10417, Tamuning, 96925. ℂ/Fax: 646-6743. E-mail: rainbow@kuentos. guam.net

Two boats; PADI and NAUI instruction; nitrox and oxygen available; equipment rental.

Real World Diving P.O. Box 2800, Agana, Guam 96932. ℂ646-8903, Fax: 646-4957. E-mail: rwdolphin@ite.net Web: www.rwdiving.com Four boats; PADI, SSI instruction; nitrox, mixed gas and oxygen available; equip-ment sales and rental; boat charter.

Scuba Company 221 Farenholt Ave., #101, Tamuning 96933. ℂ649-3369, Fax: 649-3379. E-mail: scubaco@ite.net Two large boats; PADI instruction; equipment sales and rental; Japanese language.

Accommodations

All the major hotel chains have properties on Guam, though they seem to be designed primarily for the Asian tourist trade and well-heeled travelers. Further investigation will yield more affordable alternatives. Though in the smaller hotels there is often a small surcharge, air conditioning has value everywhere you venture in Micronesia, and will often be an option upon check-in.

EXPENSIVE

Rooms at these hotels run $150/night and up. All can order tour and dive trips, and all the dive operators offer hotel pick-up. The restaurants are generally very good.

Hyatt Regency Guam Tamuning, ℂ 647-1234. Al Dente Italian stone hearth pizza, great breakfast. Meridian Room offers buffet at all three meals.

Guam Hilton ℂ 646-1835. 700 rooms, 7 restaurants, including Roy's pan-pacific cuisine (great!). Tennis, fitness center and beach club.

Guam Dai'Ichi Tumon, ℂ 646-5880. Japanese teppanyaki restaurant, Creole Coffee Shop.

Hotel Nikko Guam Tamuning, ℂ 649-8815. The Magellan Room buffet is excellent.

Pacific Islands Club Tumon, ℂ 646-9171. Lunch, dinner and Sunday brunch (expensive); live music; happy hour.

Hotel Okura Tumon, ℂ 646-6810. Flamboyant Room. Pacific European cuisine, lunch $20, dinner $30.

Onward Agana Beach Tamuning, ℂ 647-777. Built on the very beach where the Japanese invaded Guam.

Palace Hotel Tamuning, ℂ 646-2222. Chinese and Japanese restaurants. A beautiful and expensive hotel.

Pacific Star Tumon Bay, ℂ 646-9335. 435 rooms, Japanese and Chinese restaurants, sports center, more.

Guam Reef Tumon, ℂ 649-0128.

MODERATE

There are no real cheap hotels on Guam, but there are a handful of mid-level places with rooms going for $75 a night or so.

Hafa Dai Agana, ℂ 646-6542 25 rooms, on the highway near the airport.

Golden Motel Tamuning, ℂ 649-5662. 18 rooms. Simple, cheap.

Marina Hotel Agana ℂ 477-7836. A nice hotel which offers 2 restaurants, and overlooks the marina. It's a bit out of the way (in Agana) for night life.

Dining

Though you can cop out in a Denny's, McDonald's (Guam had six at last count), Kentucky Fried Chicken (four) or a Pizza Hut (ten), or any of another dozen or so U.S.-based fast food franchises, but I recommend you take advantage of the geographical position of this cultural crossroad.

There are top-notch restaurants here, offering the best in Pacific Rim dining: Vietnamese, Thai, Chamorro, Japanese, Chinese, Filipino, and Korean.

One of my personal favorites is ZoZo, a Vietnamese kitchen serving traffic-stopping imperial rolls—thin, lightly fried spring rolls which you wrap in lettuce before dipping in chili and fish sauce and asking for another. If you're thinking about grocery shopping, keep in mind that groceries are pricey in Guam. Fresh produce is insanely expensive and the quality poor—a shriveled head of lettuce cost $4.50 during my first and last foray into the supermarket!

All the hotels have restaurants, some serving excellent fare (see this page). Most offer lunchtime buffets, typically an $18–$20, all-you-can-eat type of thing. The Okura Hotel has a great little happy hour. Load up on freebies on Fridays, 5 pm–7 pm.

ZoZo (Upper Tumon, ℂ 649-1422). Vietnamese fare at great prices.

Ivory Restaurant Pan-American, French, Creole, New England, and Pacific cuisine offered here. Lunch $6–$8, dinner to $14. This place is always packed. Get there at 11:30 pm and still wait for a table. Sharp black and white decor. Watch the chefs at work.

United Seaman's Service Club (in the old USO headquarters). This fun spot is set into a park overlooking a marina. Sit outdoors under an awning and enjoy cheap eats. Hamburger $3.25, entrees $6–$9. Average standard burger fare.

Shirley's Coffee Shops Agana, Harmon, ℂ 472-2695. This is an old stand-by. Shirley's serves hearty breakfasts and lunches, and although most of the food is only fair, a New York steak for $7.75 can't be wrong. Unusual meals in a Chamorro-Chinese vein, including a world-famous fried rice. This a clean, reliable local hangout. Don't miss the finadene sauce made with soy sauce, onions and boonie peppers. It goes on everything except ice cream.

Top O' de Mar Once an officer's club, today it's open to everyone and never crowded. $6.95 lunch buffet, American cafeteria food.

Chuck's Steakhouse Upper Tumon, ℂ 646-1001. Not so hot, but if you want an inexpensive steak, what are you gonna do? The bar is not bad at all, and extravagantly air conditioned.

Jan Z's Agat Marina. A breakfast platter that feeds two, lunches and dinner from $8-$10.

Night Life

Guam, unlike most of the Western Pacific, actually has a night life. While there is certainly the seedy side often attracted by a large military presence, there is a good selection of every kind of activity to which most urbanites are accustomed, including bars, bowling alleys, movies, theaters, and major concert events—international stars traveling between Japan, Australia and the United States often use Guam as a working rest stop.

BARS

Most of the night life is focused on Tumon Bay. Bars close between 2 am and 3 am. **Onyx** and the **New Yorker** at the Sandcastle, Tumon, ✆ 649-7263. A splashy Las Vegas style dinner show twice nightly except Wednesdays. Dressy, aimed mainly at tourists. Onyx is a disco, the New Yorker is a private club on a balcony over the Onyx dance floor, where you'll find a crowd of locals.

Castaways is a rockin' little joint with drink specials and a Texas BBQ on Sundays from 4-9.

TJ's, at the Hyatt Regency, features Irish-Mexican food, loud music, and flashy lights.

Tree Bar at Guam Hilton is a fun outdoor bar with live entertainment.

Wet Willie's in Tumon ✆ 649-OWET/2WET. This beach club draws a strong local crowd—bikers, Chamorros, tourists and divemasters, all of whom feel qualified to give you expert advice on local conditions both above and beneath the surf. Sunset is the time to come here. In the center of the bar, stocked with a collection of local reef fish, is a thriving marine aquarium designed by local divemaster and colorful expat, Will McHugh. Willie's offers an unusually good selection of beers (in Micronesia, Bud is King) and puissant "island drinks," but watch the very-greasy food. The atmosphere can be a bit rowdy.

Tahiti-Rama in Tumon (✆ 646-1056) is similar to Wet Willie's, but dingier. Live music. Drink specials.

Suzie's on Serena Ave., offers alternative music, a mostly gay crowd, and the best jukebox on the island.

The People

The original Chamorran people were largely decimated by exploring Westerners and evangelical missionaries. Today, a mixture of Filipino, Micronesian and Spanish blood, they are anxious to regain their cultural heritage and reassert their traditional rights. Almost everyone is Catholic.

LANGUAGE

English is spoken by everyone; Spanish, Japanese, and Tagalog are heard as well. And, while many English and Spanish words have entered the native tongue of Chamorro, it is an entity all its own.

Chamorro Phrases

Hafa dai! Hello, how are you?
Si yus masi Thank you
Buenos dias Good day
Adios Good-bye
Que hora? What time is it?

HOLIDAYS

In addition to celebrating most American holidays, March 6 marks a fiesta at Umatac Village commemorating Magellan's landing (a little like the North American Indians celebrating the arrival of the Columbus). On December 8 there is a huge parade honoring the Virgin Mary. Each village also celebrates its own patron saints' day with a parade and feast. If you are invited, go; you'll have a great time though you might have to adjust your weight belt afterwards. July is filled with festivals, fireworks and special events celebrating Guam's liberation by the Americans in 1944.

Shopping

Guam offers every conceivable form of retail trade. The Japanese are attracted by the bargains to be found here when the yen is converted to the dollar. In the heavily populated centers of Tamuning and Tumon, strip malls, designer stores and duty-free outlets are scattered between vacant, leaning hotels and office buildings crippled by the recent earthquake. If you sift through the usual tourist junk, you can even find some interesting souvenirs.

PHOTOGRAPHIC

There is a small photo shop in the new mall that offers B/W processing, though I've never tried it and can't vouch for the results. Film prices are high almost everywhere except Kmart and Ben Franklin. The most professional shop is Tropical Color.

Tropical Color Across from ITC building. One-hour processing, good quality. The Navy and the local newspapers send work here. E-6 processing only two days a week.

The Northern Marianas

The vast majority of the visitors to this area are Japanese, and the Northern Marianas are relatively unknown to American and European travelers. There are plenty of services on Saipan, and Tinian and Rota are quiet and relaxed. Everywhere here the scenery is beautiful, and the water impossibly blue.

My Way In Saipan, what I would do is take a cab straight from the airport to the Remington Hotel, check in, then call Ben Concepcion at Ben and Ki's Watersports to set up your diving schedule. Then I'd hit Little Tokyo and have a plate of sashimi and an ice-cold beer. Make sure you tell Ben you want some special diving off Tinian, combined with a long surface interval to have a look around. Also make sure the sites in Marpi, northern Saipan, are on the schedule. On Rota, I'd simply call the Michaels at Dive Rota and have them set me up with everything I need.

General

GETTING THERE

Continental Micronesia offers frequent flights to Saipan from Guam. The plane pretty much takes off and lands in the same breath for this short flight. Japan Airlines and Northwest also serve Saipan.
Continental Micronesia ©234-6491
Japan Air Lines ©234-6553
Northwest ©234-2011
Several smaller airlines serve Tinian's airstrip and Rota from Saipan.
Freedom Air P.O. Box 239 CK, Saipan 96950. ©234-8328, Fax: 649-0729. Serves Rota, Guam, Tinian and Saipan.

Ryan International Airlines ©288-7831. Serves Tinian and Rota.
Patriot ©288-4471. Serves Tinian and Rota.
Pacific Island Aviation ©532-3893. Serves Tinian and Rota.

LOCAL TRANSPORTATION

If you have no intention of leaving your hotel and beach site except to dive with an operator (you could do far worse), you only need a pair of shoes. Day trips (more than adequate to see the sites) are available from many hotels and Continental also offers a tour of their own.

Buses operate along Beach Road from the airport to Garapan and are fairly regular. Though there are designated stops, drivers will usually pick you up if they see you waving. You'll pay a reduced price if you buy your tickets ahead of time instead of on the bus. For schedules, call the main office (©234-2789).
Taxis are plentiful and reasonable, but ascertain the price *before* you begin the ride. The taxi fares are regulated, and each driver must carry a fare card. Typically, fares start at around $3.

On Rota, everything in Songsong is within walking distance.

Car Rental

If you want to have a good look around Saipan, it would

be best to rent a car for a day or two. Traffic moves on the right, U.S. style. The speed limit is 35 mph and the center lanes are for turning. Note that the coral roads are very slippery when wet. There are a number of excellent shore access dives all over the island, which you could dive from a car, but if this is your aim please make sure you know what you're doing—it would be much better to find a guide to show you around.

Mopeds and bicycles are available, but overpriced and not worth the trouble.
Hertz At the airport, ©234-8336. Free mileage, hotel pick-up.
National Car Rental Airport, ©234-8338.
Dollar Rent-a-Car Airport, ©288-5151.

TOURIST INFORMATION

Marianas Visitor's Bureau P.O. Box 861, Saipan, MP 96950, ©234-8325. At the airport. Very helpful. Open Mon.–Sat.

CONSULATES

Japan has a consular office in Garapan (Horiguchi Bldg, ©234-7201) and the Philippines has one at the CTC Building, Susupe (©234-1848).

BANKING

ATM machines are available everywhere. The Bank of Guam (©234-6467), Bank of

Hawaii (②234-6102), and the Bank of Saipan (②234-7694) have offices here. The Bank of Hawaii is on the Plus and Cirrus systems.

MEDICAL SERVICES

Pacific Medical Center Garapan, ②233-8100

COMMUNICATIONS

International telephone calls are expensive here, as elsewhere in Micronesia. There are several communications offices; if you have trouble making connections, go to the offices of MTC, Key Communications, or Marianas Communications. There are main post offices in Saipan in Capital Hill, Garapan, and Chalan Kanoa.

Saipan and Tinian

DIVE OPERATORS

Two-tank dives generally range from $75 to $95, depending upon the operator and season. When the weather dictates diving on the eastern side of Saipan, expect to pay more and experience considerably longer trips to the site. Diving off Tinian will also cost more (about $120) as it is a bit of a haul to get there in most of the smaller boats (don't miss it, however). Most of Saipan's more than twenty operators are up for Japanese language–speaking clients, but there are a few catering to U.S. and other English-speaking divers.
Abracadabra Aquaventures P.O. Box 503851, Saipan, MP 96950. ②233-7234 and ②235-7054, Fax: 235-7055 and 233-7235.
E-mail: ejcomfort@saipan.com
Web: www.abracadabra.saipan.com
A large PADI 5-star opera-

tion. Full range of services, including mixed gas diving. American owned.
All American Divers San Antonio, in the Pacific Islands Club. ②235-7056. A full-service PADI operation offering courses, boat and beach diving, rental, sales and service. A good way to go if you are staying in the area, though they will be happy to pick you up at your hotel.

AT A GLANCE

Northern Mariana Islands
Commonwealth of the Northern Mariana Islands (CNMI)

STATUS U.S. Commonwealth since 1986
CAPITAL Saipan Island, pop. 62,000 (1999 est.)
INTERNATIONAL AIRPORT Saipan Island (SPN)
LAND AREA 14 islands comprising 184.2 sq. mi. (477 sq. km.)
LARGEST ISLANDS Saipan (47.45 sq. mi.), Tinian (39.30 sq. mi.), Rota (32.90 sq. mi.)
POPULATION 69,398 (1999 est.)
PER CAPITA GNP $8,300 (1994 est.)
CURRENCY U.S. dollar
COUNTRY CODE 670
LANGUAGES English (official), Chamorro, Carolinian, and others.
AVERAGE TEMPERATURE 78.5°F (25.8°C)
YEARLY RAINFALL 85.90 in. (2,182 mm)
NAME From "Las Marianas," coined by the Spanish priest Luis Diego Sanvitores in 1668 in honor of the Spanish queen Maria Ana of Austria (and to replace Ferdinand Magellan's unflattering Isla de los Ladrones—"Islands of Thieves"—from 1521).

Ben & Ki Watersports P.O. Box 31 CHRB, Garapan, Saipan, MP 96950. ②234-6664, Fax: 235-5068.
Contact: Ben Concepcion
Ben and Ki run a top-notch operation, the oldest locally owned shop on the island. They are a conscientious team that truly cares whether or not you have a good time (and no, I don't have stock in their business; it's just a fact). Offering a full array of activities:

diving, including YMCA-CMAS course work, waterskiing, tours (land and sea), trips to Mañagaha, fishing, banana-boat rides, wind surfing, Hobie Cat rentals, and parasailing. Their prices are reasonable and the service complete. With a veritable fleet of boats, any size group is easily accommodated. Several languages (including Japanese) are spoken.

Offshore Marine Sports P.O. Box 167, Saipan, MP 96950 ②233-2628, Fax: 233-0277. Captain Fred Reiman offers activities such as deep-sea fishing and scuba diving as well as other water sports to singles and groups.

ACCOMMODATIONS

There are no hotels to speak of on the eastern shore of Saipan; most are along the west. Always ask for the "local rate," which usually works out to about a 10 percent discount and is freely given to those visitors who live (or *say* they live) on Guam. A hotel tax of 10 percent is added to your bill, and most operators require deposits.

Expensive

The hotels listed below are all world-class. Rooms are in the price range of $160 and up per night. Especially beautiful and convenient to both diving and the heart of Little Tokyo are the Dai-Ichi, Hafadai and the Hyatt. Near the airport, the Diamond and the Grand are gorgeous. The Nikko is also huge and first class, though you might want to rent a car if you stay here.

Aqua Beach Resort Hotel P.O. Box 9, Tanapag, Saipan 96950, ©322-1234.
Chalan Kanoa Beach Club P.O. Box 356, Chalan Kanoa, Saipan 96950, ©234-7829.
Dai-Ichi Hotel Box 1029, Saipan, 96950, ©234-6411. 425 rooms, 2 swimming pools, 2 tennis courts, about a thousand restaurants.
Hafadai Beach Hotel P.O. Box 338, Garapan, Saipan, 96950 ©234-6495.
Hotel Nikko P.O. Box 152, San Roque, Saipan 96950, ©322-3311.
Hyatt Regency Hotel Garapan, 234-1234.
Mariana Resort Hotel Marpi, 322-0777.
Pacific Islands Club San Antonio, 234-7976
Saipan Diamond Hotel P.O. Box 66, Susupe, Saipan 96950, ©234-5900.
Saipan Grand Hotel Susupe, 234-6601.

Moderate

The moderate hotels in Saipan do not seem to offer much more than the lower-priced accommodations, yet cost between $75 and $100 per night. For a few dollars more, you can enjoy real luxury.

Chamorro House Hotel P.O. Box 975, Saipan 96950 ©234-8900.
Marine Sports Hotel P.O. Box 158, Saipan 96950, ©234-1462.
Pacific Gardenia P.O. Box 144, Chalan Kanoa, 96950, ©234-3455.
Summer Holiday Hotel P.O. Box 908, Saipan 96950 ©234-3182.

Inexpensive

Remington Hotel P.O. Box 1719 Garapan, Saipan, MP 96950. ©234-5449, Fax: 234-5619. Though the bar and restaurant downstairs is fun and a bit unusual, this funky hotel is for the budgeteer who doesn't plan on spending much time in his or her rather damp and well-used room. The employees are very pleasant and cordial, but the rooms are musty, even smelly. The bed is firm, there is a phone, radio, mini bar and refrigerator in each room, and the water pressure is serious (this shower is better than the one in my own home). At $49 a night, and steps from the beach, it's a bargain. With a little effort, this could be a great place to stay, but not a dollar is being put back into the business, and its threads are bare. The hotel is located on the main strip in Garapan, and it seems to be the best of the budget rooms.

There are a number of inexpensive motels between the beach and the main strip in Garapan. Don't expect much and you'll be satisfied, though most have television, telephone and honor bars. The accommodations can be small, musty and a little on the funky side. Rooms start at around $50.

Holiday In Saipan P.O. Box 5308, Garapan, ©234-3554.
Islander P.O. Box 1249CK, Garapan 96950, ©234-6071.
The Joy Hotel Garapan, ©234-8713.
Micro Beach Hotel P.O. Box 1328, Garapan, Saipan 96950, ©233-1368. Has a nifty shooting club.
Sugar King Apartment Hotel P.O. Box 1939, Saipan, MP 96950, ©234-6164.

Accommodations on Tinian

All are moderately priced, under $70 a night, except for the monster listed at the end.
Lorilynn Hotel P.O. Box 50. ©433-3256, Fax: 433-0429. 15 rooms; cash and traveler's checks; government, military, group and corporate rates. Free airport transfer. Laundry service, refrigerator in room, long distance phone booth.
Main Street Hotel P.O. Box 92. ©433-9212. 5 rooms; cash and traveler's checks; government, military, group, and corporate rates.
Meitetsu Fleming Hotel P.O. Box 68; ©433-3232 Fax: 433-3022. 13 rooms; cash and traveler's checks; government, military, group and corporate rates. Free airport transfer. Restaurant, bar, tour desk, laundry, refrigerator in room, market on site.
Tinian Dynasty Hotel and Casino One Broadway, P.O. Box 1133, Tinian, MP 96950. ©328-2233. This is a half-million square foot five-star hotel and even bigger casino that, as of press time, was under construction near Taga Beach. The Hong Kong–based developer, with an investment of $200 million, planned 100 Las Vegas style gaming tables, 500 slot machines, 412 luxury rooms, 22 suites, 7 restaurants and bars, a health club, sauna, night club, swimming pool, golf diving range, an 18-hole natural grass putting green,

tennis court, children's playground and a water slide. A planned staff of 1,400 and two ferries to run clients to and from Saipan are part of the package.

DINING

Predominantly Japanese and other Asian cuisines are to be found here, but you can also get American fast food and even Chamorran delicacies. Fish reigns supreme at the better places, and is the center of such wonderful dishes as *cadin gohan* and *escabeche*. Typical Micronesian dishes such as chicken *kelaguen*, coconut crab, lumpia and various rice plates are commonly served. Always order a side of finadene, a soy sauce with onions and hot pepper; it goes on everything and it's delicious.

Most of the Asian restaurants are good—they have to be, since they cater almost exclusively to an Asian crowd. Some of the smaller coffee shops serve excellent and quite reasonably priced food. Several restaurants serve an enormous buffet, all-you-can-eat, or multi-course lunch for around $5; ask around. The big hotels, of course, all have first class restaurants.

Saipan

Boga Boga Saipan Beer Factory Across the street from the Hotel Nikko, ©322-9191. Fun, modern and moderately priced, and it does feature its own micro brewery.
Chamorro House Restaurant Garapan, ©234-7361. This one is a bit overpriced, with good, not great, food. Unusual local dishes such as fruitbat are available. The octopus is excellent. Expensive mixed drinks.
The Ship Ashore Restaurant On the Beach Road, adjacent to the town dock, Garapan.

The name is not metaphorical. Though a typhoon convinced the vessel to lean a little to port, it's still fun. **Shirley's** ©235-4115. Killer fried rice, serious finadene. Inexpensive, dependable, hearty food.
Winchell's Garapan. This is a great doughnut shop, and they even have Chinese bao.

Tinian

Fleming Restaurant In the Meitetsu Fleming Hotel, ©433-3232. American and Japanese dishes.
JC Cafe In San Jose Village, ©433-3413. American, Filipino, Chinese, Japanese, and Chamorro dishes. Beer, wine, and spirits.
Lorilynn Restaurant In the Lorilynn Hotel, ©433-3256. Serving American, Japanese, Chinese, and Chamorro dishes. Beer, wine, and spirits.
Rosie's Gazebo ©433-3201. American, Filipino, Chinese, Japanese and Chamorro dishes. Beer, wine, and spirits.

BARS

You have officially entered Karaoke Land. Everywhere you'll find the tacky, near-miss style of Japanese entertainment. Some hotels and community houses offer native dance and Polynesian stage shows, ask. There are some neat expat bars here and there, many of which feature pool tables, western beers and cocktails. Look around.
The Gig Nite Club In a structure that would make Las Vegas blush, a Pyramid and two giant Sphinxes greet the disco man and woman into this mirrored ball palace. Don't bother looking for me here. I'll be across the way at Mom's.
Mom's Round Two, just around the corner from Ben's dive shop, is a good ol' expat bar. Brawny A/C and ice-cold

beer offer respite from the scalding Saipan sun. Locals always point the way to the best bars and this is no exception.
The bar in the **Remington Hotel** is fun. Low key, with a pool table, great juke box and lots of bar food. Real cocktails with lots of ice! A local hangout, but tourists are very welcome.

SHOPPING

Anything you need is available on Saipan. Just remember the Duty Free Shop is not a *real* duty-free shop, though this retailer has certainly done well capitalizing on semantics. The La Fiesta shopping center near the Nikko Hotel in San Roque is filled with stores and restaurants; all the hotels have upscale stores in their complexes. There are endless souvenir shops, though none really sell what one would consider "handicrafts."

LAND TOURING

The U.S. Marine's invasion beaches southwest of Saipan (and on the western shore of Tinian) are still littered with rusted artillery and abandoned equipment. Tanks and planes are scattered in the lagoon, often used by jetskiing tourists as slalom gates.
The oxidized remnants of the fierce fighting that took place on Saipan is central to the strange beauty that exists here. Sheer rock faces rise hundreds of meters from impenetrable jungle and lush rainforest; desolate white strands of beach give way to ice-blue lagoons; volcanic peaks draw a hard line against rich blue sky—this is Saipan, and you will never forget it.
Take a nice walk through Micro Park along paths landscaped with rusted artillery, past Charley Dock, where yachts are lined up in their

slips. From here you can catch a boat to Mañagaha Island with CJ Nelson and the *Santa Maria*, but there are less touristy ways to get there with the operators who work from the small huts on the beach between the Dai-Ichi and Hyatt Regency Hotels.

Climb Suicide Cliffs for a solemn visit to the scene of one of history's most tragic events. A few miles down the road is Banzai Cliff, where a similar scene was replayed, although the players were Japanese soldiers. Despite announcements and pleadings from the American forces anchored offshore, they jumped 60 meters onto the rocks and surf below.

Take a tour to the northern tip of the island. From the lookout in Marpi, you will have the ultimate postcard shot of Bird Island (called Moon Viewing Island by the Japanese), once covered with gulls, but still majestic in its stark solitude. From here you can see The Grotto across the bay. A narrow dirt road leads down to the wide and sandy beach, where you can picnic, swim, fish or lie in the sun (not for too long though).

The Last Command Post at Banadero offers an unusually close look at World War II. Cut into the rock bluff is a fort that proved quite impenetrable until an American rocket fired from a battleship cut through the cement wall and obliterated the interior.

Rota

DIVE OPERATORS

Dive Rota P.O. Box 941, Rota, MP, 96951, USA. ©532-3377, Fax: 532-3022. E-mail: mark@diverota.com Web: www.diverota.com Contact: Mark Michael

Rota's oldest dive operator. A full-service shop offering boat dives, air, rentals, instruction.
Sirena Marine Service Rota P.O. Box 1340. ©532-0304, Fax: 532-0305. Dive trips and gear rentals.
S2 Club Rota P.O. Box 1469. ©532-3483, Fax: 532-3489. Dive trips and gear rentals.

ACCOMMODATIONS

Expensive

Rota Hotel P.O. Box 878; ©532-2000 Fax: 532-3000. 30 rooms; AMEX, VISA, MC, JCB. Call for group, government, military or corporate rates. Services: airport transfer, restaurant, bar, swimming pool, tour desk, gift/sundry shop, bicycle, golf club and marine and beach equipment rental, mini-bar, BBQ dinner, currency exchange service, room service.
Rota Pau Pau Hotel P.O. Box 855; ©834-5511 FAX: 834-5512. 20 rooms; AMEX, VISA, MS, JCB. Military, government, group rates. Services: $12 airport transfer, swimming pool, bar, restaurant, sunset BBQ dinner, tour desk, gift shop.
Rota Resort & Country Club P.O. Box 938; ©532-1155. Fax: 532-1156. Email: rota.resort@saipan.com 20 rooms; AMEX, VISA, MS, JCB. Military, government, group rates. Services: $12 airport transfer, swimming pool, bar, restaurant, sunset BBQ dinner, tour desk, gift shop.

Moderate

Coconut Village P.O. Box 855; ©834-5511, Fax: 834-5512. 20 rooms; AMEX, VISA, MS, JCB. Military, government, group rates. Services: $12 airport transfer, swimming pool, bar, restaurant, sunset BBQ dinner, tour

desk, as well as a gift shop.

Economy

Bay View Hotel P.O. Box 875; ©532-3414, Fax: 532-0393. 9 rooms; Cash, personal or traveler's checks. Government and group rates. Airport transfer, laundry service, restaurant, room service.
Blue Peninsula Inn Rota, MP 96951; ©532-0468, Fax: 532-0841. 14 rooms; traveler's checks, cash. Airport transfer, room service, laundry service, restaurant, bar.
Coral Garden Hotel P.O. Box 597; ©532-3201, Fax: 532-3204. 18 rooms; JCB, Diners MC, VISA, AMEX, Carte Blanche. Government, military group rates. Airport transfer, room service, laundry service.
Jotina Inn P.O. Box 887; ©532-0500, 532-0499, 532-0392, Fax: 532-0703. 10 rooms; JCB, VISA, MC, AMEX, Diners, Carte Blanche. Government rates. Airport transfer, room service tour desk, mini-mart, deli.

DINING

As Paris Restaurant (©532-3356) located in Songsong Village
Bay Breeze Snack Bar (©532-7575) across the street from Dive Rota
Chamorro Restaurant (©532-2233) in Songsong Village
Cool Spot (©532-3414) Songsong Village
Del Mar Restaurant (©532-2000) in the Rota Hotel
Figueroa's (©532-2337) Songsong Village
Hibiscus (©532-3448) in the Coconut Village Hotel
Pacifica (©532-1155) in the Rota Resort
Plumeria (©532-3561) in the Pau Pau Hotel
Tokyo-En (©532-1266) Songsong Village

Palau

This is the most famous of the Micronesian destinations. There are excellent, experienced operators here, and three fine live-aboards. Hard-core divers might find live-aboards the best deal, but do not leave Palau without experiencing at least some of its outstanding land-based beauty and charm.

My Way There are so many very satisfying ways to "do" Palau that it wouldn't be fair to name just one. I suppose if you pressed me, I would say you should simply come back more than once. I love the Palau Pacific Resort. A few nights alone on a deserted isle can be mind-altering. A week on a live-aboard is heaven. Of course there's always a funky downtown hotel where you can plant your feet on terra firma, your face in a plate of sashimi and your lips around the end of a nice cool Bud.

General

GETTING THERE

Continental Micronesia flies between Guam and Airai airport daily, stopping in Yap three times weekly. You can (and should) take this free stopover. Major airlines offer service to Guam from points in Asia, Australia and the United States. Palau imposes a $10 departure tax. Airai airport (ROR) is on Babelthuap Island, about eight miles from Koror.
Continental Air Micronesia Koror ✆488-2448.

TO PELELIU AND ANGAUR

For a day or weekend trip to Peleliu or Angaur, I recommend the *Nippon Maru* which you can catch at the Fisheries Coop Dock in Ko-

ror. The trip costs $3, takes only two hours and offers a rainbow of local color as well as a perfect vantage point from which to view the full chain of Rock Islands. For around $30, Palau Paradise Air also makes this short trip, but I prefer the boat. Palau Pa-

cific Airways also offers a sightseeing trip for small groups at around $300.
Palau Paradise Air P.O. Box 488, Koror. ✆/Fax: 488-2348. Flies Airai–Peleliu–Angaur (Ngaur) and back twice a day Mon., Tues., Thurs., Fri., and Sun., and once a day Sat.

No flights Wednesdays. Baggage limit is 20 pounds, $2/lb. for overweight. They take you to and from Airai for free from their Koror office.

LOCAL TRANSPORTATION

Taxis are plentiful in Koror. The ride from the airport to downtown costs approximately $15. From downtown to the Palau Pacific Resort costs $5. The speed limit is 25 mph. Gratuities seem to be included.

Car Rental

Renting a car is hardly neces-

AT A GLANCE

Republic of Palau

STATUS sovereign republic since 1994
CAPITAL Koror, pop. 12,299 (1999 est.)
INTERNATIONAL AIRPORT Airai (ROR) on Babelthuap
POPULATION 18,467 (1999 est.)
LAND AREA 343 islands covering 177 sq. mi. (458 sq. km.)
LARGEST ISLAND Babelthuap (153 sq. mi.)
PER CAPITA GNP $8,800 (1997 est.)
CURRENCY U.S. dollar
COUNTRY CODE 680
LANGUAGES Palauan (official), English
AVERAGE TEMPERATURE 80.9°F (27.2°C)
YEARLY RAINFALL 146.8 in. (3,728 mm)
NAME One sometimes sees "Belau" for Palau, which better represents the local pronounciation. "Palau" is the official spelling, however.

sary here, but if you want one they're certainly available. Prices are reasonable. Watch your speed on Palau, they take the posted limit very seriously. Slow is the word. **DW Rent a Car** At the DW Motel, ℃488-2641. **Toyota Rental Cars** P.O. Box 280, Koror, 96940. ℃488-1550. More expensive than DW.

SEASON

Winter is usually recommended as the best time to dive Palau, with December through April offering the best diving conditions. But the summer months can still be excellent. The dramatic blues, greys, and blacks of a summer sky bring out the poet in everyone. Mile-wide columns of steamy rain bridge sea and sky and rolling swells grace the sea. Rain falls for a few minutes each day, and can be a pleasant respite from the heat. One year, the rainy season forgets to show up, the next it floods.

The water can be slightly rougher in the summer and visibility can suffer, but the higher tides often allow access to areas that are often inaccessible in the winter. Temperature varies little from season to season, with air and water hovering around 28°C. Soothing trade winds temper the heat.

TOURIST ASSISTANCE

There is an annex of the Palau visitors authority at the airport. Stop there upon arrival and pick up some of their handy brochures listing hotels and restaurants. The main office is in Koror. **Palau Visitors Authority** P.O. Box 256, Koror, Republic of Palau, 96940. ℃488-2793, Fax: 488-1453.

EMBASSY

U.S. Embassy Topside, Koror. ℃488-2920.

MEDICAL

Be careful—very careful. The currents in Palau are completely unpredictable and unrelenting. If you do get in trouble, the good news is that there's a new recompression chamber in Koror. The bad news is I've heard they're not that good at operating it, yet.

There is a good hospital just outside of Koror on Arakabesan. Dr. Victor Yano operates a clinic there (℃488-2688).

COMMUNICATIONS

Telephone

Across from the large playing field is the telcom office. They offer you the facilities to complete international telephone calls, faxes and messaging. As of this writing, the minimum for overseas calls was a painful $3 per minute (and that is to FSM).

Up on the hill, near the hospital, is the PNCC Overseas Comm office, open 24 hours a day. From here you can call anywhere in the world, but bring your wallet—figure $12 for a three-minute call to the States.

Post Office

In the middle of town, just past the civic center. Open 8 am to 4 pm.

BANKING

The Bank of Hawaii (℃488-2602), Bank of Guam (℃488-2697), and Bank of Palau (℃488-2638) have offices in Koror. They are all open Monday through Friday with extended hours on Friday.

HOLIDAYS

Youth Day March 15
President's Day June 1
Nuclear-Free Constitution Day July 9
Christmas December 25
New Year's Day January 1
Thanksgiving late November

PHOTOGRAPHIC

Just across the street from West Plaza Desekel is an all-purpose photo lab. At Palau Pacific Resort, Photo Palau offers excellent service at a fair price. They'll also let you use their light board and give you productive tips on how to improve your U/W photos.

KD Photo Shop, run by photographer Kevin Davidson, offers a full line of photographic services. He's also good for advice.

Dive Operators

There are many dive operators in Koror, though Fish 'n Fins, Neco Marine, and Carp Tours seem to be the biggest and most popular. The Palau Pacific Resort also offers diving trips to all the same dive sites the other boats serve, though their gourmet lunches allow them to sharply inflate their fees.

In line with the rest of the region, a two-tank dive costs $80 to $95. While Sam's Tours tends to be the most reasonable, most operators offer three-day and/or weekly packages that bring the cost down. If you like to dive four or five times a day, a liveaboard actually offers the most bang for the buck. **Fish 'n Fins** P.O. Box 142, Koror, Palau 96940. ℃488-2637, Fax: 488-5417. E-mail: fishnfin@palaunet.com Web: www.fishnfins.com This is the oldest dive operation in Palau, founded by Francis Toribiong, who is responsible for the discovery of many of the shipwrecks in these waters. The shop is near the Palau Marina Hotel, and is today owned and operated by Navot and Tova, who also run the *Ocean Hunter*. They use stable and roomy 26 ft. power boats that carry 6–8 divers each. Ask for divemaster and diveguide Maurice Tudong. From time to time, Fish 'n Fins advertises a great bargain: for around $130/person, double occupancy, they offer two dives, room, tax, airport transfers, breakfast and lunch. Sounds good to me.

On May 1, 2000, an expedition organized by Fish 'n Fins and led by owner Navot Bornovski found the USS *Perry* at its resting place, 70 meters deep, 700 meters south of Ngaur. Navot and instructor Jeff Wonnenberg were the first to dive the newly found wreck. Some 56 years ago, on September 14, 1944 the *Perry* (a destroyer-minesweeper) hit a mine and sank.

Neco Marine Corporation P.O. Box 129, Koror, 96940. ✆488-1755, 488-2009, Fax: 488-3014.
E-mail:
necomarine@palaunet.com
A full service dive center, with a fleet of dive boats and a new photo center run by ace lensman, Ken Davidson.

Sam's Tours P.O. Box 7076, Koror, Palau 96940. ✆488-1062, Fax: 488-5003.
E-mail: samstour@palaunet.com
Web: www.samstours.com
While small, I believe Sam's Tours to be the friendliest, most helpful and most reasonably priced of all the dive operations in Koror. Located in Koror's busy harbor. Sam Scott's decision to stay smaller than some of his competitors serves the diver well. I was never in a group larger than four, and was occasionally the only diver on the boat. Sam picked me up and dropped me off at my hotel each day, and locked my equipment in a storage container to save me the trouble of lugging it back and forth. A limited amount of equipment is available for rental. The two-tank dive day costs $85, including lunch and frequent side trips.

Sam is a favorite among American and European divers. He prides himself in escorting divers to dive spots not frequented by some of the other operators.

Splash P.O. Box 847, Koror, 96940. ✆488-2600 ext. 485, Fax: 488-1741, 488-1606, 488-1601.
E-mail: splash@palaunet.com
Web: www.panpac.com
This is a 5-star PADI facility associated with the Palau Pacific Resort (see page 229). They are well-equipped with two large and fully-loaded dive boats. Splash caters almost exclusively to Pan Pacific guests.

Live-aboards

Live-aboard diving, the new mainstream in dive travel, is becoming extremely competitive. Charters are booked many months in advance and operators are adding more and more luxury in the quest for your dive travel dollars. In some parts of the world expectations are not always met—we've all heard reports of (and maybe even lived through) nightmarish experiences. Divers have been poisoned, bent, abandoned or just plain skunked by operators, chefs, or mother nature.

There is no danger of disappointment with the three live-aboards operating in Palau. All three adhere to the highest codes of safety and service. All three are competitively priced and all put you on the same dive sites at optimum times.

They do offer slightly different angles on the theories of diver comfort and activity. Whereas the *Sun Dancer* may not seriously encourage night diving, the *Aggressor* doesn't bring a hot mug of coffee to your cabin in the morning. While the *Ocean Hunter* may charm you with its nautical feel and intimate accommodations, the *Sun Dancer* will make you forget you're even on a boat.

All three boats visit the same sites, though occasionally, one operator will offer a special charter. The *Sun Dancer,* for example, may visit Kayangel, a largely unexplored reef system several hours to the north, or *Angaur,* the beautiful and interesting monkey-inhabited island to the south. The *Ocean Hunter* will accept special request charters anywhere in the archipelago for groups as small as four divers.

I will try to give you an objective overview of the distinguishing characteristics of each boat so that you can decide which experience might fit your personal idea of the perfect Palau dive vacation.

Of course you do not have to dive from a live-aboard. But the alternative, day diving with the land-based operators, can quickly become expensive for a diver interested in spending the maximum time underwater.

Consider a week-long stay on-island: at $95 for a two-tank diving day, plus hotel, transportation, long rides to the dive sites, and food (diving gives you credit for bento box lunches with Spam), you are looking at an expenditure of probably $2,000 for only fourteen dives.

For about the same amount of money, a live-aboard will

put you right on top of the sites, handle all your equipment, serve you extraordinary meals and snacks, wait on you hand and foot, and allow you a complete escape from all your cares. And you will be making at least 30 dives, not 14. There is clearly no comparison.

The only possible drawback from being on a boat for ten days is that you will miss the many interesting sights, restaurants, shops, and the wonderful vibe of Palau on land. The solution is simple: tack on an extra couple of days at the Palau Pacific Resort or the Carolines Beach Resort, so you can look around a bit while degassing before your long plane-ride home.

Legendary Palau is becoming quite crowded these days; I have seen as many as 14 boats moored or anchored to the reef at Blue Corner. The pressure put upon the ecosystem in Palau is visible everywhere. Broken coral, fewer—and more wary—fish, and garbage floating in the water.

These developments are disappointing, but make no mistake—the diving is still spectacular. Do visit soon, however. Who knows how much stress these waters will be able to stand? Maybe I'm setting off a false alarm, but I've seen it happen in the Red Sea, Jamaica, Cayman and elsewhere. While you still have a chance, dive Ngemelis Wall, Blue Corner, Blue Holes, The German Channel, Peleliu Corner, the Express, Big Drop-off. You'll never forget it.

Delivering five dives a day is not easy—many of the dives can be lackluster, and your day can become too rushed. But each crew functions like a well-oiled machine to make it all work. On a live-aboard

there is virtually no traveling time to the dive sites, no hotel hassles, no rental cars, no schlepping back and forth with heavy dive bags, no negotiation of every expense, no discussion of where to eat, no unwanted surprises; only easy-going surface intervals during which your every need and desire is catered to, balanced with exciting, unrivaled underwater experiences.

The *Ocean Hunter*, *Palau Aggressor II*, and *Sun Dancer II* are all world-class operations with conscientious and professional crews. I would be hard-pressed to recommend one over the others. The five-foot picture windows on the *Sun Dancer* made for spectacular views, but the *Aggressor*'s hot-tub was sublime, and the old-fashioned nautical feel of the *Ocean Hunter* is unique in today's dive world. The *Aggressor*'s hydraulically-launched jetboat was the coolest contraption I'd seen, but the *Sun Dancer*'s chase boat was much more comfortable, and the *Ocean Hunter*'s ability to forego skiffs entirely is ultimately convenient. The *Aggressor* has a relaxed, casual style; the luxury of the *Sun Dancer* is intoxicating; the *Ocean Hunter* offers the most dives for the dollar. Whichever you choose, you'll find yourself immersed in luxury, constantly exploring some of the best diving in the world.

OCEAN HUNTER

In 1986, Navot Bornovski and Tova Har-El Bornovski worked on Palau's first liveaboard, the proverbial *Sun Tamarin*. Tutored in the intricacies of these difficult waters by scuba pioneer Francis Toribiong himself, Navot now offers a serious dive operation for the serious diver.

Built by Spencer Yachts

and professionally managed by underwater legend Carl Roessler, the *Ocean Hunter* is one of a large fleet of sister ships operating worldwide. Sixty feet with a 16-foot beam, this sloop comfortably sails six divers and a crew of three to the less-traveled reefs in Palau, offering seven full days of diving with an average 5-6 dives daily, though you may dive even more.

This is a charming, family-owned business operated by people whose love of the sea pervades everything they do (their newborn son is even named Liam: Hebrew for "my ocean"). These days, Tova stays in Koror caring for their three beautiful children (all divers, of course) and rarely accompanies the charters. She is active in shore duty, happy to fulfill errands and last-minute business for guests who have their hands full diving on this boat.

Though the *Ocean Hunter* is a motor sailer, with twin 175-hp diesels pushing her along at a comfortable 7 knots, she is almost never under sail. Drawing just five feet of water, the ship is able to easily skirt the tricky reefs of Palau, allowing divers to forego a chase boat completely. Unlike the larger boats, 100 percent of the diving here is done from the mothership (although a skiff is always ready to go should the unpredictable currents cause you to finish your drift dive away from the pack). Access to the water is effortless, with the extra-wide teak dive platform and waist-high tank holders that automatically grab your tank/BC as you simply back into them. A warm shower awaits you right on the deck.

The entire bow is a shaded teak deck, serving as a lounge. Extra gear is stored underneath benches; wetsuits hang

Palau Live-aboards

	Ocean Hunter	Palau Aggressor II	Sun Dancer II
LENGTH	60' (18.3 m.)	106' (32.3 m.)	138' (42 m.)
BEAM	15' 6" (4.7 m.)	30' 6" (9.3 m.)	26' (7.9 m.)
DRAFT	5' 6" (1.7 m.)	4' 6" (1.4 m.)	8' (2.4 m.)
CRUISING SPEED	7 knots	18 knots	10 knots
DIVER CAPACITY	6	16	20
CABINS	3	8	10
CREWMEMBERS	3	8	10
LAUNCH DATE	1993	1995	1994
PHOTO SERVICES	on shore	onboard	onboard
RENTALS	on shore	onboard	onboard
ELECTRICITY	110/220 VAC	110 VAC	110 VAC
AIR CONDITIONING	all areas of ship	all areas of ship	all areas of ship
DIVES PER WEEK	35+	27	22
DIVE FORMAT	from ship	chase boat	chase boat
FOOD RATING	excellent	very good	excellent
EXTRAS	unlimited diving	hot tub	sit-down dinner
	no chase boat	open bar	open bar
PRICE PER WEEK	$2,795-$2,995	$2,395	$1,795-$2,195
NITROX 32% ADD-ON	$199	$100	N/C

here and there's another warm-water shower. If it's a tan you're after, the sun shines bright on the mid-deck between the mast and wheelhouse.

Wood accents every turn and corner of the interior, and portholes look out over the sea. Private baths, cozy beds and ample closet space round out the accommodations. 110VAC *and* 220VAC are provided. The salon is fully equipped with TV, VCR, CD, cassette and a full selection of diving guides, marine books, and trashy novels. Two 500 gallon-a-day desalinators ensure free-flowing water, both hot and cold with strong pressure. At 30 tons, the ship is a very steady sailer, and extremely quiet.

While this newly refitted yacht certainly takes care of creature comforts, she is no Queen Mary with a compressor—*diving* is the focus of this operation. Whereas many boats advertise "unlimited diving," the Ocean Hunter is truly an unlimited-dive vessel. I casually mentioned to Navot one afternoon that I had never seen a reef at 2 am, and ten hours later found myself yawning into my regulator, that is until I witnessed hundreds of hyperactive pelagics hunting for post-midnight snacks.

You can dive as often or as seldom as you like, but before lunch is served, you'll have had the opportunity to descend onto these lush reefs *three times*: notorious Blue Corner, a healthy breakfast and then, Blue Holes, and German Channel, for instance. After lunch, the first afternoon dive is briefed and executed. An hour and a half later, after absorbing all that Big Drop-off has to offer, a delicious, rehydrating fresh fruit shake is served along with "boatmade" cake. Now it's time for dive five; the guests have asked for Peleliu, so away we go.

"There are no limits on the *Ocean Hunter*," says Navot. "It's your boat; you're going to be on it, you make the most of it. With the exception of removing things from the reef, there are no 'no's.'"

At dusk, in the intimate salon, the evening meal is served, and the food is superb. Chef Solomon Viray offers the best of Mexican, Chinese, Japanese, continental and island cuisines, keeping away from heavy, greasy foods. Falafel, hummus and couscous reflect the owners' Mediterranean heritage. The soursop sorbet is a boat specialty, and heavenly. We enjoyed tortillas, smoked oysters, sashimi, tempura, ceviche and steamed fresh fish—tuna or wahoo—either caught from the *Ocean Hunter* or delivered daily by passing fishermen (it is their strict policy to not remove any fish from the reef). It's always amazed me how rarely fresh fish is served on a live-aboard. Other live-aboards always seem to serve *frozen* fish which is like bringing eggrolls to Chinatown. Diving is not an aerobic sport, so though you'll eat like a king, you may not feel the need to visit a health spa at the end of this charter. Beer, liquor, and canned soft drinks are available, at a nominal charge. Fresh fruit juices and delicious fruit shakes are free and served all day.

After dinner, you may dive again once, twice, three times or more as the evening draws its star-studded canopy over the Palauan sky. It was 11 pm when I savored one of the most amazing dives of my career. *Fifty* slipper lobsters marched across the floor of the cavern at Blue Holes. Through the natural shaft cut into the reef, the full moon, clearly visible at 50 feet, sailed across the eastern sky and cast its light upon thousands of silversides gracing the reef. This is night diving at its finest and it is etched into my memory. We overnighted near Peleliu's Camp Beck Dock and in the morning were treated to a fascinating land tour of the island and its historic battle sites. Our guide showed us large battle photos while we stood at the same scene fifty years later. This was a great sidetrip that was not offered elsewhere.

The *Ocean Hunter* offers 7- and 10-day charters. They spend more time on the eastern side of Palau than the other boats, and never dive the same site twice, unless the guests desire a return to a favorite reef. The *Ocean Hunter* does not offer any on-board PADI courses, photographic services or dive equipment rentals, but all can be arranged through one of several land operations working in conjunction with them.

Ocean Hunter P.O. Box 964, Koror, Palau 96940. ℃488-2637, Fax: 488-5418 and 488-1725. E-mail: Ocean.Hunter@palaunet.com Web: www.oceanhunter.com Package rates for 2001: 7 days, $2,795–$2,995; 10 days, $3,993–$4,278. For unlimited Nitrox 32% add $200.

PALAU AGGRESSOR II

The world's largest fleet of live-aboards recently sailed its newest and most advanced boat to Palau. Peter Hughes' Aggressor fleet spared no expense in outfitting this behemoth with all the latest gizmos—what's novel is that they all seem to work. Naturally, there were some growing pains as the crew got used to the boat and the boat to Palau, but the only evidence of whatever trials they went through is a very smooth operation.

This 106-foot power catamaran is fast, comfortable and *huge*. The advanced Z-hull cuts through chop and swells, ensuring an incredibly smooth ride even during the rainy season, while drawing only a four and a half feet of water. Triple-decked with a vast 31-foot beam, this boat hides passengers so well, you'll find yourself wishing you had a buddy *between* dives.

Rich wood panelling covers the boat. Guest quarters are modern, clean and comfortable with two beds, private head, sink and glass-enclosed shower. Two 1,200 gallon-per-day reverse-osmosis desalinators ensure a never-ending supply of fresh water. Hot water is plentiful, too, as is air conditioning, easily adjusted with individual controls in each cabin. A large window offers a view of the incomparable Rock Islands right from your firm queen-sized bed.

A few steps aft is the dive deck, again huge, centered around a two-tiered camera table equipped with high-pressure air. Photo pro Gui Garcia is patient, experienced and knowledgeable. A full complement of Nikonos equipment is available for rent; E-6 processing is done daily and there are several light tables around which guests gather to gawk at each other's artistry.

The shining gem of the *Aggressor* is the ingenious hydraulic lift carrying the 30-foot skiff, *Aggressor 2Ω*, used to run divers to the shallows above the reefs surrounding the Rock Islands. 95 percent of the diving is done from this skiff, which is boarded at the dive-deck level. An arm eases the entire unit into the sea, and the two-engine, 500-hp jetboat flies to the reef at a blinding 50 mph. We dove all the great spots: Blue Corner, Blue Holes, German Channel, Turtle Cove, Iro Maru, Yellow Wall, Peleliu Corner, Ngemelis Wall, Ulong Channel and more. The fact that this skiff can operate in an impossible 6 inches of water ensures minimal damage to the ecosystem. It should also be noted that many of Palau's more frequented dive sites have finally been rigged with moorings to reduce the need for anchoring and the resultant reef destruction.

Anything you can imagine has already been taken into

consideration on the *Aggressor II*. it is a measure of how well it all works that I never had to consider the routine equipment storage, after dive showers, tank refills, towels, though they all were taken care of. Captain Buck Beasley and his crew were practically invisible in their effort to make everything seem easy. Long before each dive briefing, your BC is connected to a fresh tank on the skiff, waiting for you to slip it on and roll over the gunwale.

Lavish meals are served in the second floor dining room/lounge, a beautiful, and of course, spacious room. Here is also a 24-hour bar stocked full of beer, wine, soft drinks and every liquor imaginable, all included in the package price. The galley is well-equipped with two huge freezers and a large walk-in pantry so the menu is not reliant on the often limited variety and quality of groceries in Koror. Chef Irwin cooks three good (if overly hearty) meals every day, and always has a snack ready after every dive: Chinese steamed dumplings, bao, lumpia, zucchini bread, grilled sausage. Breakfast is cooked to order with your choice of eggs, bacon, ham, waffles, cereal and fruit. After the second dive, you'll find a hot lunch waiting: massive Irwin Burgers ("Bigger than a burger, smaller than a meatloaf!"), Greek salad, world-class lasagna, wahoo salad, sandwiches. Dinner is a banquet spread with chicken korma, Chinese beef, Indonesian chicken, Indian rice with cashews and raisins, fried bananas, seafood risotto, pork tenderloin, duck a l'orange, beef tenderloin with black pepper sauce, potato soufflé—you get the idea! Irwin will happily accommodate special dietary requirements.

In the lounge, a state-of-the-art entertainment center equipped with VCR, CD and cassette broadcasts music to any selected corner of the boat. A well-stocked library of novels, dive and marine books aids fish and reef identification. There is also a "boatique" where you can buy clothing, toiletries and souvenirs. On the aft deck is a patio with a barbecue, more seating and a large hot tub, always ready to soothe you at a scintillating 104°F.

The third floor is a soccer stadium doubling as a sundeck. With chaises, tables and chairs, the immense 30 foot by 60 foot platform offers a beautiful perch from which you can watch the Rock Islands drift by. In the evening, bring a cocktail up here and all your worries are gone. (Note that it is all the ships' policy that if you consume alcohol during the dive day, you become a snorkeler until the next day.)

Upon questioning the other guests, I could elicit no negative responses. I sought their impressions of the crew, the diving, the food, the quarters, even the weather during this "rainy season," and I received not one discouraging response.

Palau Aggressor II P.O. Box 1714-P106, Koror, Palau, ©488-6075, Fax: 488-6076. Toll-free booking for Aggressor fleet (US/Canada): 1-800-344-5662. Also: Aggressor Fleet, Ltd., P.O. Drawer K, Morgan City, LA 70381 USA. ©(504) 385-2628, Fax: (504) 384-0817. E-mail: paggressor@palaunet.com or info@livedivepacific.com Web: www.pac-aggressor.com Package rates for 2001: 7 days, $2,395, per person, double occupancy. Nitrox 32% additional $100.

Six-thirty a.m.—a knock on my cabin door, usually grounds for justifiable homicide, signals the arrival of Captain's Coffee Service. Captain's Coffee Service? Extra-thick Oscar de la Renta terry-cloth robes? A liveaboard staff in naval uniforms? Tablecloths at a five-course sit-down dinner? Peter Hughes' *Sun Dancer II* is clearly going after a totally different live-aboard experience, and it's possible they've found it.

With its clean lines, brushed aluminum paneling and color schemes reflecting Palauan sunsets, Peter Hughes, has outfitted the fourth and most glorious member of his fleet of luxury yachts as though he were planning to make it his permanent home. At almost 140 feet long, *Sun Dancer II* is steady in all but the most severe conditions. Beginning its life as a crew boat, in 1994 Hughes outfitted it for live-aboard service in Palauan waters with stabilizers, two reverse-osmosis desalinators, twin generators and a spare skiff.

With four accessible decks, *Sun Dancer II* is spacious even with a full complement of 16 divers. In the hull is the photo lab/video editor, light table, lounge, library, boatique and Owners' Suite. (Note: When booking your trip, you may request this suite. Though it's larger and has a bathtub, I prefer the huge picture windows of the standard cabins.) The main deck holds the very comfortable guest quarters, with an assortment of bed configurations, each with private bathrooms.

A few steps aft of your room is the dive deck, equipped with two freshwater showers and equipment baths and a camera table. There's ample storage for all your extra dive and photo gear. Watch the on-board E-6 processing; I had several rolls developed and ruined by burned-out chemicals. I would recommend you bring your undeveloped film home, or have it developed by Photo Palau (488-2600) at the Palau Pacific Resort; they'll do a nice job for you and they offer same-day service. A full line of well-maintained Nikonos U/W equipment is available for rent as is dive equipment and accessories. A full range of PADI courses is available, though I can't imagine an inexperienced diver on most of these sites.

The *Sun Dancer II* puts you on the reefs using its own 30-foot state-of-the-art chase boat, the *Safe Dancer*, piloted by charming Second Captain John Blair, an Australian who doubles as ship troubadour, entertaining guests on the "moon deck" with bawdy Aussie folk songs on those legendary Palauan nights. Mr. Blair and his lovely wife, Dot, are well-known for their tenure running Palau's first live-aboard, the classic and fondly remembered *Sun Tamarin*, ten years ago. (Today, Dot manages the brand-new and quite wonderful Caroline's Beach Resort in Koror, a perfect place to unwind after your exhaustive dive trip.)

The *Safe Dancer* is the fastest, most comfortable skiff I've ever been aboard. Recently built at a cost of $200,000, it is used to bring the dive sites nearer to the *Sun Dancer II* as she lies in snug harbor, ensuring guests' uneventful sleep. It works; thanks to the captain's excellent instincts. Most nights, I forgot I was even on a boat.

Although the *Sun Dancer II* only offers four dives a day, I didn't feel like I was getting less. With the slightly lighter schedule, the captain was able to put us on each reef at an optimum time and tide, and each dive was perfect. During dinner, guests are asked to vote on several different diving scenarios for the following day, within the limitations of schedule, location, weather and tide conditions. Since the diving here is so diverse, this was a nice way of pleasing everyone. There is a rather irritating bell signaling dive briefings, but it's a good way to make sure no one sleeps through a dive.

The sit-down dinner makes it logistically difficult, but I would have liked to have seen more attention paid to putting us in the water *after* dark. Three times a week at 5:30, the crew briefs a "twilight dive," but there is no real night diving offered.

Speaking of dinner, chef Sylvia Eiley prepared some of the most varied and interesting food I've ever seen on a live-aboard. Meals were sumptuous and satisfying. Sushi, tender steak marinated in papaya, Belizean chicken, grilled black snapper, crunchy salads, shrimp cocktail, Indonesian pork roast, coconut fish soup, and grilled marlin were prepared with expertise. After-dive snacks were always comforting: homemade brownies, oatmeal chocolate chip cookies, seafood pates and creamy salads. All beverages, including liquor and beer, are included in the package price.

Sun Dancer II P.O. Box 487, Koror, Palau 96940. ℗/Fax: 488-3983. Main office: Peter Hughes Diving, 5723 NW 158 Street, Miami Lakes, FL 33014, USA. ℗(305) 669-9391, Fax: (305) 669-9475,

Toll-free (US/Canada): 1-800-932-6237.
E-mail: dancer@peterhughes.com
Web: www.peterhughes.com
Package rates for 2001: 7 days, $1,795–$2,195; 10 days, $3,095–$3,295. No charge for Nitrox 32% (at time of this writing).

Accommodations

Many hotels grace Koror, in a price range to fit any budget. Camping (though not in Koror) is also an option, though you will want to return to Koror for a bit of civilization from time to time. Vacancies don't seem to be a problem, and you can usually wait until you arrive to choose the accommodations that appeal to you. The best game in town, by far, is the Palau Pacific Resort, but other less expensive hotels are also available, and the dive operators will pick you up anywhere.

EXPENSIVE

Caroline's Beach Resort This beautiful, terraced bungalow accommodation is the new kid on the block. They are on the crest of a ridge just above the Pan Pacific Resort. AC, fan, refrigerator, modern bathroom, big shower (great water pressure), comfortable queen-sized beds, balcony, even night lights. Manager Dotty and her nephew Paul (Australians both) know how to make you comfortable. Continental breakfast, $6. $110 per night and you can use Pan Pacific's facilities—they'll even scoot you down on a golf cart! Soon to come are the Japanese gardens, a restaurant and a bar at the summit of the hill.
Hotel Nikko Palau P.O. Box 310, Koror, 96940. ℗488-

2486. Nikko is located on Babeldaop, near the airport, which is inconvenient for divers. This is a beautiful hotel set high on a hill that offers a great view. The rooms are so-so. The swimming pool is occasionally filled with water. They cater mainly to Japanese tourists and businessmen. The overpriced restaurant here isn't particularly good, but local businessmen meet here for Palauan power lunches. **Marina Hotel** P.O. Box 142, Koror, Palau 96940. ✆488-1786. Situated on a jetty in Koror harbor. From here, Francis Toribiong operates the Fish 'N Fins and Marina Divers, and staying here makes for a convenient set-up. The Southern Cross Restaurant has quite good food, but the service stinks and it's pricey. In the evenings, I like to come here for cocktails and feed bar snacks to the dozens of trumpetfish and parrotfish lolling in the water below. The town dump is located on the access road to this hotel, and they've done a rather inadequate job of concealing it behind a long broken wall. Don't let the ubiquitous wild dogs worry you. They're basically shy and tend to mind their own business. **Palau Pacific Resort** P.O. Box 308, Koror, Republic of Palau 96940; ✆488-2600, Fax: 488-1606, 488-1601. E-mail: PPR@palaunet.com Web: www.panpac.com This is a world-class resort offering 160 gorgeous rooms offering either ocean or garden views. The Palau Pacific was built on the site of a World War II Japanese seaplane base near Koror, and offers all the facilities you'd expect from an international resort that cost its owners, the Pan Pacific chain, $40 million, plus one of the most spectacular sunsets seen anywhere.

Ice-cold tropical daiquiries, stuffed lobster, sashimi, and sake happily delivered to your room. Stingrays, lionfish and pyramid butterflies swim in a pond. Thick terry cloth robes, luxurious baths, private terraces. The Palau Pacific successfully achieves the elusive balance between nature and luxury. You will rarely if ever take your wallet out of your pocket (until you check out, of course). The resort is so perfectly integrated into its surroundings that it is actually difficult to capture the main building in a photograph. Experts have tried and failed.

The sunset, cocktails, restaurant, gift shops and pool are open to all. Even if you don't hang your hat here, it's certainly worth visiting for a snack and a drink.

The Palau Pacific offers easy access to the live-aboard operations. Each operator picks you up and delivers you to the resort. PPR offers live-aboard customers a day-room and full use of their facilities—in case you arrive early or are departing late—for a nominal fee of $15.

It is a lovely place, offering the best of everything. Standard rates, which vary with season and view: $210–$320 S, $210–$320 D, $400–$675 suite, $190–$595 international corporate rate. **Sunrise Villa** P.O. Box 6009, Palau, 96940. ✆488-4590, Fax: 488-4593. Thirty-four spacious rooms overlook the lagoon. This once-lovely hotel is a bit threadbare, but still very comfortable. Conveniently located just a few miles from the dock, it is situated high on a hill, where the air is a little cooler.

MODERATE

DW Motel Box 738, Koror,

Palau 96940. ✆488-2641. Twenty decent air-conditioned rooms, equipped with lots of hot water and a refrigerator make this a popular bed. Very reasonably priced. **Carp Island Resort** P.O. Box 5, Koror, Palau 96940. ✆488-2978. Popular with the Japanese, Johnny Kishigawa's Carp Island is unique. Set on the shore of Ngercheu Island, it is a convenient spot to roost if you want to avoid long boat rides to the dive sites each morning. A little rustic, the cottages here are fun and reasonable. The food can be quite good, but it ain't cheap. **West Plaza Desekel Hotel** P.O. Box 280, Koror 96940. ✆488-1671. I highly recommend the West Plaza, located right in the middle of the erratic capital, Koror. A modern, clean room with all the usual amenities plus a VCR, refrigerator, microwave, A/C, cable TV, (complimentary slippers that come in handy in camp), and charming view of a parking lot (you can't have it all) can be had for $40 a night. Staff is very helpful, very friendly. There are two other branches of this hotel in Koror, one down at T-Dock and the other in Ngerchemel, all similar.

Some low, low budget hotels are also available, such as the **T-Dock Guesthouse** (P.O. Box 178, Koror, PW 96940. ✆488-2369). A quick walk through town will yield other guest houses and lower-end motels.

Dining

On a live-aboard, you'll eat till you explode. If you stay in town, you have to work a bit harder at it, but there are dozens of restaurants in Koror, serving a multitude of different cuisines. With the exception of one or two sushi bars, most are very inexpensive and quite good. Though I enjoy many, the **Carp Restaurant** in Malakal (an island connected by bridge, only a mile from downtown Koror), remains my favorite. For five dollars, I couldn't eat another bite of the freshest fish and vegetables anywhere. The first time I found the Carp, all the patrons were sitting on the steps and in the patio, enjoying their lunch. A hostess offered me a plate and pointed me to the buffet which was spread with sashimi, fried chicken and fish, Japanese dumplings, a light and tender cold cabbage salad, steamed tapioca, several styles of potatoes and yams, ice cold sugar-baby watermelon, fresh mandarin oranges and of course, Budweiser. I ate well. When I asked for the check, we were mutually surprised to discover that I was not with the wedding party! They graciously offered no bill and accepted no money. I congratulated the bride and groom and returned the next evening for dinner, which was also impressive, served on the breezy veranda built on a pier over a particularly beautiful inlet of the main harbor.

For Japanese food, I recommend **Furusato Restaurant** (℃488-2689), where you can get a beer, lumpia, sashimi, coffee, desert, tip and tax for $12. They serve both Japanese and American food, and feature some local favorites, as well. The sashimi is excellent. Locals gather here for "power breakfasts." There are a number of good Japanese, Korean, and Filipino restaurants along the main drag of Koror. You can safely take your pick.

Across the small bridge, near the Carp Restaurant in Malakal is the **Storyboard**

Lounge which features a bar carved deeply with one of the most beautiful and detailed (and spicy!) Palauan legends. Decent bar food with a special or two.

Marina Hotel (in the Marina Hotel) Local, Continental, American cuisine; moderate for this area, casual. Try the Fish Grand Meuniere.

Philippine Orient (℃488-3114) is a wonderful restaurant out on the main drag, serving Philippine and Asian cuisine. The staff is cordial, even warm; the food is excellent and quite inexpensive. Casual, local hangout; open 7 days, 7 am to 10 pm, entrees $5–$12.

Aoshima (℃488-1947) good food, always busy, always hot. You can get coconut crab here, but it will cost you upwards of $25. 11 am to 10 pm, closed Mondays.

Emiliano's (℃488-1034) for a bit of Italian food, located right behind the Air Mike office in the middle of town. Not bad, considering Rome is half a world away.

Arirang (℃488-2779) is a cute little spot serving mainly Japanese food, though you can pick up a sandwich here for $3.50. Korean and Japanese specials are served for lunch. They'll cook you a fruitbat for $30.

Rock Island Cafe (℃488-1010) is a hopping joint that features pizza, burgers, fried fish and sashimi. Casual, inexpensive; very popular with the locals.

For fresh fruit, vegetables and a cold drink, stop into **Yano's** just next to the WCTC mall. **Pirate's Cove** (℃488-2349) is another favorite of mine. The parrotfish and wahoo sashimi here are top-notch, as are most of the other entrees. Depending upon the catch, you can get giant clam, octopus, squid, marlin and a host

of other locally caught fish. Lots of ice cold beer.

Night Life

There are several nightspots in Koror that offer everything from one-man-bands to jukeboxes. Feel free to enjoy them, but it was often suggested to me that I not stay late because the young men of Palau can be boisterous, to say the least. Fights between them are frequent, though the combatants are refreshingly unarmed. I never actually saw any real trouble, and felt very comfortable most of the time.

Karaoke is offered in many lounges, most of which serve light bar snacks with your Budweiser. The **Royal Belau Yacht Club** on the Fisheries Coop Dock lends a new meaning to the phrase "Yacht Club," but do check it out. It is an easy-going pub with ample air conditioning. It's safe and filled with a variety of tourists. The **Peleliu Club** and **Kosiil's Landing** cater more to locals, but they can be fun and interesting (don't stay too late). All the bars and restaurants close at midnight, whereupon you're allowed an hour to get home until the curfew kicks in.

The **Marina** is wonderful at night, with a lively outdoor bar and a terrace from which you can feed the many fish in the lagoon below. The beer is cold and the nights are warm; what could be better? The **Storyboard Bar** is also nice— that beautiful bar, cable television and strong AC. The food isn't bad, either.

And, there's always something going on at the **Pan Pacific Resort**: theme nights, dancing, drinks at the gazebo bar, a midnight swim in the pool or lagoon, or just swinging in a hammock.

Yap

This is a quiet and traditonal corner of Micronesia, and tourism is new enough here that services can still have a quirky, slow-moving charm. There are a couple of experienced dive operators, and two comfortable hotels, and you won't do wrong by sticking with these.

My Way If I were to dive Yap, I would go straight from the airport to the Pathways Hotel high up on the hill, overlooking the village of Colonia, Chamorro Bay, and the harbor below, and book a room. Then I would unpack, and head down to the Marina Restaurant.

While my order was being prepared (it can take a while) I'd walk ten steps next door and set up my diving schedule with David and Jesse at Beyond the Reef.

I'd tell them I want to dive with the mantas (they'll pick the optimum channel for the tides and season), and also to dive the walls both in the south and the north. Then, back to the Marina where I'd toss back a few cold ones, while watching the meticulous inactivity in the main harbor.

Sometime during my stay I'd be sure to visit one of the traditional villages, and get a ride out to Dalipebinaw, on the west coast of the main island, to see the stone money.

General

GETTING THERE

Continental Micronesia offers 7 flights per week, three originating in Guam, four in Palau (The Yap stopover is free on a Guam–Palau ticket). The airport is four miles from town. There is a $10 departure tax.

Continental Micronesia ℡350-2127. In the same building as the Marina restaurant in the middle of town and easy to find, although their hours are awfully hard to figure out.

AT A GLANCE

State of Yap
Federated States of Micronesia (FSM)

STATUS Self-governing federation in free association with the United States; constitution in effect 1979, full independence 1986, admitted to UN in 1991.

FSM CAPITAL Palikir, Pohnpei Island

FSM POPULATION 131,500 (1999 est.)

FSM LAND AREA 607 islands comprising 271 sq. mi. (702 sq. km.)

FSM PER CAPITA GNP $1,760 (1996 est.)

FSM CURRENCY U.S. dollar

FSM COUNTRY CODE 691

YAP STATE CAPITAL Colonia, on Yap Island, pop. 8,900 (Wa'ab, 1999 est.)

YAP STATE AIRPORT Yap Island (YAP)

YAP STATE POPULATION 13,500 (1999 est.)

YAP STATE LAND AREA The five islands of Wa'ab, together with 15 outlying islands comprising 45.72 sq. mi. (118.4 sq. km.). Largest islands: Wa'ab, 38.69 sq. mi.

YAP LANGUAGES English (official), Yapese

YAP AVERAGE TEMPERATURE 81.4°F (27.4°C)

YAP YEARLY RAINFALL 121.5 in. (3,087 mm)

NAME The traditional name for so-called Yap Proper, the state's main island group, is Wa'ab. "Yap" is probably a corruption of this name, although one story has it that when the first Europans asked the islanders who had paddled out to meet them the name of their island, the Yapese held up their paddles and said "yap" ("paddle") thinking that was the object whose name the strangers sought.

LOCAL TRANSPORTATION

Taxis are privately owned; there are no meters, but the average price of a trip in town is $1 or so. Call Wanyo Taxi (℡350-2120), Island Mutual (℡350-3401), or Midland Taxi (℡350-2405).

There are buses that connect the outlying villages with Colonia, but the schedules are a bit difficult to ascertain. Hitchhiking is accepted and effective. It's customary for your hotel operator to pick you up at the airport, so that's one less thing you'll have to worry about.

Car Rental

Rental cars are available, but I can't see the purpose. Rates are approximately $40 per day plus 10 percent tax. You can also get an hourly rental, if you prefer. Be especially wary of "sand traps" cut into the roads by village chiefs to catch speeders.
ESA Hotel ℡350-2139
Island Rentals ℡350-2566
Target Car Rental ℡350-3275

OUTER ISLANDS

Visiting any of the outer islands of Yap State is allowed only with permission from the island's chief. See the Office of Outer Islands Affairs at the Governor's office. If you're interested in Yapese culture, by all means, don't be put off by this. Permission is usually granted, and the trip is worthwhile. You have to be specific about the areas you want to visit.
Office of the Governor State of Yap, Colonia, Yap, FM 96943. ℡350-2108.

SEASON

Diving is good year-round in Yap, but the trade winds die in the summer, allowing greater access to the channels in the north. I've always had better luck with the mantas from October through May.

It never gets even remotely cool in Yap, so pack lightly. Remember that despite a tradition of toplessness, bikinis are shocking—modest dress is expected. Short shorts and the like are inappropriate. A very light waterproof jacket might be in order, but I prefer to just let the rain cool me down.

TOURISM OFFICE

Yap Visitors Bureau P.O. Box 988, Colonia, Yap FM 96943. ℡350-2298, Fax: 350-7015. Located next to the Bank of Hawaii in downtown Colonia.
E-mail: yvb@mail.fm
Web: www.visityap.com

MEDICAL

It is best not to get too sick in Yap, but, since 1979 the Yap State government has owned and operated a 150-bed hospital. There is no intensive care and only limited surgery performed, but rates are reasonable. It is not safe to drink directly from the tap in Yap. Bottled water is available at all the grocery stores.
Hospital ℡350-2110
Ambulance ℡350-3446

COMMUNICATIONS

International calls to anywhere in the world can be made from the Telecommunications Corporation, next to the land resources office in "downtown" Colonia. Rates are a bit cheaper in the evening and at night. The Colonia post office is open weekdays from 8:30 to 4 pm.

BANKING AND MONEY

The Bank of Hawaii (℡350-2129) and the Bank of FSM (℡350-2329) have outlets in Colonia. Do not depend on credit cards in Yap. The dive operators, the larger hotels, and Continental accept them, but most businesses do not.

Tipping is not a common practice in Yap. Use your own discretion, but a couple of dollars for a service well-rendered are appreciated.

ELECTRICITY

Standard 110 VAC, U.S.-style outlets.

PEOPLE AND LANGUAGE

It is not common for Yapese to start conversations with strangers. They are not shy, but the Yapese believe that keeping to oneself is a virtue. In fact, the Yapese are very friendly—just say, "Hi," and you will open the floodgates to friendly conversation.

Three of the eight known Micronesian languages are spoken here: Ulithian, Yapese and Woleian. English is widely spoken and many of the elderly speak Japanese.

Some Yapese phrases
Mogethin Hello
Kammagar Thank you
Rib mangil Very good
Kefel Good bye
Beer Beer

PHOTOGRAPHIC

Bring lots of film. If you cannot wait to process it at home (always the best bet) Bill Acker has opened Manta Visions, a complete U/W photo and video center in the lobby of the Manta Ray Bay Hotel. He offers a full range of services, including E-6 processing, video editing, photography courses, rentals, and sales.

Many Yapese, especially children, are delighted to have their picture taken, but some, particularly older people, object to cameras. *Ask permission before taking someone's photograph.*

Dive Operators

Like in the rest of Micronesia, diving is not cheap in Yap. All three operators offer almost exactly the same rates, starting at $95 for a two-tank day of boat diving. **Beyond the Reef** P.O. Box 609, Yap, FSM 96943. ℂ350-3483, Fax: 691-350-3733. E-mail: beyondthereef@mail.fm Web: www.diveyap.com This outfit has been in business for five years now. They offer a bit less luxury than the original operator, Yap Divers, but more personalized service. Owners David Vecella and Jesse Faimaw specialize in small groups, usually four divers or fewer.

Beyond the Reef offers a full line of PADI courses, and rents high-quality gear and 35mm cameras. They have a full-service dive shop. From their own pier, they run three boats, two fast, smooth 22-footers (maximum four divers) and one 17-footer (three divers). They also have three larger boats available if necessary, up to a 32-footer with a capacity of eight.

They dive all of the well-known sites as well as a smattering of secret sites that Jesse, a native Yapese, has been visiting since he was a boy.

The lunch provided on day trips is always made from local foods—crab, lobster, grilled fish, chicken, veggies and roots, such as taro, breadfruit, tapioca and potato. It is all delicious. Jesse will be happy to arrange cultural tours to traditional Yapese villages, as well as other sightseeing tours throughout the main island. Boat trips through the mangroves, the German Channel and to outlying islands can also be easily arranged.

Dive packages are available

with both the Pathways and Rai View Hotels, so do inquire when booking your trip. Repeat customers get 10 percent off diving and the purchase of accessories. With five days of diving, you also receive a 10 percent discount. Hotel pickup and drop-off is included. They offer safe storage, fresh water equipment baths and dockside rinse shower for divers.

Beyond the Reef is very environmentally conscious, and offers no reef fishing, but they will take you trolling offshore for yellowfin tuna, mahimahi, bowrunner, wahoo and skipjack. A one-day (5-hour) charter will only set you back $95 and includes bait, tackle and refreshments; a full day is priced at $130 per person.

Single day of boat diving, two-tanks, $95; additional tank $35; single-tank night dive $60. **Nature's Way** P.O. Box 238, Yap, FSM 96943 ℂ/Fax: 350-3407. E-mail: natureswasy@mail.fm This outfit was founded in 1993 by the late John B. Iou, who had served as Chief of Marine Resources Management for Yap State. They offer a range of diving, kayak tours, and village tours. Basic NAUI instruction.

Single day of boat diving, two-tanks, $95; three tanks, $130; single-tank day boat dive (on request) $60; single-tank night dive $50. Various village and snorkeling tours, $20–$55. **Yap Divers** P.O. Box MR, Yap FSM 96943. ℂ350-2542, Fax: 350-3407. E-mail: yapdivers@mantaray.com Web: www.mantaray.com This is the original operator, the one that put Yap on the diving map. Yap Divers is a fully-accredited PADI facility offering a full complement of

diving activity and instruction. Owned by Bill Acker, they have five boats, including a sleek new 250-horsepower flat-top which cruises at a breathtaking 20 knots. Their boats can accommodate four to 20 divers, and the larger ones are equipped with freshwater showers.

"It never occurred to me that anyone would be interested in the mantas," Bill told me, "A friend suggested I publicize this phenomenon, and that's how it all started." Since Bill arrived here with the Peace Corps in the 1960s, he has made himself quite comfortable, having opened the first hotel and dive operation in Colonia.

Along with a full dive shop, gift shop, rental station and dock, Bill offers guests some very attractive dive and tour packages. Just tell him what you want, and he'll try to arrange it. "Recently, a couple wanted to be wed on an outrigger canoe," Bill said. "So, I dropped a dime and called the island chief, who had a canoe paddled to Colonia from an outlying island and the couple began their life together."

They offer packages with the Manta Ray Bay Hotel (which they own, see next page), daily dive trips, night dives, PADI instruction (including the world's only PADI manta specialty), a full-service photo and video center, equipment for rent or sale, and nitrox and oxygen fills.

Single day of boat diving, two-tanks, $95; additional tank $35; fourth tank, $30; single-tank night dive $60. Nitrox 32% additional $10 per tank.

Accommodations

Remember that Yap is a very quiet and relatively new stop

on the tourist's itinerary. Amenities here are thus a little odd, but interesting and even fun in that way. With the exception of the Manta Ray Bay Hotel and the Pathways, all the hotels are a bit primitive in design and service. All are just a three-minute walk from anywhere. Colonia is a very small capital.

Manta Ray Bay Hotel P.O. Box MR, Colonia, Yap, FSM 96943. ℂ350-2300, Fax: 350-4567 and -3841. E-mail: yapdivers@mantaray.com
In Yap's main town of Colonia, the center of diving activity on the island, you will find only one modern hotel, owned by the hospitable American expat Bill Acker and his lovely Yapese wife, Patricia, the operators of Yap Divers.

Bill came to Micronesia in 1974 with the Peace Corps, laying low in the north. He left for a short time, returning in 1990 when he blended his knowledge of the island with a generous helping of good old Western entrepreneurial drive and parlayed his way into the hotel business, overseeing the construction of one of the most comfortable and luxurious hotels in Colonia—the first to be opened here in 22 years.

The 23 air-conditioned rooms are gorgeous. Decorated in wicker and pastel, some feature water beds, some have panoramic views of Tamil Bay (not an especially picturesque bay) and the ocean. The bathrooms are unexpectedly spacious and they have water pressure unlike anything I've seen anywhere in Micronesia with the exception of Talofofo Falls. The rooms are equipped with VCR, color television and well-stocked mini bars.

Each room is cutely named after an underwater friend — The Clownfish, Angelfish, Shark, Manta, etc. Framed U/W photography is everywhere, and best of all, the soaps are shaped like traditional stone money, holes and all. Also in this complex is the Manta Ray Restaurant (see listing below under Restaurants). The price for this charming luxury does not seem unreasonable, running $115 to $225.

New Rai View Hotel. P.O. Box 488, Colonia, Yap 96943. ℂ/Fax: 350-3527. Clean and cheap. Owners Lonnie and Rose Fread, cordial, hard-working transplanted Americans, offer spare but comfortable rooms for a fraction of the price available from neighboring innkeepers. Water pressure is a bit on the weak side, and the pump goes off at midnight, but unless you're planning late-night water sports, this should present no problem. The walls are thin, so if it's a wild night of passion you're intending, this may not be the place. This is *not* a luxury accommodation but prices are reasonable, with singles starting at $55.

Ocean View Hotel P.O. Box 130 Colonia, Yap, FSM 96943. ℂ350-2279, Fax: 350-2339. Friendly staff, but a bit cramped. $40S, $50D.

Pathways Hotel P.O. Box 718, Colonia, 96943. ℂ350-3310, Fax: 691-350-2066. E-mail: pathways@mail.fm. This group of 15 breezy bamboo cottages built into a hillside jungle is my personal favorite on Yap. Each room has a king-sized bed covered with a lacy mosquito net, although rarely in these islands will you find insects to be a problem. (Between the bats, birds, and ocean breezes, Micronesia is not a mosquito's idea of a good time). Each room is supplied with purified water, and ice is also available. Laundry is washed at $3 per load. TV/video is offered for rent at $5 per day. The Pathways is owned and operated by the charming Stan and Flora Fillmed and their son John. Traditional building methods were used in constructing the buildings, and they are on a slope overlooking Chamorro Bay. Each cottage has a private balcony (smoking is not allowed in the cottages). A restaurant and bar are situated in the main house. I love sitting in the open-roofed bar under the rainforest, enjoying an ice cold glass of vodka. Highly recommended. $95 for a cottage with air conditioning; $85 without.

Dining

The Public Market is where the populace come to meet and buy, trade or sell their produce, fish and meat. The fruit and vegetables are exotic and fresh; there's even a cooler stocked with fresh-cut coconuts ready to drink—yours for a quarter. Along with your change, the cashier offers you a machete with which you're expected to hack off the top of your coconut, exposing a small hole through which you sip nature's perfect cocktail. It's definitely worth a visit, as early in the morning as you can get there. Yapese oranges are among the best I've had.

Next door is Colonia's huge general store, converted from a refurbished World War II airplane hangar. Offering everything from fresh and frozen fruitbat to phosphorescent Fruit Loops, it also serves as a meeting place for the citizenry.

A terrace at water's edge, overlooking tranquil Colonia

harbor, the **Marina Restaurant** (©350-2211) has few walls. Located just behind the Continental Micronesia office, the Marina serves breakfast, lunch and dinner. An inexpensive menu offers everything from great burgers to Yapese food, and the beer is cold and fresh. When I reflect upon my travels, I often remember "happy hours" here watching the sun fall in the west, my ice-cold beer sweating in the heat while we nibbled on platters of wahoo and skipjack served with searing *wasabi* and cooling ginger. Later, the waitresses turned up the stereo and coaxed us out to dance in the warm Pacific night. Take me back.

The **Slacktide Restaurant** (©350-2319) in the Manta Ray Bay Hotel is also a nice restaurant, though prices seem a bit high. They carry the stone money theme all the way to their pizza which, you guessed it, has a hole in the middle. Chef and all-around good guy "2C" oversees a menu that offers a good variety of local selections (including my favorite—parrotfish with coconut), as well as stateside fare—three eggs over easy with bacon and home fries. Do not miss the home-baked banana bread. This restaurant has another view of the marina, and if you can forgo the AC, there's a warm, swift breeze blowing through the outer dining room that goes very well with the ice-cold beer. The **Slacktide Saloon** (same location and number) is a nice place to enjoy a cocktail. Main attraction is if you can corner Bill into a conversation. Prices are moderate.

The **Pathways** has a beautiful and well-stocked bar, cut into the jungle itself. Ask Flora to pour you a tall one! At the other end of the complex is a restaurant serving breakfast and lunch, though at the time of this writing, a dinner menu was being planned.

NIGHT LIFE

Plan on retiring and waking early on Yap. While you can have a nice evening enjoying dinner and cocktails in the cool night air under a glittering sky, there is no real night life here. Colonia is so small that your experience will vary widely depending upon who else happens to be there.

In 1993, when a colorful captain friend of mine and his faithful crew were stranded here while having their bowsprit rebuilt, half the town rocked late into the evening at the Marina Restaurant. On the other hand, I've been here when the hotels were filled with honeymoon couples, and Colonia turned into a ghost town at 8 pm.

Land Touring

There is much to see and do in Yap. Though modern currency is now the accepted rate of exchange, the 7,000 pieces of stone money that still exist are of real value to the Yapese, and may be seen in every corner of Yap. Donut-shaped so that a pole can be slid through to enable two men to carry the lighter pieces, the largest pieces measure three meters across and require the backs and shoulders of fifteen men when it is (seldom) moved. It's absolutely forbidden to stand or sit on stone money.

In the villages outside Colonia, traditional songs and dance are frequently performed not only for the edification of visitors, but to commemorate holidays and keep their fragile culture alive. Dance is the most developed and complex art form in Yap, and definitely worth seeing.

Shopping

A stop at the tourism office elicited an odd response from the Director of Tourism who, when asked to recommend a source for keepsakes, told me, "We really don't make high quality souvenirs in Yap."

This is an uncommon display of humility, but not entirely true. You can pick up some unusual island mementos in the Women's Craft Center, which is located just up the street from Yap Divers. Inventory changes depending upon what the local craftmakers decide they want to work on, but you can usually find nice examples of *lava-lava* as well as many items made from shells.

Just before the last time I left Yap, my plane was on the tarmac when I decided I wanted to bring my girlfriend a *lava-lava*. The ticket agent told me I had fifteen minutes to board, so I picked out the most daring cab driver I could find (look for youth, raging eyes, dice hanging from the mirror, mud on the fenders) and headed back to the Women's Craft Center, only to find they had sold out for the day.

Taking the gross national product into his own hands, this driver sped me to his house, ran inside, and retrieved his sister's skirt! Though he adamantly insisted it was a gift and not a sale, I tipped him well.

The plane had to be stopped as it headed toward the runway where the stairs were lowered from the tail section so that I could board. Head carried low in shame, I walked through the gauntlet of impatient passengers towards my seat, carrying my trophy well-concealed under my T-shirt.

Chuuk

The islands of Chuuk are a bit dirty and charmless, and the hotels are only now creeping upward from dismal. But it is a unique place, and the people are not as gruff as they are made out to be. If good diving, good food, and a good night's sleep is what you want, then you are best to book a live-aboard.

My Way Double check your equipment. Book a trip on the SS *Thorfinn* and leave the rest to Captain Higgs and his wife, Narinta. Dive deeply and take long, long, long safety stops.

General

GETTING THERE

Continental Micronesia stops here Sundays, Mondays, Wednesdays and Fridays on its eastbound route and Mondays, Wednesdays and Fridays, westbound. Flights are often full on this popular stop, so book early and reconfirm diligently. **Continental Micronesia** ℂ330-2424, open 8am–6pm.

LOCAL TRANSPORTATION

Among the rare pleasures Chuuk has to offer are cheap taxis. Just stand on the road and a small pickup filled with people will invariably offer you a ride. Let the driver know where along the main road you want to hop off, and he will stop—or at least slow down a little (wink). When you get out, give him a dollar and he will thank you. Renting a car here is a bad idea.

For trips to the outer islands, call the **Truk Shipping Company** (ℂ330-2455). The *Micro Trader* and *Micro Dawn* both circumnavigate the Mortlocks, Western, and Hall Islands.

These are not typical tourist ventures. Accommodations are rough and so, usually, are the crossings. Further information can be found at the Transportation Office (ℂ330-2592).

SEASON

September through April are optimum, but I've had great experiences here all year round. The weather is more predictably calm during these months, and less rain causes less sediment to be washed into the lagoon.

TOURIST ASSISTANCE

Chuuk Visitor's Bureau P.O. Box FQ, Chuuk, FM 96942. ℂ330-4133 **Truk Travel Unlimited** P.O. Box 546, Chuuk State, FSM, 96942. ℂ330-4232, Fax: 330-2286.

MEDICAL

Chuuk's hospital is not really to be recommended. Be careful, and be responsible for yourself. Save the daring adventures for islands better equipped for medical emergencies.

Chuuk was the scene of a widespread cholera outbreak in 1982, probably caused by water contaminated with sewage. The danger is past, but it is best to be very careful with whatever you ingest. Bottled water only, please, and peel your fruits and vegetables.

COMMUNICATIONS

There is a 24-hour Telecommunications Center, near the airport, and the post office is downtown.

MONEY AND BANKING

The Bank of Guam (ℂ330-2331) and the Bank of FSM (ℂ330-2353) are both in Weno. Few operations here take credit cards.

PHOTOGRAPHIC

I've never found any film processing on the mainland. And if you're on a live-aboard, it might be advisable to take your exposed film home rather than chance any of the E-6 developers onboard.

Black and white is becoming popular and can be a dramatic way to shoot the wrecks, since light is at a premium and shadows are in abundance. Double strobes can be useful, but some of the most striking photos I've seen have used available light and creative angles. Wide-angle lenses tend to deliver a greater sense of the enormous size of many of these ships.

PEOPLE

Half the population of the Federated States of Micronesia resides in Chuuk State, with at least 50,000 living on the islands bordering the lagoon.

Throughout history, the Chuukese have gotten a bad

rap as an aggressive, warlike, even cannibalistic people, but they are as friendly as any of the Micronesian islanders. It is better to avoid a group of drunk Chuukese teenagers, but where in the world would that not be true?

For many years, in fact, prohibition was enacted here. As Budweiser became the opiate of the people, women voters grew tired of their husbands spending all their money on liquor before coming home to rough them up. Nightly rumbles on the docks were so frequent they were called "Free Movies." So, they pressed for and enacted government sponsored abstinence.

Today, community life has toned down a bit, and while it is not sold everywhere, beer and liquor are easily obtainable. In many bars, Chuukese even smoke marijuana, but it is best for the tourist to forego this indulgence; there are many places to better pass your vacation time than in Weno's jail.

LANGUAGE

Chuukese is widely spoken and most islanders are familiar with English. A few, especially among the elders, are able to converse in Japanese, though they may not be willing, since they were not treated well by the soldiers of Empire. "Good day" in Chuukese is "Ran annem."

Dive Operators

Make sure your equipment is in top working order. Bring extra everything. Because of all the sharp edges on the sunken steel hulls, protective gear is recommended. On land, short shorts, miniskirts and bikinis are inappropriate, but loose fitting cotton cloth-

ing is perfect for this climate.

Diving on Chuuk costs in the vicinity of $90 for a two-tank dive, about par for Micronesia. Live-aboards are the best deal for hard-core divers. A visitor's dive permit for Chuuk now costs $35. **Blue Lagoon Dive Shop** P.O. Box 429, Chuuk, FM 96942. ℂ330-2796, Fax: 330-4307. Blue Lagoon was founded in 1973 by Kimiuo Aisek, the father of Chuuk diving, and is now operated by his son Gradvin. Blue Lagoon is highly regarded with respect to their knowledge of the lagoon and the expertise of their guides, most of whom have

eight years or more of experience diving these wrecks. Using simple wooden and fiberglass boats, Blue Lagoon does a good job of finding the right balance between their guests' ability and the difficulty (read "depth") of the wrecks. Rates: $90 for a two-tank day of diving, single tank night dives $45.

Micronesia Aquatics P.O. Box 57, Weno, Chuuk, FM 96942. ℂ330-2204. Located just inside the grounds to the Blue Lagoon Resort. Owner Clark Graham has a rule that renders some dives impossible and which many divers find hard to accept—maximum depth of 40 meters. But they've been in business here for 20 years and are certainly experts on Truk Lagoon. Clark and his Chuukese bride, Chineina, are extremely knowledgeable about Chuuk's wartime history, and will offer to include a tour to one of the islands' war sites during a surface interval in a two-dive package.

Micronesia Aquatics is a leader in environmental protection and historic preservation, regularly donating profits to the Society for Historic Investigation and Preservation (SHIP). They have a new 10-meter boat, which is very comfortable—ample space for cameras and gear, generous shade, and easy entry. Other watersports such as windsurfing and water-skiing are also available.

Sundance Tours and Dive Shop P.O. Box 85, Weno, Chuuk, 96942. ℂ330-4234, Fax: 330-4451. This, the newest operator in town, is located between the airport and the Blue Lagoon Resort. Japanese and Chuukese guides. Catering to the Japanese market. Seven boats. Prices similar to Blue Lagoon.

LIVE-ABOARDS

Though it's not really necessary in order to access most of the wrecks in Chuuk, a live-aboard does offer you a chance to escape the dreary restaurants, marginal hotels and dusty day-to-day life in Weno. Though you will not get as clear a sense of life in Chuuk, a live-aboard's accommodations, food and fun are far superior to what you'll find on the mainland. Remember that diving is deep in Chuuk. More than three and especially four dives a day can be extremely dangerous. Don't necessarily take advantage of any unlimited diving offers, unless you are absolutely sure you know what you're doing. You might be better off at the Chuuk jail than at the Chuuk hospital. And the nearest chamber is in Palau.

S.S. Thorfinn Operated by Seaward Holidays Micronesia, Inc., P.O. Box 1086, Weno, Chuuk, FM 96942. ℂ330-3040, Fax: 330-4253. Ship's phone: 330-4302. E-mail: Seaward@mail.fm Web: www.thorfinn.net

Captain Lance Higgs' *Thorfinn* is one of the most enjoyable boats I've been on. One of the first of the Pacific sport-diving live-aboards, the *Thorfinn* was refitted in December 1995 at a cost of over $500,000. It is clean, modern, and everything works well. This is not a boat so much as it is a ship; it's *huge* at 55 meters and it's steam powered which makes it very quiet. No more sleepless nights while your diesel live-aboard ferries you across the sea.

Each of the eleven oversized rooms has a queen and single bed, private bath and toilet, multi-system VCR, CD, and cassette stereo. In the salon is a beautiful aquarium and HDTV set. The food is excellent, if hearty. The *Thorfinn* is now equipped with satellite communications for telephone, fax, and e-mail. Captain Higgs is very knowledgeable about Chuuk, both in and out of the lagoon, and is expert on the wrecks he will show you. The *Thorfinn* uses moorings and chase boats instead of anchoring near or directly to the sunken ships. Though the ship accommodates 24 divers, multiple dive sites are accessed simultaneously using four large tenders in order to keep the dive parties small—no more than six divers per dive.

Complete photographic and video rental and video editing system on board. Keep in mind that the *Thorfinn* boasts a toasty Jacuzzi from which to gaze at those star-clustered Pacific skies. This and a bottle of champagne and you'll practically drown in bubbles.

Standard cruises are 7 1/2 days and 7 nights, five dives a day. $2,195 double occupancy. Extension days $314, Non-divers $1,695.

Captain Higgs also sails the *Thorfinn* to Yap, through the outer islands of Chuuk and Yap States, on a special "Pan Micro Cruise." This is remarkable exploratory diving, and a really special event. You can join on either Yap or Chuuk, and are let off at the other island. The cruise takes 14 days, and runs $3,495 plus an additional $800 for boarding fees, village elder fees, and the like, which must be paid in these hinterlands.

Truk Aggressor II Aggressor Fleet, Ltd. P.O. Box 1470 Morgan City, LA 70381. ℂ1-800 348-2628 (US/Canada toll free), ℂ504 385-2628 Fax: 504 384-0817 E-mail: info@aggressor.com *and* okeanos@aggressor.com Web: www.aggressor.com

The Aggressor Fleet has a fine boat operating in Chuuk. Captained by Buck Beasley, the *Truk Aggressor II* is a 107-foot (33-meter) aluminum yacht, completely air conditioned and carpeted, offering all the amenities you can imagine. Built in 1988 and thoroughly refurbished in 2000, with a new stateroom on the upper deck, and a new hot tub for the deck, and a satellite phone system, for worldwide telecommunications and e-mail. Ten sumptuous cabins, each with private shower, sink and bath, accommodating up to 18 guests.

The oversize salon/dining area features a wet bar and entertainment center. Topdeck is for suntans and barbecues. Luxury is what the Aggressor fleet does best, and the *TA* is no exception. Full camera and video facilities and rentals; on board E-6 processing (make sure you request fresh chemicals). You will never touch your equipment if that is what you choose. Just "Eat, Sleep and Dive" (mostly eat, with diving running a close second!).

Standard cruises are one week, Sunday to Sunday, with 5 1/2 days of diving. $2,395 double occupancy, with "Deep Week" runs an additional $500.

Accommodations

Blue Lagoon Resort P.O. Box 340, Chuuk, FSM 96942. &330-2438, Fax: 330-2439. International Reservations: Castle Resorts and Hotels, 1150 S. King Street, Honolulu, HI 96813 USA. Toll-free (US/Canada/Guam/Saipan) &1-800-367-5004, Fax: 1-800-477-2329. &808 591-2235, Fax: 808-596-0158. E-mail (headquarters): reservations@castleresorts.com E-mail: BLResort@mail.fm This is the best game in town (if not the only game). Built on a former Japanese seaplane base, many of the 56 rooms face the ocean and the majestic sunsets. The grounds of this hotel are inviting, and the formerly damp, musty rooms have undergone a renovation. Although the best on Chuuk, it is not really luxurious. This used to be the Truk Continental (owned by Continental Airlines) until they sold it to the Blue Lagoon Dive Shop who then sold it to the Hawaii-based

Castle Hotel chain. $125 standard room, $132 superior room, $175 one-bedroom suite.

Christopher Inn P.O. Box 37, Weno, Chuuk FM 96942. ©330-2652. E-mail: xstore@mail.fm I only mention this place so you'll be sure to avoid it. It is awful. The staff is rude and will take advantage of you. Overpriced and depressing.

Chuuk Pacific Resort P.O. Box 123, Weno, Chuuk, FM 96942.©330-2723 and 330-2736, Fax:(691)330-2729. E-mail: GOCPR@mail.fm Faces the water, but concrete slab construction. 24 rooms.

Chuuk Star Hotel P.O. Box 1230, Weno, Chuuk FM 96942. ©330-2040 through 2044, Fax: 330-2045. Email: chuukstar@mail.fm Relatively inexpensive, functional, damp, and musty. Bring slippers.

Island Motel P.O. Box 728, Weno, Chuuk FM 96942. ©330-4220, Fax: 330-2926. Damp, a bit run down, but the rooms are large with A/C, color TV, refrigerator and 24 hr. hot water. Very inexpensive—singles at $40.

Pacific Gardens P.O. Box 494, Weno, Chuuk FM 96942. ©330-4639, Fax 330-2334. Inexpensive, in the $50 range.

Truk Stop Hotel P.O. Box 546, Weno, Chuuk FM 96942. ©330-2701 Fax: 330-2286. E-mail: TrukStop@mail.fm Actually, since its recent renovation, this small (23 rooms) hotel isn't all that bad. It's clean, modern and fiercely air-conditioned. Cable TV, refrigerator, private baths. Car and moped rental available. 24-hr power and hot water. Decent restaurant. Not great, but recommended. Rooms in the $70–$90 range.

Dining

In Weno, there are a few decent places to eat, though none can be considered memorable. If you feel adventurous and want to try some truly native food, ask for *oppot*, a traditional Chuukese staple. Breadfruit is well-pounded before being buried in a pit lined with banana leaves. After a year, it is removed, and kneaded into dumplings or loaves before it is boiled or baked. *Oppot* has a yeasty, alcoholic flavor that will stay with you long after your wetsuit dries. Not for the meek.

Takarajima Japanese Restaurant, near the Blue Lagoon is very good and possibly the best restaurant on the island. I highly recommend the sushi, but all the selections are good. It seems a bit expensive for the locale, but there ain't much choice in Weno.

The restaurant at the **Blue Lagoon Resort** is also pretty good. They serve breakfast, lunch, and dinner. I recommend you select an entree off the menu here for your lunch stop.

The restaurant in the **Truk Stop Hotel** is also good, serving burgers, pizza and other western fare. It's right downtown along the main, dusty drag.

As with accommodations, avoid the Christopher Inn and its **Roof Garden Restaurant.** There *is* a bakery at the Christopher Inn called the Rainbow Coffee Shop that's not bad for bread and pastry.

Night Life

There is no night life in Chuuk. After 10 pm you are very lucky if you can even find a taxicab. Though citizens passing by will often offer you a ride, you won't see many of them, either. Next to the airport are a couple of bars whose names change too often to mention. One is in a rundown ranch-style building. The bartender and owner make sure the customers are nice to one another, so feel reasonably safe here. It's good for an ice cold beer or staunch cocktail. Otherwise your best bet is the bar at the **Blue Lagoon Resort**, where divers congregate.

Land Tours

Among and between the piles of garbage and mountains of empty aluminum cans are a few interesting sites to see. There are certainly a couple of satisfying hiking tours you may follow; one leads you to the United States Civil Action Team (CAT) headquarters atop Mt. Tonachou (230 meters) from which you will be rewarded with a postcard view of Chuuk Lagoon and most of the surrounding islands.

On the western coast of Weno, at the village of Epinup, the road ends and doesn't pick up again until Sapuk. The connecting path offers a fascinating walk through the jungle, and shouldn't take more than a couple of hours. Morning is the best time for this, to avoid either the direct sun or the danger of running into darkness.

One of my favorite escapes from dusty downtown Weno is to grab a ride to Peniesene in the north and walk one kilometer south along the Wichoun River to the Wichoun Falls, a nice break from the salt water and bone-cracking heat. When you return to the main road, continue east to Sapuk, where you can sight along a

few 200mm cannons that are aimed out across the lagoon. They appear to have been manufactured in Italy, though they were used in attempting to defend the lagoon in 1944. Nearby is the Japanese lighthouse, which, for a small fee, you can climb for another extraordinary vantage point.

Across the lagoon to the southeast is Tonoas Island, site of the infamous Japanese hospital, where cruel doctors performed experimental surgery upon unanesthetized American prisoners-of-war. Within the 15 sq. km., there are numerous remnants of the Japanese occupation including caves and cannons. At high tide, you can snorkel across to Eten Island. Look for a submerged Betty Bomber (known as a "flying cigar") in just 3 meters of water. This Betty crashed in 1944, just meters short of the runway. Many of the day boats take their lunch stops on Eten. During World War II, 30,000 people lived here.

Fefan Island, also in the lagoon, is a nice day trip which can include a pleasant hike and a visit to a wonderful garden market. The infamous smoking tobacco, Supanchuuk, is grown here. If you smoke, this ought to do it for you.

Shopping

You can certainly find the usual assortment of Micronesian souvenirs in Chuuk—storyboards, carvings, grass skirts, T-shirts—but it is better to take home something uniquely Chuukese instead. When natives lived in pandanus huts, the pubescent boys would carve long sticks with personal designs. At night, they would stealthily walk to the hut of the object of

their desire. Outside, they would poke these love-sticks through the seams in the walls, entangling them in the hair of their intended.

The girl would wake at the annoyance and, feeling the individual pattern carved into the stick, give one of three signals: if she pulled, he was to come in; if she shook the stick, he was to await her outside; and, if she pushed the stick back out, he was to understand that he was being rejected. You can buy one of these unique items for about a dollar. They make great conversation pieces, and are quite attractive when mounted on a wall.

Chuuk is the only island in Micronesia where war masks have been carved and used. Though they are now cut from the fibrous hibiscus tree and no longer sculpted from hardwoods, some of these *tapwanu*s are quite beautiful.

Handbags, satchels, grass skirts, war clubs and wooden jewelry are also available, but of marginal quality. Stick to the love-sticks; the challenge of getting them home in one piece through a half dozen crowded airports will certainly test your patience. I succeeded only to have my girlfriend soon after sit on both of them, breaking them in half.

Be aware of your home country's importation laws before attempting to buy any products made from turtle, black coral, crocodile, etc. You don't want to risk fines, jail or bad karma.

There are many small grocery stores selling all kinds of strange and unusual canned and bottled foods as well as ice cream, soft drinks, bread, meats, cold cuts and in some cases, beer. A huge warehouse in the center of town sells everything from cotton candy to coffins (really).

Pohnpei

Few tourists—particularly dive tourists—visit this island, which is just as well for those of us who do. The operators are competent, and the accommodations are charming. The reefs are healthy, and the island even has a fun, old-style expatriate bar scene.

My Way Make a reservation with Patty Arthur at the Village Hotel. They'll pick you up at the airport and whisk you to their hilltop aerie. The rooms are beautiful and reasonably priced. Their dive operation is good, though you might want to be sure of where you want to dive. If you insist upon a divemaster being on board, this isn't for you. Make sure you dive off the shore at Balikir.

Dinner here is luxurious; the double prime rib is suitable for any cave-man and -woman. At night, visit the Senyavin bar and ask for Jimmy or Ricky. With a little prodding, they might escort you to a *sakau* market, where you will experience a true Pohnpeian ritual.

If you imbibe conservatively, you may experience only mild effects. This will afford you the opportunity to see how it's done and be able to leave with some dignity. Otherwise, plan on a long crawl through the mud to your car.

A nice walk through town will last about two hours, and there is lots to see. The post office maintains a philatelic center where you can buy unusual stamps (some are quite large and make nice souvenirs and gifts). Pohnpei is also one place that bothers to offer a good selection of beer. If you've tired of Budweiser by now, you will find other more palatable brands here.

General

GETTING THERE

Continental Micronesia stops here westbound and eastbound. Air Nauru also services the island. Pohnpei is a duty-free port, but expect to have your baggage inspected on arrival to help keep plant and animal pests and diseases out of the island. The airport is on Takatik Island, a couple miles north of Kolonia. Departure tax is $10.

Air Nauru At the airport,

AT A GLANCE
State of Pohnpei
Federated States of Micronesia (FSM)

STATUS Self-governing federation in free association with the United States; constitution in effect 1979, full independence 1986, admitted to UN in 1991.

FSM CAPITAL Palikir, Pohnpei Island

FSM POPULATION 131,500 (1999 est.)

FSM LAND AREA 607 islands comprising 271 sq. mi. (702 sq. km.)

FSM PER CAPITA GNP $1,760 (1996 est.)

FSM CURRENCY U.S. dollar

FSM COUNTRY CODE 691

POHNPEI STATE CAPITAL Kolonia, pop. 8,800 (1999 est.)

POHNPEI AIRPORT Takatik Island, Pohnpei (PNI)

POHNPEI POPULATION 44,100 (1999 est.)

POHNPEI LAND AREA One island and 8 atolls, comprising 133.3 sq. mi. (345.4 sq. km.). Largest island: Pohnpei, 129.03 sq. mi.

POHNPEI LANGUAGES English (official), Pohnpeian

POHNPEI AVERAGE TEMPERATURE 80.1°F (26.7°C)

POHNPEI YEARLY RAINFALL 193.6 in. (4,917 mm)

NAME Until 1984 Pohnpei was officially rendered "Ponape," and one still sees the old spelling in references and maps. One also still sees the name "Senyavin Islands," for Pohnpei and its two nearby atolls, which comes from Captain Fedor Lutke, who named them in 1828 after his ship *Senyavin*.

©320-5963. Flies once a week Nauru–Pohnpei–Guam–Manila.
Continental Micronesia At the airport, ©320-2424. Stops in Pohnpei between Hawaii and Guam.
Pacific Missionary Aviation P.O. Box 517, Kolonia, Pohnpei, FM 96941. ©320-2796, Fax: 320-2592. Once a week this small airline flies to the outer atolls of Pingelap and Mokil, for about $80 each way.

LOCAL TRANSPORTATION

Taxis are inexpensive in Pohnpei. Any trip is $1 or $2 (tipping is not expected), except to the Village Hotel and some of the more far-off sites, including Nan Madol, which are $5. The fares are per head, and the taxis pick up other passengers as available. There is no reason to rent a car here.

SEASON

More important than the particular season you choose is the time of day and tide condition. The same site can be completely different if you hit it at anything other than optimum tide position.

TOURIST SERVICES

Pohnpei Tourist Commission P.O. Box 66, Kolonia, Pohnpei FM 96941. ©320-2421, Fax: 320-2505.
Iet Ehu Tours ©320-2959

HEALTH

Water is okay in the village of Kolonia, but, as usual, better to invest in bottled water. The hospital, just outside of town, is primitive. For medical emergencies, call ©320-2213.

EMBASSY

Maryalice Eperiam at the U.S. Embassy (whose husband, Emensio, operates Iet Ehu Tours) is accessible and very helpful should you have any problems while on Pohnpei.

COMMUNICATIONS

There is a telecommunications office on the main thoroughfare in Kolonia. From here you can place international calls, though many hotels also offer international calling. The post office right along the main street in downtown Kolonia. Across the street is a philatelic center, where you can buy nice collectors' items, including many stamps that feature underwater life.

PEOPLE AND LANGUAGE

An intricate system of class and social structure are the backbone of this matrilineal culture. However, the traditional chiefs—*Nahnmwarki*—still wield political and cultural power.

Pohnpeians are generally friendly and approachable, but proper respect is always the order of the day. Both Polynesians and Micronesians also inhabit this island group. Pohnpeians speak two native languages, Polynesian and Pohnpeian. English is widely spoken.

One phrase you should know is "Kaselehlia," an all-purpose greeting that means "Hello," "Goodbye," and "Welcome to Pohnpei," among others. (It is also the name of a great shampoo.)

Dive Operators

A number of operators have developed here. The prices are more reasonable here than in most of Micronesia, running about $65 per two-tank diving day. All those listed below are good, although we prefer Iet Ehu and the Village Hotel services.

Blue Oyster Tours and Dive Shop P.O. Box 1402, Kolonia, Pohnpei FM 96941. ©320-5117, Fax: 320-5227. Contact: Mr. Edgar Santos.
Iet Ehu Tours P.O. Box 559, Kolonia, Pohnpei, FM 96941. ©320-2959, Fax: 320-2958. Contact: Mr. Emensio Eperiam. On the main town road. This is a small but classic dive operation. They are well-connected, and well-versed in underwater Pohnpei. Recommended.
Joy Ocean Service P.O. Box 484, Kolonia, Pohnpei FM 96941. ©320-2447. At the Joy Hotel.
Phoenix Marine Sport Club (PMSC) P.O. Box 387, Kolonia, Pohnpei FM 96941. ©320-2362 and 2363, Fax: 320-5678 and 5679. Phoenix Marine is the biggest operator on the island, and have the biggest boat. With their hot pink boats and garish wetsuits, they are not exactly subtle. They offer a rather regimented dive tour, and the price is a little high. They cater to large groups of Japanese tourists, and, therefore, are usually more crowded than other operators.
Pohnpei Aqua World P.O. Box 535, Kolonia, Pohnpei, FM 97941. ©320-2134, -2995, or -4220; Fax: 320-4221. Contact: Lynn Kilara or Misko Edwin.
Village Hotel Tours P.O. Box 339, Kolonia, Pohnpei FM 96941. ©320-2797. The Village Hotel also runs an excellent dive operation, staffed by conscientious and knowledgeable native Pohnpeians who will do their best to get you to the best spots at the best times. Recommended.

Accommodations

Harbor View P.O. Box 1328, Kolonia, Pohnpei, FM 96941. ©320-5244. Fax: 320-5246.

Near the airport. The Harbor View is locally owned, and the rooms are really not bad, if a little damp and dingy. Water pressure is like a fire hose with ample hot water. Color TV, fridge, telephone in each room. There is no view, better to keep your curtains closed. Bring slippers. The restaurant serves a fantastic garlic crab for $18. Give yourself a bib and a good two hours to eat it. The bar here is strictly seventies disco—tacky and mostly for locals. It can even get a bit rough at times. Relatively inexpensive at $50–$60.

The bar is a favorite watering hole for the colorful residents of this unusual island. Here, you might meet Professor Russell Brulotte, editor Sherry O'Sullivan, or writer Gene Ashby. Sunsets are perfect from this open perch; tropical drinks, piña coladas and rum punches are magical. The restaurant serves up healthy portions of expertly and imaginatively prepared foods. 20 bungalows, $90–$110 depending on occupancy and view. **The Joy Hotel** P.O. Box 484, Kolonia, Pohnpei, FM 96941. ☏320-2447. Fax: 320-2040. Clean, yellow, and functional. In the middle of town. Each room has a small terrace, but not much of a view. Offers diving through Joy Ocean Service. 10 AC rooms with fridge and TV, $75S, $95D. **Village Hotel** P.O. Box 339, Kolonia, Pohnpei FM 96941. ☏320-2797. Run by the beautiful and charming Patti Arthur and her husband Bob, is the perfect Pacific island getaway. In my opinion, there is nowhere else that even comes close. Individual thatch bungalows, airy and cool, are built high off the ground. Furnished with queen beds draped in gossamer mosquito netting, each

is very spacious, rustic, romantic and exceedingly comfortable. I'm a water pressure nut, and this place has never let me down. Flower-lined jungle pathways planted with banana and breadfruit run between the cabins and down to the main buildings.

Dining

The restaurant at the **Village Hotel,** with a nice, open-air view, and the restaurant at the **Harbor View Hotel** are both excellent. The **Sei Restaurant,** near the U.S. Embassy, offers a Viking Smorgasbord on weekends that features all-you-can-eat sushi, barbeque, chicken, lumpia, and the like. Much of its menu is Japanese, and it is a very good value.

Night Life

Pohnpei offers a fun night life, with karaoke, dancing, live music and cocktails. The **Sonato, Flamingo, Senyavin** (the Ocean View Bar), and the **Tatooed Irishman,** the bar at the Village Hotel, all offer fun evenings with bands, cocktails, DJs, and dancing. I've always had a great time at Senyavin and the Tatooed Irishman in particular.

At sunsets, Sherry O'Sullivan keeps her back to the wall at the Tatooed Irishman. She has a wealth of knowledge about FSM politics. Look for Canadian expat and archaeology professor Russell Brulotte at happy hour and beyond. A plate of wahoo sashimi and ice cold beer never hurt a sunset. This is where you'll find me. The tropical cocktails can't be beat.

Pacifia Starlite, on the outskirts of town, is modern and very touristy. The **Palm Terrace** is as much a part of

Pohnpei as Kolonia itself—funky, even dingy, at happy hour this is the place to be. The bar is a Pohnpeian classic and filled with interesting expats who play pool and ping empty Budweisers against an aluminum can. It can get a little rough after nine, but I wouldn't worry.

Land Tours

Some of the only true ancient ruins in Micronesia can be toured at Nan Madol. The *Nahnmwarki* (high chieftain) will grant you the necessary permission for $3, which allows you to tour this Venice of the Pacific. Located on the southern shore of Madolenihmw Harbor, these impossibly huge basalt foundations, built along hundreds of acres of canals cut into the coral flats, are evidence of the 10th-century Saudeleurs' ability to quite literally move mountains. The nearest possible source for the basalt used to build Nan would have been Sokehs Rock, 25 miles to the north, inaccessible by land. The task would be difficult in 1999, much less 999!

In a whirlwind ten-minute tour of downtown Kolonia, you can see the ruins of Fort Alphonso XIII, the Spanish Wall, the German graveyard and the graves of those who died in the Sokehs Rebellion.

Iet Ehu Tours will take you to hike and/or camp on top of Sokehs Mountain, Nahna Laud, Black Coral Resort, Heg's Island or Ahnd. There are numerous waterfalls offering fresh-water bathing and skin-replenishing mists near Nan Madol, Kepirohi and east of Kolonia along the Nanpil River. Locals are very helpful and will happily point you in the right direction, no matter what it is you are looking for.

Kosrae

The resorts on this quiet little island are both beautiful and ecologically sound. One is fully equipped for disabled travelers, including disabled divers. Here you can sleep in comfort, nestled in the mangrove forest, and dive on what is Micronesia's best-kept reef.

My Way Check into the Kosrae Village Resort. Have a cold drink at the bar and leave the rest to them. Katrina and Bruce will do everything they can to show you the best of Kosrae.

General

GETTING THERE

Continental Micronesia stops in Kosrae six times weekly. The airport is at Okat, a few miles west of Tofol. There is a $10 departure tax.
Continental Micronesia ©370-3024. Open 8am–4pm Mon. and Wed; 9 am–4 pm Tues, Thurs, Fri.

LOCAL TRANSPORTATION

While there is no public transportation, there is a taxi company (**AA Taxis**, ©370-2639) and a limited number of rental cars. If you want to do without the fuss, an outstretched thumb will always get you a ride into town and back. Dive and tour operators will always pick you up at your hotel. Bicycles are also available and provide the perfect speed with which to tour this small island.

SEASON

Some part of the reef is always accessible on Kosrae, though from May through November you will most likely be diving the leeward side of the island.

Seas are usually calm year round and though it rains frequently, typhoons and tropical storms are rare.

TOURIST ASSISTANCE

The tourist office (©370-2228) as well as most government offices, the hospital, the post office, the high school, and the FSM Telecom Corporation office are located at Tofol, Kosrae's administrative center, about four kilometers from Lelu.

MEDICAL

Water and ice at restaurants is generally safe, but the tap water on Kosrae is not. A few places have purified water on tap, but don't risk it. Substitute beer and bottled water.
Hospital In Tofol, ©370-3012.

COMMUNICATIONS

Call anywhere in the world from the FSM Telcom building in Tofol. Local calls are free, international calls are reasonable. The post office is in "downtown" Tofol, and is open from 8 am to 3:30 pm Monday through Friday, and 8 am–11 am Saturdays.

BANKING

The Bank of Hawaii (©370-3230) and the Bank of the FSM (©370-3225) both have branches in Tofol.

HOLIDAYS

Liberation Day (Sept. 8) is

wonderful on Kosrae. Months are spent in preparation for the one-week holiday (I think they begin preparing for the following year's festivities the day after Liberation Day). Young men carve outrigger canoes from scratch in much the same manner as they've been made for centuries, and race in fierce competition. A restorative choir competition rounds out the week. There is lots of food.

SUNDAYS

Kosrae is very serious about keeping the Sabbath. You are not supposed to work, cook, dive, fish, or drink on Sundays. Churches are packed on this day, and shops and offices are closed.

PHOTOGRAPHIC

As of this writing, there is no E-6 processing available on the island.

Dive Operators

Kosrae Nautilus Resort P.O. Box 135, Kosrae FM 96944. ©370-3567, Fax: 370-3568. E-mail: inquiry@kosraenautilus.com Web: www.kosraenautilus.com Dive sites are reached via a 27 foot dive boat with full shade cover and a 250 hp motor. Daily trips (except Sunday, of course). Convenient night diving in front of the resort.

Prices similar to Sleeping Lady.

Phoenix Marine Sports Club P.O. Box PHM, Kosrae FM 96944. ©390-3100, Fax: 370-3509. Just beyond the Civil Action Team base, toward town. Phoenix offers a complete facility with compressor, tanks, gear and very pink, comfortable dive boats. Caters to a predominantly Japanese clientele. Prices similar to Sleeping Lady.

Sleeping Lady Divers at the Kosrae Village Resort, Kosrae FM 96944. ©370-3483, Fax: 370-5839.
E-mail: Info@kosraevillage.com
Web: www.kosraevillage.com
The most comprehensive dive resort on Kosrae. Three 22-foot motorized catamarans speed you anywhere along the fringing reef. Two large compressors and a 12-tank bank system guarantees a good, fast fill. Nitrox available. All boats are fully equipped with safety equipment, including oxygen, binoculars, flares, radio, and PFDs. Dive guides are experienced local divers who must be certified rescue divers before they can begin leading tours. Operating out of all three harbors, the boats are limited to six divers each.

A 5-star PADI dive center with staff providing instruction ranging from introductory training to Assistant Instructor. Fully-equipped classroom (including training slides and tapes, current instructor's manuals and class outlines) is available for group leaders and instructors use at no extra charge. This operation is NIAAD (National Instructors Association for Divers with Disabilities) certified, and the diving and resort are fully accessible to the disabled.

Scubapro, US Divers, and Mares dealer and Kosrae's only factory authorized repair center. Repair technicians are certified to repair and maintain most major brands of equipment. Complete line of rental equipment (including computers). Two-tank dive day, $80. Single-tank night dive, $55.

State of Kosrae
Federated States of Micronesia (FSM)

STATUS Self-governing federation in free association with the United States; constitution in effect 1979, full independence 1986, admitted to UN in 1991.
FSM CAPITAL Palikir, Pohnpei Island
FSM POPULATION 131,500 (1999 est.)
FSM LAND AREA 607 islands comprising 271 sq. mi. (702 sq. km.)
FSM PER CAPITA GNP $1,760 (1996 est.)
FSM CURRENCY U.S. dollar
FSM COUNTRY CODE 691
KOSRAE STATE CAPITAL Tofol, area pop. 3,200 (1999)
KOSRAE AIRPORT Okat (KSA)
KOSRAE POPULATION 9,600 (1999 est.)
KOSRAE LAND AREA One island comprising 42.31 sq. mi. (109.6 sq. km.)
KOSRAE LANGUAGES English (official), Kosraean
KOSRAE AVERAGE TEMPERATURE 81.0°F (27.2°C)
KOSRAE YEARLY RAINFALL 175.9 in. (4,466 mm)
NAME Kosrae—pronounced "ko-shrye"—was in the past rendered "Kusaie," and one still sees this on maps and in texts.

Accommodations

Coconut Palm P.O. Box 87, Tofol, Kosrae FM 96944. ©370-3181, Fax: 370-3567. Currently under renovation, Coconut Palm may soon offer office space, and long term, apartment-type accommodations.

Kosrae Nautilus Resort P.O. Box 135, Kosrae FM 96944. ©370-3567, Fax: 370-3568. E-mail: inquiry@kosraenautilus.com
Web: www.kosraenautilus.com
Just a stone's throw from their own private beach. Friendly staff and comfortable surroundings. The resort is a 16-room complex surrounded by tropical gardens. Very good restaurant and bar facilities. The only swimming pool on the island. All rooms are air-conditioned and furnished with 2 double beds, video movies, mini bar, tea/coffee making facilities and daily room service. Rates $80–$95.

Kosrae Village Resort Kosrae, FM 96944. ©370-3483, Fax: 370-5839. In the United States (CA): ©(510) 370-1246; Fax: (510) 370-6756.

E-mail: info@kosraevillage.com
Web:www.kosraevillage.com
Kosrae Village Resort, run by the mercurial Bruce Brandt and his wife Katrina Adams, is the most beautiful, eco-conscious, and politically correct resort in Micronesia, if not the world. The resort and dive operation have made it a point that their facilities be accessible to disabled travelers and divers. Nestled among five acres of coconut, banana, citrus and pandanus trees are twelve bungalows with walls of plaited reeds. Steep thatched roofs are built high, ensuring a cool breeze delivered by the trade winds and augmented by graceful ceiling fans and wide screened windows. In the magnificent rooms floored with ruddy, polished wood, queen beds are draped in white gossamer netting. A comfortable dressing alcove, refrigerator, charming lamps and spacious bathrooms offering fierce water pressure and unlimited hot water round out the rustic, yet luxurious accommodations. $70S, $95D, $120T.
Pacific Treelodge P.O. Box 51, Lelu, Kosrae FM 96944. ©370-2102, Fax: 370-3102. E-mail: asigrah@mail.fm
This unusual resort consists of six duplex bungalows nestled right into the mangrove and fronted by pristine swimming waters. Lots of birds here. Rooms are very private with modern furnishings, private phones, queen and twin beds, hot and cold showers, AC, TV, and VCR. The restaurant is set atop the Mutunnenea channel. Rates a reasonable $58S, $75D.

Dining

For the most part Kosrae is a good place to start a diet, but

there are a few exceptions. There is no night life in Kosrae. Only the resort restaurants serve drinks.
Inum Restaurant In the Kosrae Village Resort. This place has a reputation as one of the best not just in Kosrae, but in Micronesia. Local and international dishes. The dinner menu changes nightly, depending on the availability of fresh local produce, chicken and fish. Try the mangrove crab—it's delicious. In addition to fine meals and excellent service, the restaurant is a focal point for various community activities such as Thursday cultural night, and Monday night movies (both open to the public at no cost). Once or twice a month a local band will be invited to play on a Saturday night. The Inum's large dining room is easily subdivided to set up dedicated conference space, leaving a small dining room available to the public.
Kosrae Nautilus Resort Restaurant Excellent food served in an air-conditioned, smoke-free dining room. Typical American breakfast priced from $2, lunch less than $5. Varied international cuisine includes lasagna, grilled fish, and Asian specialties, all under $10. Beer, wine, spirits available. Don't miss the house special margaritas, made with fresh Kosraen limes.
Pacific Treelodge Restaurant In the Treelodge Hotel. A lovely spot. Dine al fresco in a mangrove swamp, on typical international fare, including teriyaki dishes, for under $5. Slow service, so don't be in a rush.
Bill's Restaurant P.O. Box 87, Lelu. ©370-3181, Fax: 370-3084. This place is a Kosraen standard, and locals have been eating here for years. Varied menu with Asian

specialties, including ramen and grilled fish, most under $6. Killer sashimi for less than $4. If you're really nice, Bill might send someone to catch and cook you a mangrove crab.
Islanders Restaurant P.O. Box KHC, Lelu. ©370-3075. Good local joint, particularly for breakfast or lunch. Reasonable.
Webster's Market A good spot for grocery and general supplies, including canned goods, bottled water and snacks.

Land Touring

The Wiya Bird Cave, a towering 20-meter deep abyss in the western palisades is home to tens of thousands of island swiftlets, who flock in black clouds as you drive past. In the south, 12-meter Sipyen Waterfall and the smaller Saolung Falls (permission necessary) are only short walks from the road and spill into cool bathing pools.

Walung Village still maintains the cultural traditions of Kosrae. Cut off from the rest of the island by jungle, Walung is only accessible from the sea, by boat or canoe. Permission is needed if you choose to visit this lovely village, with no telephones, cars or electricity (conservative clothing is required).

The largest village is on Lelu, a small island connected to Kosrae proper by a causeway. Lelu flourished as the feudal capital of Kosrae from 1400 to 1800. The Lelu ruins, made up of criss-crossed hexagonal basalt logs, bear a striking resemblance to Pohnpei's Nan Madol. The ruins have recently been cleaned up, and the state has set aside money for their continued preservation.

The Marshall Islands

Although Kwajalein's Ebeye town is a tiny, ultra-crowded raft of cardboard, tin, and duct tape, the people are charming and the dive operator is a good one. This is the most convenient wreck diving in the Marshalls. Further afield in this nation of atolls are Arno, Mili, and especially Bikini.

This section lists practical information on Kwajalein Atoll first, then contacts for diving and lodging on the other atolls in the Marshalls with diving: Arno, Bikini, Majuro, and Mili.

My Way For diving Kwajalein, just contact Steve Gavegan at Kwajalein Atoll Dive Resort and leave it all to him.

General

GETTING THERE

Continental Micronesia stops on Kwajalein. Don't let the reservationist bully you—you certainly are allowed to *land* on Kwajalein, and without anything but a passport. You can't stay there, so make sure someone is waiting for you on the dock after you pass security clearance and pick up your luggage. Because of the nature of this base, you will be thoroughly checked and your bags sniffed and re-sniffed by a phalanx of dogs and guards.

LOCAL TRANSPORTATION

Shoe-leather express is all you need on tiny Ebeye.

TOURIST ASSISTANCE

Marshall Islands Visitors Authority (MIVA) P.O. Box 1727 Majuro, MH 96960. ©625-3206, Fax: 625-3218. E-mail: tourism@ntamar.com

HEALTH AND MEDICAL

Don't get hurt or sick on Ebeye. The U.S. armed forces maintains a decompression chamber on Kwajalein, although they don't publicize this. It will, of course, be available to you should you get in trouble. There is also a hospital on Kwajalein, probably among the best in Micronesia, but it is not generally accessible except in an emergency.

AT A GLANCE

The Marshall Islands
Republic of the Marshall Islands (RMI)

STATUS Constitutional government in free association with the United States since 1986 (parliament)

CAPITAL Darrit–Uliga–Delap (D-U-D), Majuro Atoll, pop. 20,000 (1990 est.)

MAIN INTERNATIONAL AIRPORT Majuro (MAJ)

POPULATION 65,507 (1999 est.)

LAND AREA 870 reefs, 29 atolls, and 5 separate islands (1,225 islands total) comprising 69.94 sq. mi. (181.1 sq. km.). Largest islands: Kwajalein Group, 6.33 sq. mi.

PER CAPITA GNP $1,680 (1996 est.)

CURRENCY U.S. dollar

LANGUAGES Marshallese and English (both official)

AVERAGE TEMPERATURE 80.4°F (26.8°C)

YEARLY RAINFALL 135.6 in. (3,444 mm)

COUNTRY CODE 692

NAME From Captain John Marshall (English), who charted the islands in 1788

WATER

A large Israeli-designed desalination plant has been recently completed on Ebeye, but it does not allow continuous running water. Every day for a half hour the water comes on, and residents fill up their tanks. During the "water hours," water is collected in the many cisterns for use after the flow is stopped. While the water purified by the plant is as clean and fresh as it gets, you have to rely upon the cleanliness of the cisterns. My advice is to buy it bottled.

COMMUNICATIONS

There is a telecommunications center in the municipal building (there is only one) on Ebeye. On the main road on the lagoon side is a post office.

HOLIDAYS

Constitution Day, May 1, is big in Ebeye. Singing, dancing and canoe races are among the featured activities.

USEFUL PHRASES

Yokwe   Hello
Kommol   thank you

PHOTOGRAPHIC

There is no photo processing on Ebeye.

Dive Operator

Kwajalein Atoll Dive Resort, Inc. (KADRI) P.O. Box 5159, Ebeye, Kwajalein, MH 96970. ©329-3100, ©329-3102 and ©329-1220; Fax: 329-3297. Reservations (US/Canada toll-free) 1-800-846-3483.
Owned and managed by Steven M. Gavegan, a transplanted American. A good and attentive operator. KADRI offers PADI Courses (Open Water to Assistant Instructor) and runs three boats—two 40 foot dive boats w/450 hp cats and a ferry boat to retrieve customers from Kwajalein.
Full service dive and watersports, snorkeling, fishing, sailing, sailing on a hobie cat or sunfish, and windsurfing. You'll certainly enjoy the company and guidance of Yoshi, Albon ("Cowboy") and Joab (the "Cisco Kid"). Accommodation and dive packages available. Rates: $85 for a two-tank diving day.

Accommodations

Kwajalein Atoll Dive Resort, Inc. (KADRI) (see contact information this page) offers eight duplex cottages, hot and cold running water, large dining room and bar. The restaurant serves fresh fish and coconut crab. 26 air conditioned rooms, some with kitchenettes. MasterCard and Visa accepted. Rate: $95.
Anrohasa Hotel P.O. Box 5039, Ebeye, MH 96970. ©329-3161. Though it is modern and has great potential, I found this place disappointing. The help was surly, my room was never made up, the carpets were musty, the water stank of sulphur, the sheets were stained, nothing worked, and the staff acted like they were doing me a big favor just to respond to the slightest request. 21 rooms. Rate: $90.
Midtown Hotel P.O. Box 159, Ebeye, MH 96970. ©329-3199. 10 rooms.

Dining & Night Life

The restaurant at the **Anrohasa Hotel** is not bad, and the prices are average. Service can be painfully slow, but, hey, you're in Ebeye, so you're not going anywhere, anyway. Jimmy the cook is expert and will prepare your catch any way you like.
There are no blue laws on Ebeye. The bars only close when the proprietors don't feel like working. The bar at the **Anrohasa Hotel** looks like any you would find at a small airport, but it's the main spot for locals and tourists alike. You can choose between ice-cold Budweiser or ice-cold Bud Light, except that they are always out of the Bud Light. Snacks are avail-

able from the hotel's restaurant. The TV is tuned either to major sporting events or one of a great selection of B-movies.

Land Touring

The Marshallese exhibit that certain quality of islanders everywhere. Here, it's called *jaba*—"hanging out"—and island life goes on, peacefully, if uneventfully. I won't lie to you; there is not much to do here, except dive and fish. The tour of Ebeye will take about 45 minutes on foot, so your second hour on island is going to be a challenge.
A drive through the five islands that make up this atoll can be interesting. You'll be using the new coral road started by the U.S. Army Corps of Engineers and almost completed by a private concern. Ask someone for a tour. The beaches are quite lovely and vary considerably from one side of the island to the other. The lagoon side is calm while the ocean side can become rough and wild—I prefer the ocean side myself.
You'll pass the New College of Marshall Islands extension from Majuro high school, and a thatch "convention center" used by government officials (and their cousins).
It's interesting to attend one of the many daily church services, as the full gospel singing can be quite inspirational.

Shopping

There is nothing to buy on Ebeye, but the airport has a small yet surprisingly well-stocked gift shop featuring items from all of Micronesia. It's really hard to figure out when it is open, but if luck is with you, you'll find a good assortment of souvenirs here. Look for the fascinating wooden "stick charts," and pandanus hats, skirts, belts, purses and the like. Beautiful carvings of sharks, fish and canoes are highly polished and rather unusual, though quality varies considerably.

Other Atolls

Kwajalein offers some of the best and most convenient wreck diving in the Marshalls, but there are some other fine dive sites here as well. Majuro, the capital of the islands, has some good, although perhaps not great diving. At tiny Arno, adjacent to Majuro, things get much better, and and the diving can be spectacular at Mili, a short plane flight away.

The current star of Marshall Islands diving is Bikini Atoll, whose lagoon contains within it perhaps the most spectacular collection of wartime wrecks in all of history, including the world's only diveable aircraft carrier, the USS *Saratoga*, and the *Nagato*, the flagship of Japan's World War II navy.

Bikini, the site of the famous post-World War II atomic tests, opened its attractions to visitors only in mid-1996 and has since taken the diving world by storm.

Although stunning, Bikini is not for everybody, however. The ships here lie very deep, and only divers experienced with long decompression dives should think about a trip here.

Marshalls Dive Adventures offers diving in Majuro, Arno, and Mili, and has the exclusive on Bikini Diving. Marshall Islands Aquatics also offers diving in Majuro and Mili.

OPERATORS

Marshalls Dive Adventures Robert Reimers Enterprises, Inc., P.O. Box 1, Majuro, MH 96960. ☎625-3250, Fax: 625-3505.
E-mail: mdabikini@hotmail.com
Web: www.rreinc.com
This is the largest operation in the Marshalls, and they run diving at Majuro Atoll, Arno Atoll, Mili Atoll, and Bikini, as well as sportfishing excursions, general tours, and even giant clam farming. Hotel accommodations for Majuro-based diving are offered at **Hotel Robert Reimers**, next to Marshalls Dive Adventures. A comfortable resort with 39 rooms and bungalows. Divers rate: $75 room with lanai, $150 bungalow. Add $5 for double occupancy.

Majuro

Here the outfit maintains its main base. They run a fast custom dive boat with freshwater showers, camera table and a swim platform to sites off D-U-D. They offer PADI and NAUI instruction, and authorized Scubapro sales and service. Rates: two-tank boat diving $90, single-tank boat diving $60.

Arno

This small atoll is just one hour from Majuro, and diving here is handled from the outfit's Majuro base. Rates: two-tank boat diving, $120.

Mili

This is a remote atoll a short flight from Majuro. Marshalls Dive Adventures maintains a small resort (with 7 thatched huts) on tiny Wau Island here near their giant clam farm. There is some excellent diving here, especially in the passes. Contact them for availability of packages and prices,

which include the flight to Mili, accommodations on Wau, and diving.

Bikini

Marshalls Dive Adventures offers one-week packages to Bikini. The flight from Majuro is on an Air Marshall Islands twin-engined commuter plane, and the accommodation in Bikini is at lodging run by the operator.

As we mentioned earlier, this is serious diving, and they require you show proof of accident insurance and, if over 35 years old, proof of a doctor's exam.

The package is $2,750 for 12 (deco) dives, although the price goes down for groups— $2,350/person for eight, $2,000/person for ten.

This does not include airfare, either to Majuro or to Bikini, the first night at Majuro, or gratuities, so this can wind up being an expensive trip (though your first glimpse of the 880-foot *Saratoga* might make it all worth it).

Marshall Islands Aquatics P.O. Box 319, Majuro, MH 96960. ☎625-0567 and ☎625-6267, Fax: 625-3669. Contact: Matt Holly. Operates in Majuro and Mili.

AGENCY PACKAGES

Packages, including air tickets, accommodation, and diving for the Marshall Islands operators can be booked through the following agencies.
Central Pacific Dive Expeditions (CEN PAC) 29 Blazing Star, Irvine, CA 92714. ☎1-800-846-3483 (US/Canada toll-free), ☎(714) 551-1167, Fax: (714) 851-3111
Mad Dog Expeditions 132 East 82nd Street, New York, NY 10028. ☎(212) 744-6763, Fax: (212) 744-6568.

Index

Page numbers in boldface indicate the main section on that topic; page numbers in italic indicate photographs

Map Index